The Money Changers

The Money Changers

by

John G. Fuller

THE DIAL PRESS   NEW YORK   1962

PROLOGUE

It was bound to happen, and it did. The date was May 28, 1962. The fact: a paper loss of 20.8 billion dollars in five and one-half hours and nearly ten million shares worth of trading. The dollar loss was the greatest in history; it was double the loss of the blackest day in 1929.

More eloquently than words could say it, this single day on the stock market stated plainly: The stock market is overwhelmingly vulnerable. It has profound weaknesses. The weaknesses must be corrected.

The market in general can be observed only as a continuous line which fluctuates. Any observation about what the stock market will do or won't do at any given moment or period of time is bound to be of ephemeral value. There is no such thing as saying what the stock market *is*. The only statements which have validity are those which tell what the stock market *was*.

In spite of the fluctuations of the market, which are the only things that can be relied on, there are general principles which any observant human being, expert or not, can detect. They are, in fact, timeless clichés. The amazing thing is that they can be forgotten so readily by professional and amateur alike. It is known universally that you can't get something for nothing—or that if you do, the chances are that you're going to lose it fairly quickly. It is almost a cliché to say that anything bought on emotional impulse is bound to look tarnished or faded in the cold light of later reason. It is obvious to a sailor that when he is on a rocking ship, he must walk accordingly; he doesn't jump off a ship because it is rocking.

The financial and industrial world often becomes so absorbed in its own activity that it is unable to see the most important basic problems, which if not faced and solved can produce severe damage to its own well-being. Because some of the most brilliant and intelligent minds in business become so preoccupied, they lose their sense of awareness when it comes to the relationship between their own institutions and the general public. Their public relations programs become apologia for existent practices rather than dynamic inquiries into what can be done to improve the entire structure of their enterprise so that it can continue to grow and remain fruitful. This practice can lead only to its destruction.

The health of the financial market depends on two very basic things: a market in which the investor is safer than he is or has been; and a market in which the large bulk of the public is able to participate in realistic rather than token terms. Unless these fundamentals are given the highest priority of attention, the financial community will continue to founder.

The crash of May 28, 1962, as drastic and dramatic as it was, was only a symptom. Behind it were many currents and crosscurrents—some of which this book tries to examine frankly from the point of view of the outsider looking in. Most of the book was written during the peak bull market of 1961, many months before the May 28 debacle. The strange thing is that there was so little to change in the light of what happened later. To an outsider, it seemed that May 28 was long overdue. At a cocktail party, the nondrinker is often fascinated as he watches the manic buoyancy of the extra-dry martini drinker. A roseate haze of well-being wells up in the atmosphere, which brings the participants to a point stopping just short of levitation. It is unreal, of course, but it is pleasant. The hangover which follows is also unreal, because it is temporary. But somehow it often comes as an unpleasant surprise.

What was behind the 1962 crash, how it happened, what can be done to prevent another in the future, are all questions which can never be answered fully. But the fundamentals—the principles—stand out clearly in the jungle.

With the undergrowth cut away, they may have a chance to mature and prosper.

The Money Changers

"The Stock Exchange is an essential link in the chain of the nation's business life. . . ."
—STATEMENT BY THE NEW YORK STOCK EXCHANGE

CHAPTER I

On September 3, 1946, sixteen years before the 1962 thump, the sun rose at 6:24 A.M. and set at 7:25 P.M. Between those hours of mild and seasonable weather came the worst break in the stock market in the previous fifteen years.

As usual, the parkways had been jammed with Labor Day fugitives, sweating their way home to New York. Mayor O'Dwyer was reassuring a nervous public that there was no famine in sight, even though the first general trucking strike in six years was tying up the city's food more than a six-car accident on a Long Island parkway. The Railway Express Agency refused to accept any merchandise for movement within the city limits, a necessary step to prevent its facilities from being overloaded in the face of the strike. In addition, a general maritime strike was threatened within hours, which would tie up every merchant ship on all the coasts.

But aside from this, the news was relatively quiet. The Republican State Convention at Saratoga Springs was plugging for "mediation and conciliation rather than governmental interference and compulsion," and the Democrats were slamming Dewey's record and praising the late FDR's record with enthusiasm and just a touch of chauvinism. Oddly enough, the Democrats (meeting in somber Albany compared to plush Saratoga Springs) were covered by a *New York Times* reporter by the name of James A. Hagerty. Equally incongruous was the fact that the United States joined Soviet Russia in pressing for an investigation of Ukrainian charges against the Greeks, the latter being accused of threatening the peace of the Balkans. All Paris was talking about a grisly "Existentialist" murder, in which a pre-Beatnik habitué of the Latin Quarter was found in a hut, badly bloated and burned. Frederic Wakeman, who had written his best seller *The Hucksters* in a month, was in the process of moving to Bermuda to beat the housing shortage, and claimed to have several novels in his head. *Time* was reporting that 8,000,000 U.S. citizens were neurotic or worse, and that there was an acute shortage of psychiatrists. Olivia de Havilland was being married for the first time, and "Hurry Up" Yost, the football great, had just died at the age of 75. Van Alstyne, Noel & Company was cautioning investors that there was danger ahead if they clung to the hope of getting rich quickly. The Hearst newspapers were pounding their chests in a series of advertisements claiming that they had always protected the pocketbook of the U.S. investor, listing their vigorous editorial warnings in the years of 1908, 1912, 1914, 1920, 1931, 1936, and 1946. Conspicuously missing was the year 1929.

The market break of September 3, 1946, took place some 17 years after the 1929 Crash. When the bell rang on the floor of the New York Stock Exchange at 10:00 A.M., a good percentage of the gentlemen there wore healthy Labor Day tans, along with that let-down feeling that comes with the end of vacation and the beginning of a long year's routine ahead. On the fringes of the arena at 11 Wall Street, which houses the New York Stock Exchange, the clerks of the member firms were standing by to push telephone earpieces against their sunburned ears for an endless succession of phone calls coming in on wires from all over the country. On the floor, over 1,000 members—specialists, floor traders, odd lot dealers, floor brokers (known anachronistically as $2.00 brokers), commission-house brokers, and their squires pushed into action to start the day off. Each member (holding an equally anachronistic "seat") had paid anywhere from $17,000 to $625,000 over the years for the privilege of yelling through his days on the floor in the bedlam which follows the 10 A.M. gong. So frenzied does the action appear from the visitors' gallery that one onlooker was overheard to say: "If a man from space were to drop in here on his arrival, he wouldn't even bother to ask to be taken to the Leader."

As on most any other day, member firms from Kokomo to Keokuk had opened their doors to admit the hopeful but often neurotic battalions who inhabit their board rooms (or funeral parlors, as they are sometimes called) to watch the name and number of each and every stock as it would click on the board in front of them. Emotionally, they would have all the enthusiasm of a Yankee fan on the Fourth of July. On the surface they would remain bland and inscrutable, almost motionless, as the boards clicked with the sound of a thousand crickets. There for most of the day they would sit and stare hypnotically at the high, low, previous day's closing, and latest sale price of their favorite stocks.

The doctor in Portland, Maine, and the little old lady in Portland, Oregon, which the Stock Exchange likes to use as the perfect illustration of a perfectly balanced transaction, were probably on hand at two of these funeral parlors on this day; or if not, they were close to their phones and ready to chatter with their local brokers, who probably wished they would let up for a peaceful moment.

As on any other day, the bell at 11 Wall Street would ring on the south wall, and the sound and the fury would begin at the 18 trading posts on a floor not much bigger than a good-sized basketball court.

There would be no running on the floor, of course. A $50 fine would take care of that. And no smoking on the floor either. Too much paper, including the inevitable paper gliders which cruise the floor at odd moments for no reason whatever.

By the time the first yells of "How's Steel? How's Motors? How's duPont?" hit the floor that post-Labor Day morning, some old-timers felt something in the air.

SEC reports and Dow-Jones averages had indicated that stock prices had been moving slightly but nervously downward up to the last of July, then had bumped upward in mid-August, only to hit another downdraft at that time. The Dow-Jones industrial average—a composite average of a handful of stocks—had dropped over 15 points between the middle of August and the beginning of the Labor Day weekend. The SEC reported that there had been tough sledding for new issues for several months.

Most important was the fact that the late August drop had carried prices to the so-called Dow resistance level, which would immediately give the signal to the large herd of lambs who follow the Dow theory to sell as soon as they could push their brokers to the telephone.

The Dow theory was devised by Charles H. Dow, who was the first editor of the *Wall Street Journal,* not as a speculating wind sock, but as a serious method of tracing fluctuations in business. Only indirectly was the theory supposed to predict what was about to happen in the stock market. But the herd instinct of the lambs, bulls, and bears very shortly pounced on the theory as a sure-fire way of predicting what the market was going to do, and together they have been putting hard-cash bets on its efficacy since the turn of the century.

History has shown the Dow theory to be right on 45 major occasions, and wrong on exactly the same number—which should indicate even to the layman that he's not exactly in a favored position by following the theory's tenets. But the Dow theory continues to be worshipped as an infallible prophet by an unaccountable cult of board room addicts.

Basically, the Dow theory breaks the spasmodic movements of the stock market into three types: tides, waves, and ripples. The tides are supposed to be those major trends, either up or down, which take place over a period of years. One of these long-term tidal movements can last anywhere from nine months to two years, and can go in either direction: up or down. The "waves" in the Dow theory are just like the waves in the ocean. They are shorter in duration than tides, but considerably greater than ripples. And you can usually measure between the peaks. Dow considered the ripples to be the nervous, day-to-day variations in stock prices, and admitted that they were absolutely unpredictable—unless, of course, there was manipulation going on in the market.

But on September 3, 1946, the wave-watchers (stock market variety) were alert and sensitive, if nothing else. They were watching, of course, for the Dow-Jones average to break through the "resistance level" of 186.02. They were watching like hawks, as subsequent events were later to prove.

The "resistance level" on this particular day happened to be at 186.02, because at this point in the chart the trough and cap of the wave would fail to equal the previous trough and cap. This, according to Dow purists who depend on the theory to speculate, is the point at which you must sell, come hell or high dividends.

Strangely enough to an outsider, it would make no difference whatever to the Dow-crested Board-watchers' Society that the general corporate earnings and dividends had increased all through 1946. Income after taxes, in fact, had reached an all-time high in the second half of the year. The speculative members of the cult pay little attention to such trivia as sound earnings and corporate stability. Apparently the trick is not to be interested in owning stock as a means of furthering production in return for a reasonable profit, but to get on and off the band wagon at those precise moments when the music is playing best.

Further, the speculative Dow cultist seems to be equipped with built-in psychological blinders which irrationally convince him that he is the *only* possessor of the single key to profits. The blinders seem to shield him from recognizing that by his very own actions he is influencing the market along with a large crowd of fellow Dowists (pronounced the same as the mystic Taoists whose total acceptance of Life and the Inevitable is the exact opposite of the frenzied board-watcher) to such an extent that he is destroying the very thing he wants to foster.

On August 30, the last trading day before September 3, the Dow-Jones industrial average had closed at 189.9. A drop in these same averages of slightly more than 3 points was all that was needed for the jumping signal. Only a few days previously, some Dow theorists who used a slightly different system from that of the Dow purists decided that a "resistance level" had been reached, and they had jumped off a little early. As a result, the market dropped a measurable 5.95 points. This was August 27, and there were apparently not enough Dowists wearing this particular plaid to disturb the market further than this. A drop of 5.95 points, however, is not inconsiderable.

If you will, for a moment, picture a long line of workmen carrying an enormous steel girder, and visualize what would happen if a large percentage of the workers decided to let go suddenly when the lunch whistle went off, you can get some kind of idea of what could happen to the stock market when the Dow cultists saw their "resistance level" being pierced. For a while, the remaining workmen would struggle to hold up the girder, but since the weight would be too much for them, they would inevitably stumble, fall, and let go themselves. In the process, some of them would be hurt. It would also be obvious that as much as some of the workmen wanted to hold on to the girder, they could not possibly do so after the whistle-jumpers had left the scene. In addition, there might be among the workmen a good percentage who knew in advance that a certain portion of their fellow workers was going to let go at the precise moment the whistle went off, and this group would probably let go at the same moment so that they wouldn't get hurt. This would leave only the innocent and the conscientious holding the girder, who would take the biggest shock.

Standing by on the floor of the Exchange, on this pleasant September morning in 1946, were the corps of liquid and financially responsible gentlemen known as specialists. About 25 per cent of Exchange members fall into this category, and they specialize in "making a market" for one or more stocks on the Exchange. Every stock listed on the Exchange has at least one specialist bird-watching it. It is his job to maintain a "fair and orderly market" for the stock or stocks he represents, and he must be willing to stick his own neck and wallet out to do so.

He does practically no business directly with the public. But he does trade for his own account in order to keep this fair and orderly market in hand. He makes his money out of commissions which other brokers split with him, and out of any profits he might make by the inventories of stocks he accumulates through trading for his own account.

He is continually in the spotlight. Since he buys stocks and holds them, he is a dealer as well as a broker. He accounts for somewhere around half of all the transactions on the Exchange of the stocks he deals in.

His bible is a slim, narrow book, neatly ruled, with the left hand page labelled BUY and the right hand page labelled SELL. He has a page for each reasonable dollar price, and down the margins on the page are the gradations between, say, 80 and 81, indicated in stock market custom as $1/8$, $1/4$, $3/8$, $1/2$ and so on. On these pages, he lists whatever orders have been given him, opposite the amount his fellow brokers want to buy or sell. For instance, at $80\frac{1}{2}$, he might have several orders to buy, and at $80\frac{7}{8}$, he might have several orders to sell. He lists these in the order in which he receives them, and in effect, the buyers and sellers stand in line in his book. If a fellow broker comes up to him and says: "How's Smith-Jones?" the specialist might reply: "$80\frac{1}{2}$ to $80\frac{7}{8}$," meaning the high price bid is $80.50, and the lowest price offered is

$80.75. At this point, it's up to the broker to try to get the stock somewhere in between, but the chances are he'll have to settle for 80⅞, because this is the lowest price available for Smith-Jones stock at the time.

If one of the specialist's colleagues on the floor wants to sell some Smith-Jones stock, he again asks: "How's Smith-Jones?" and the specialist will again tell him that the market stands at 80½ to 80⅞. The selling broker will make a couple of attempts to unload at a higher price, but failing that will take the highest bid at the time, which is 80½. The specialist and the selling broker will check each other's badges, send a report to their respective customers, and the sale is completed. Within a few moments, the sale will appear on the tape simultaneously in board rooms all over the country, and a new "market" has been set.

There are many complex functions of the specialist, including the listing of "stop" orders, which simply means that a customer has put in a request to his broker that if a stock reaches a certain lower price level, he is to sell it to prevent further losses. There are also stop orders on the buying side, in which a specialist will reserve a requested amount of stock if a potential buyer requests it, at a given price level, in case a stock is on the rise.

A specialist faces not only a great deal of responsibility, but also a great deal of temptation. The Securities and Exchange Commission has pointed out that he enjoys competitive advantages over the general public, along with other members on the floor, and because of the information he carries in his little book, he has a large fund of knowledge which, if abused, could result in out-and-out manipulation.

The specialist knows, for instance, how many orders for his assigned stock there are directly below the sea level of the current market price. This is handy information to have, because the market isn't likely to drop below a certain point, at a given time at least, because of the backlog of "buy" orders standing in line and waiting. He knows also how many people there are standing in line, ready to sell at offerings above the market. As a result, the specialist is faced with a situation which might shatter the nerves of a reasonable and prudent man. On the other hand, he faces strict regulations on the Exchange itself, to say nothing of a formidable list of SEC regulations which could cause him acute embarrassment at the flicker of the ticker tape. With a few outstanding exceptions, there has been little evidence of extensive manipulative activity on the part of specialists since the Securities and Exchange Act of 1934.

The specialist also faces considerable conflict of interest in serving both as a dealer, who has his own stock to buy and sell, and as a broker, who must carry on transactions for others and give them the best possible break in price. The Twentieth Century Fund has observed that it may be possible, but it would be extremely difficult, for the specialist to trade without prejudice to the best interests of his customers. The main problem has been indiscretion on the part of the specialist in handling his customers' business while trading for himself. During a milk strike, the milkman is quite likely to feed his own children first.

The regulations which surround a specialist on all sides are considerable. The SEC tries to see to it that he doesn't disclose the contents of his book to anyone other than strictly qualified officers from the Exchange and the SEC. Speculators could have a field day with the specialist's book of an active stock. He, of course, is prohibited from manipulation under both SEC and Stock Exchange rules, and under both rules he cannot buy or sell for his own account unless the transaction is "reasonably necessary to maintain a fair and orderly market." But these and other regulations leave considerable leeway, and put on the shoulders of the specialist a burden which would be hard for a saint to carry. And, as several recent cases on the American Exchange have shown, there have been some who are far less than saints.

On September 3, 1946, the specialists on the Stock Exchange prepared themselves, as on any other day, to open the market. Under their obligation to maintain the market, and keep it as close as possible to the previous business day's close, the specialists combed through their orders, which had piled up from August 30, so that some kind of orderly prices would be arrived at, in line with the objective of keeping an even, continuous market.

Around a good many trading posts, "crowds" had already gathered, anxious to find out just what kind of day it would be. On the books of the specialists there were comparatively few limit orders—orders which could be executed at a specified price or a better one—to buy stock below the market or to sell stock above the market. There were considerably more orders to buy than to sell. In general, the feeling around the Street was bullish, and had been for the past few days at least. In London and Amsterdam, where the exchanges had opened several hours earlier, prices were firm and steady.

There were 945 stocks traded on the New York Stock Exchange that day, and at the opening gong they averaged $39.35 in price. At exactly 10:01, a total of 3,200 shares had been sold in a total of 12 transactions. One transaction was made on an "up-tick" (higher than the previous price), three were made on "down-ticks" (lower), and eight were made at the same price as previously established. The specialists made a total of two purchases and six sales. The floor traders —those members of the Exchange who have the luxury of buying and selling for themselves—were standing by and watching the circus. Broker-dealers—those who provide the facilities for the Board-watcher Society—accounted for only one selling transaction for their own firm account. The odd-lot dealers (those who buy and sell stocks in the meager quantities of less than 100 shares) participated in one buying transaction. Investment trusts bought in seven transactions. Banks sat out the first minute of trading, while foreigners made three sales to one buy—an action which was to be repeated by this group with drastic consequences in the seconds and minutes which were to follow. The public was vacillating in general, not quite knowing whether to buy or sell, and ended up in the first minute with 20 purchases and 24 sales. The net result of all this activity, which covered exactly sixty seconds, was to drop the average price of the particular stocks traded in that short time about 7¢ per share. This was insignificant, but it was also prophetic.

By 10:04 A.M., just three minutes later, some 30 transactions were made on down-ticks, and the average price of the stocks traded on the Exchange in that time had slumped about 8¢.

By 10:15 A.M., the average price of the stocks traded up to that moment had dropped down 12¢, and the board room addicts summoned up enough energy to lean forward in their chairs. However, since the Dow-Jones average still hovered in the neighborhood of 190, they didn't take too much action to unload. That magic breakthrough figure of 186.02 was still a distance away, and many Dow theorists prefer to see what the close of the market says. Strangely, the most important influence on the market during those first fifteen minutes were a couple of hefty foreign accounts, Dutch and Swiss mainly, who for some unknown reason were unloading. Up to 10:15, the specialists were standing by their guns, and for the most part they were buying and maintaining the market.

At 10.45 A.M., the stock prices began to nose down in earnest. Volume began increasing, and by 10:59 the average price of all stocks had reached the level of $39.17, a fall of 18¢ from the opening level of $39.35. The average price drop of the stocks which had been in action up to this time was even more alarming: they had fallen 29¢.

Specialists and floor traders, the insiders on the Exchange, were obviously getting nervous during this sharpest decline of the first hour. For the most part, they were selling, and selling fast—accounting for 30 per cent of the total sales which took place during this time, and only 15 per cent of the purchases. And for the most part, the public was buying.

This is a typical situation. The experts, the insiders, the

members are constantly doing exactly the opposite of what the public does. They know, at least, that stock market prices are created only by what the bulk of the stock traders are doing, that the prices are as ephemeral as a rainbow, and that each action creates an entirely different market picture from the one on which a decision to buy or sell is made. It is perhaps this quality above all that the outsider fails to recognize. He studies the tape, observes a set of prices, makes a decision to buy or sell. But the very act of his carrying through that decision changes the entire premise on which his decision is based. And if others are doing approximately the same thing he is doing, his order will meet an entirely different set of circumstances when it is executed on the floor.

From 11:00 to 11:30, the members of the club, their wives, dependents, and discretionary accounts (accounts which have been entrusted to professionals to handle as they see fit) began selling even more furiously, as the public gobbled up the opportunity.

And at exactly 11:16 A.M., the Dow-Jones average pierced the "resistance level" of 186.02, signifying to all those tutored and initiated into the Dow theory clan that a bear market, a falling market, was dead certain.

It is impossible to tell just how many of the Dow theorists stop to think that if they *believe* there will be a falling market, there is bound to *be* a falling market, simply because their beliefs are strong enough to make them sell, which in turn lowers the price and gluts the market with offerings from other members of their own cult. Their situation forms a picture of a mutual back-scratching society in which the members suddenly lose their fingernails.

Regardless of this, the breakthrough happened sharply at 11:16, and strangely enough, nothing immediately happened.

Up until 11:30, the insiders were the chief selling group, but the public didn't join in until after 11:30. One reason for the late public reaction was the fact that Dow-Jones didn't print the news that the industrial average was near its February low until 11:38, and it was not until 12:12 P.M. that the noon average of 184.24 was printed, nearly two points below the "resistance level."

In its massive and detailed study of this day at the market, the SEC reports that approximately 20 per cent of the public selling was affected by followers of the Dow theory, starting with the first sharp break, especially between 11:30 and 11:59 (after the insiders had the information) and from 12:30 to 1:14 (after the funeral parlors got the flash).

Interesting was the fact that the piercing of the Dow theory "resistance level" not only affected its devotees, but a great many other investors as well. These included those who held no brief whatever for the Dow theory itself, but surmised that a lot of stock owners were going to unload because of it, and consequently that the market was going to tumble. The sellers also included a great many stock owners who were worried by the general drop in the market, and who wanted to get out while the getting was good. In this way, the cumulative effect was to create a far greater landslide than the followers of the Dow theory alone provided.

All through the day, the average price of the 945 stocks traded on the exchange that day declined in the profile of a ski slope. From 10.00 A.M. to 11:00 A.M., the decline was mild enough, but from 11 A.M. to noon the drop went from $39.17 to $38.28. After a gentle downward slope from noon to 12:45 P.M., the slope dipped again, not giving the skiers a chance to catch their breaths until 2:00 P.M. The slope still ran down hill after that, closing at a low of $36.79—a drop of $2.56 per share. This meant that the total value of all stocks listed on the New York Stock Exchange dropped over three billion dollars in a single day. Although this was peanuts compared to the crash of 1962, this amount is roughly equal to the entire receipts of the U.S. government in 1934.

All this happened in an atmosphere of reasonable optimism. Just prior to this date, the investment advisors were singing a happy tune, while member firms of the stock exchange were joining in with them. The financial publications couldn't have been happier about the outlook. Between August 26 and September 3, exactly 146 broker-dealers came out with letters saying that the market was on the upswing and everything was rosy. Only six broker-dealers cautioned their customers about a possible bear market. Those profound and omniscient gentlemen known as investment advisors came out with a total of 61 letters, of which 54 told their clients *without qualification* that the market was going to be bullish.

After the day began rolling, a great many factors influenced the public in their stock maneuvering. By 10:15 A.M., 900 shares were sold because the traders felt the prices seemed to be declining. Others sold varying amounts of shares at that time because they needed money, they wanted to take a tax loss, and they felt the market was too high. A single broadcast by a radio commentator was directly responsible for ten different round lot sales by public traders during the day, totaling 6,200 shares. Other reasons given SEC investigators included the influence of the brokers, the suggestions of investment advisors, the advice of others, the foreign situation, the domestic situation, the summer price decline, the Dow theory, other chart systems, forced liquidation, and so forth.

But most significant is the fact that not a single seller of this particular group sold stock for anything that had anything to do with the prospects of the company involved. For all intents and purposes, the stock certificates might just as well have been lamb chops, Green Stamps, pine caskets, or jelly beans. What's more, a total of only 17,949 members of the public took part in this downhill ski contest, which caused a temporary paper loss of over three billion dollars to the nation's economy. This group is considerably less in number than the population of Ashtabula, Ohio. Their actions, however, flashing on the giant tote board of the Stock Exchange and piped out over the entire country, caused enough psychological palpitations during the day to last for a decade—and to affect millions of people.

On September 4, 1946, *The New York Times* reported

that stocks had nose-dived, that duPont had dropped 17 points, and that the sudden drop was lacking in visible cause.

"Wall Street could find no basic reasons for the assault on prices," the *Times* said. "Brokers had returned from the holiday weekend fairly confident that the sell-off of last week would find no immediate repetition. The scope of the decline, which left only thirty-two out of a total of 1,075 issues dealt in during the session on the higher side, was felt to be the result of something more than the intangibles present during the last three weeks. The mere fact that quotations for securities of the elite industrial organizations could crumble with such ease and without attracting any real support to stem the tide indicated to financial circles that developments not yet clear were in the making. . . ."

Arriving back in Washington on September 4 of that year, Secretary of the Treasury John W. Snyder was at a loss to explain the stock break. His remarks were confined to suggesting that a lot of people decided to have a "fresh look" at the market after returning from the Labor Day weekend. He emphasized that he thought that nothing in the international situation could have caused the trouble.

Snyder also remarked that he had talked with several experts, and that each expert gave him an entirely different set of reasons for the slump.

On Wall Street, the experts stumbled around trying to find some explanation. Emotionalism was one thing singled out, although this theory had little support generally. At that time, the Dow theory crowd got little attention from the press as a possible cause of the break. The public, in general, was taking a dim view of the over-all economic picture, as far as the long-term outlook was concerned. Sixty per cent of the respondents to a Gallup poll felt certain that there would be a major business crack-up within the next ten years. Only 20 per cent felt that a serious depression could be avoided, and 1951 was picked by the average respondent as the date for the crack-up. David Lawrence, writing about the market break of September 3, summed it up in a statement which should have received some kind of reward for oversimplification: "It is human nature to overlook the obvious, and that is why in America we have depressions."

It took the SEC nearly a year to make a detailed study of this red-letter day on the stock market. Every transaction, minute by minute, was traced on the New York Stock Exchange in an attempt to find out the causes of the collapse. The activities of public buyers, foreigners, banks, investment trusts, odd-lot dealers, member and nonmember firms (including their transactions for either the firm or individual accounts, and for their wives and dependents), floor traders, and specialists were compiled to create the most comprehensive picture of a day's market ever presented.

The findings indicated that there was no evidence of manipulation of the market which caused the stocks to skid. Pool, wash, or fake sales seemed to be entirely missing from the trading.

One observation made by the SEC seems to indicate that the "in" group on the floor of the Exchange has the information and the capacity to act quickly to take advantage of a trend before the public catches on and can get orders through to the floor before the picture changes. The stock market is at times like a crowded auditorium with insufficient exits. When someone yells "Fire!" the people nearest the door get out first. Regardless of how many safeguards are provided by Exchange regulations and the SEC to protect the public, the members are stationed nearest the exits, and have a distinct advantage over the general public.

There seems to be evidence of this advantage in the two major periods of sharp decline during that tumultuous day. When the first sharp drop began to hit, most of the members on the floor began selling, and selling fast. All through the early stages of the drop, the "ins" were selling and the "outs" were buying. By the time the public sniffed the trend, the positions immediately reversed, and the "outs" sold while the "ins" bought. The same activity took place in the second sharp break of the day. The pros, it seems, always work against the crowd.

In spite of the painstaking work done by the SEC to attempt to trace the *raison d'être* of the break, the official announcement of the study states: "[The report] . . . reaches no conclusions." And the SEC goes on to say: "As refined as the study is it does not, in our view, afford a basis for any assured generalization about the effect of trading by any group on either the whole character of the September 3 market, or its character at any given period of the day."

This statement is worth study.

If, through the expenditure of so much talent, experience, and energy, the SEC cannot come up with any specific conclusions, how can the occasional investor—the man off-the-street, so to speak—expect to come out any better than if he played every horse at Aqueduct across the board?

The nearest thing to a conclusion the SEC was able to reach was the fact that the devout followers of the Dow theory threw the market into a cocked hat when the Dow-Jones average punctured the "resistance level." But, it wasn't only the followers of the theory who took action at this point. It was those who knew that the Dowists were going to unload, and who thought *they* had to unload because the market was sure to fall. The pushing and the crowding at the fire exits at times like these   and other times—gives an objective observer of all this maelstrom cause to stop and think, study, examine, reflect, and wonder just what all this is accomplishing for the economic health of the country.

In 1961, 15 years after the 1946 debacle, the Dow theorists are still having at it. "STOCK BOOM COMING IN THE NEXT 30 DAYS?" a two-column advertisement by an institution known as Dow Theory Forecasts asked. Then it went on to say:

"Is there another stock boom ahead . . . one that will see prices go up and up and up? Or is this a temporary rally, with declining prices to follow . . . the famous Dow Theory has been calling the major stock market turns for over 60 years . . . Once again the time for action approaches! Will you get the word in time? . . ."

The ad goes on to report what the company has done for

its subscribers—and what it can do for YOU.

Let's assume for a moment that every stock buyer decided to subscribe to this service. Let's also assume that this army of new subscribers followed religiously the suggestions offered by the service. Moving in tidal concert, everybody would immediately decide either to sell at one time or buy at one time. Result: Total chaos.

There is no mention in the 1961 advertisement of Dow Theory Forecasts that the SEC indicated in its report that the Dow Theory sellout might well have been the largest single contributing *cause* of the 1946 crumble. No mention that throughout its history, the Dow theory has been wrong the same number of times it has been right. No mention that if stock prices go "up and up and up," they've got to stop somewhere.

The automatic scoreboard furnished daily by the Stock Exchange helps make this giant sweepstakes possible and encourages people to join the lottery, if only for the kicks it gives them. But as far as fostering a stable economy where venture and stable investment capital can contribute to a better life, there are some penetrating questions which can be asked.

There is no doubt whatever about the extension of stock ownership being the most important step in the development of an enlightened and dynamic capitalism. That some people should own more stock is the best answer to Left Wingers, and to that segment of labor unions which is unscrupulous and machine-run, and those who would demand that the government establish a free-lunch, free-handout policy.

There is also no doubt about the desirability of having liquid stocks which can be converted into cash when the need arises.

There is no doubt about the desirability of maintaining a free market in securities, with as little arbitrary government interference as possible.

There is little question that the New York Stock Exchange is a desirable catalyst to the economy, provided its dominance is kept in check enough to prevent millions of untutored speculators from facing east every morning at 10:00 A.M., eastern time, and bowing low on their stock certificate prayer rugs. It might be a stimulating link, if its tendency to create stampedes to the fire exits could be checked. It might be a regenerative link, if it could inspire mass motivation to save intelligently, and could help new industry to get on its feet and established industry to produce profitably at fair prices.

But many of these desirable ends are difficult to achieve. Would, for instance, the three-billion-dollar loss on September 3, 1946, or the greater drop in 1962 have occurred if the constant quotations on the chattering ticker tape circulating throughout the country, flashing all kinds of signals to all kinds of people, were less dominating and influential in the investor's psyche? Does it make sense that a group of Dow lovers, working on stock charts as if they were Ouija boards, racing forms, or astrology charts, should start a stampede to cause such a gargantuan loss? What possible economic health are these people creating? Does sitting in a funeral parlor for the sole purpose of speculating and watching an endless flow of figures go by add anything to the stature of the country? To its art, its science, its beauty, its progress, its spirit? Such an occupation is not only unproductive and noncreative; it is downright destructive when a loss like this occurs. What's more, the motivation engendered by such an attitude can be nothing but degrading both to the individual and the economy as well. Does it seem sensible that the 17,000 people who traded that day in 1946, and who could fill barely one-third of the seats in Yankee Stadium, could have such a far-reaching influence?

Every business day in the year, millions of people—stockholders or not—scan the high-low-last-and-net change on the financial pages with something which amounts to a mass obsessional neurosis. There are unfortunately no major and profound psychological studies of the stock mania which seizes the best of the people when they least expect it, yet the chances are that Wall Street paranoia would not set in so heavily if the constant advertising of losses and gains on the ticker tape were not so persistent.

The average investor might have a more tranquil, happier life if the score-board conditions of the current scene were not so violently prominent. With minute, hour, and daily tabulations constantly rolling out of the mill, the temptation to follow them is almost impossible to resist.

The figures on the financial page, which look so neat, so methodical, so clear, and so definite, fail to suggest much of the motivation which caused them to be what they are. Far from being bookkeeper's figures on stable items, they represent a gamut of emotions, often fiery ones based on rumor, hunches, hot tips, and misinformation, which create greed, fear, envy, and despair.

A good, healthy gambling instinct in most of us can't be avoided. But must it be so accentuated when it comes to the heart and pulse of the nation's economy? Would it not be better for those who can't resist the instinct to concentrate their efforts in the office baseball pool or the races? Losses here might be damaging to the individuals involved, but they would not cause panic, anxiety, and uncertainty when it comes to the life blood of the companies which provide most people with the way of making a living.

The New York Stock Exchange, of course, does not create this condition, nor does it urge gambling and speculation. But by its very force-in-being, it stimulates emotional action and psychological pressures which the public itself generates and carries to absurd proportions.

If an average couple were paying off the mortgage on their $20,000 home, and discovered that it was on a daily quotation sheet, their sleep might be fitful, and their outlook jaundiced.

Suppose, for instance, that a young householder picked up the paper some morning, and read this fictional listing in the financial section:

Range		*(000 omitted)*		*(000 omitted)*			
High	*Low*	*Property*	*First*	*High*	*Low*	*Last*	*Net Change*
21½	14½	24 Dover St.	20	24	12	12	—12

The chances are that his scrambled eggs would stick to the roof of his mouth. He might be stuck by firm contract with his house, for which he had paid $20,000. For no apparent reason, the value had slumped down to $12,000 by the end of the day's market. For months, we'll assume, the value had been holding steady. Maybe down ¼ one day . . . up ½ the next, but no major vacillation. Now he discovers that his house is worth about half of what he paid for it. On his way to work that day, he goes through a red light and gets a ticket; he gives his secretary holy hell, can't keep his lunch down, and comes home and gives his kids a sound thrashing with his mortgage papers. All because this imaginary Real Estate Exchange we've created has seen fit to publish the ephemeral values of the day about his house.

If homes all over the country were listed like this on a daily basis, the family hearthside would turn into a hotbed of acrimony. Certainly, real-estate values fluctuate, and people do lose money in the real-estate market. But they are not constantly being reminded of it, and they are not under steamy psychological pressure hourly and daily about it.

Yet this is the frame of reference the Stock Exchange sets up for all those who want to buy the listed securities it handles. Psychologically, it is a wonder that more September 3, 1946, or May 28, 1962, incidents don't happen. The id, the ego, and the superego are extremely sensitive to those factors which affect pride, survival, and lust. When securities are purchased, they have a direct bearing on all three impulses. When a chosen stock goes up, it can create magnificent delusions of grandeur. When it goes down, it can create delusions of persecution, deep floating anxieties, and a dozen other syndromes which don't exactly make for a jolly, adjusted individual.

Since the daily listings of the New York Stock Exchange

dominate the scene (the American Exchange, the over-the-counter market, and the local exchanges are large in total, but have nowhere near the effect on the mass psyche), its own psychological make-up is of vast importance to the millions of people it influences. And how would a psychiatrist diagnose this rumbling giant? One quick look at the patient's chart over the years would quickly establish the Exchange as suffering from the acute form of manic-depressive pathology. The evidence is unmistakable. But what's the cure?

To get at the cure, you must get at the cause, the roots, and determine the etiology of this monster. And when you do this, you find at the base of the pathology all the causes of psychoneurotic behavior of millions of individuals the monster digests to keep alive: frustration, emotional immaturity, anger, anxiety, *angst,* fear, insecurity, lust, and guilt. In other words, the Stock Exchange is a giant mirror held up to its participants, and their manic-depressive pattern is its own. The positive impulses of the ego and superego are conspicuously lacking: love, loyalty, and unselfishness. They have no place in the speculator's language, as long as he's on that particular subject.

Because the Stock Exchange is a mirror, it cannot exactly be blamed for reflecting the true image of those who peer into it. This does not mean to suggest that those who do look into this influential mirror are all emotionally immature, anxious, and lustful, by any means. But it does suggest that *at the time they are involved with the operation,* these impulses are brought to the foreground and exaggerated.

Since the Stock Exchange is a manic-depressive neurotic, created by negative emotions, its daily influence in the press can be anything but comforting. Yet it remains there in a prominent spotlight, a monument to instability. If it could perform its function of providing a stable market and adequate liquidity for the trading of stock without inducing the not infrequent mass mania, it would be serving an extremely useful purpose. But because of its very make-up, it is unable to do this. As an essential link in the chain of the nation's business life, it becomes a very weak one.

Aiding and abetting the neurotic (and nonessential) palpitations of the Stock Exchange is the flood of books recently swamping the public, showing everyone from Brownie Scouts to octogenerians how to make an unbelievable fortune in the stock market.

One look at the titles is enough to create a severe attack of fiscal indigestion. Nicholas Darvas, the dancer-wizard, offers his *How I Made $2,000,000 in the Stock Market* as a tempting bait for thousands of people who have been inspired to think that they can do as well. On the cover of the paperback edition, you read, "The Book That Shook the Financial World! . . . The Book They Tried to Suppress! . . . The Book That May Change Your Future!"

The list goes on. The back cover of Louis Engel's *How to Buy Stocks* claims that the book "tells you all you need to know to invest successfully in the stock market . . ." It reminds you that you don't need to be rich or live in a big city to invest in stocks and bonds—and reminds you that ANYONE CAN DO IT ANYWHERE!

Making Profits in the Stock Market, by Jacob A. Kamm, flaunts Dr. Kamm's "FOUR SURE FIRE METHODS OF MAKING PROFITS IN THE STOCK MARKET" in front of the thirsty neophyte whose appetite has been on the rise, as it was back in 1929. And the book throws in a full section on "What Every Woman Should Know About Stocks," as if sex made some kind of mystical difference.

Kiplinger and his staff join the parade with *Your Guide to a Higher Income,* and his paperback edition is so set typographically that the title appears to be "Make More Money in the Boom Years Ahead."

"Don't stand by," screams the back cover, "shackled by uncertainty, while others, with no more resources than you have get ahead and make more money."

In the background, ready to handle the appetites of readers of such books, is the New York Stock Exchange. Without trying to, or even meaning to, it stimulates by its daily tabulations the illusion that millions of people can get rich quick without working for it, without producing anything, without creating anything, without contributing anything. As the leader and the symbol of the entire stock market, its influence is felt everywhere—not only in its desirable functions, but in its mania-producing function as well.

Wall Street is bounded on the west by Trinity Church, on the east by the East River, by frenzy on the north, and by hysteria on the south. A casual visitor to the New York Stock Exchange Building at 11 Wall Street finds that he has to go around the corner to the visitor's entrance, where he will be greeted cordially by a tall, willowy blonde, who will act as his guide in a group of about 40 other onlookers as they dutifully follow her out onto the balcony which overlooks the trading floor. Here the guide picks up a hand microphone and proceeds to detail the procedures which enable the elite companies of American industry to keep their stocks in constant view of the public.

In spite of the running commentary so earnestly articulated by the girl guide, the picture on the floor is confusing. To the left and right are giant annunciator boards, where continually flapping metal plates are signaling floor brokers by number. Along with the buzz and constant ripple of the voices on the floor, the metal flappers contribute a steady sound similar to that of a wet mop hitting a tin roof.

One anonymous latter-day Samuel Pepys described the scene from the balcony in this way:

". . . & thence to the Stock Exchange, where I did witness all manner of behavior, of men of seasoned years indeed but acting in concert with the actions and strange movements most ascribed to small boys upon the cobblestones engaged in fanciful play. Upon this floor the fortunes of many men have been made and lost, but such bedlam and confusion so reigned upon my witness that I felt sore aggrieved that this were so. If progress has it thus I would forsooth return to older tymes, where man's good fortune or his ruin rest on more sobriety, and his failure, if it comes, arrives in wraps of dignity . . ."

It is not that the Stock Exchange is lacking in attempts at dignity. If anything, the temper of the offices off the floor tend toward that stuffiness which arrives with any institution when it becomes The Authority in its given field. Gradually, the warehouse becomes a temple, and a certain amount of worship is required.

In addition to being a pathological manic-depressive case, the Stock Exchange is also schizophrenic. Its violently split personality is reflected in the pontifical tones of its public statements, and its literature tries to say, in its schizophrenic way: "You, too, can be a millionaire—but of course you must be a gentleman while you are doing so." Constantly, its publications must at once persuade the little fellow to risk his money—but at the same time must warn him that it's dangerous. It must try to create endless, growing sales and commissions for its brokers, and at the same time must try to keep in check the easily stirred passion for getting rich which characterizes everybody from an orthodontist to a crane operator.

The position of the Public Relations department of the Stock Exchange puts it into a spot where it must rationalize as much as it must reason, and as a result the phrases of the public statements and booklets pouring out of the Stock Exchange constantly border on doubletalk.

The titles of the booklets use all the organ stops of the skilled pamphleteer: THEY WERE SURPRISED WHEN I TOLD THEM I'D INVESTED THROUGH M. I. P., WE'RE PUTTING PART OF OUR PAYCHECK IN STOCK EVERY MONTH, DOES IT MAKE SENSE FOR ME TO BUY STOCKS, and HOW TO INVEST FOR GROWING INCOME AND FAMILY SECURITY are just a few of the titles which paint a rosy, tempting picture for the neophyte investor.

What's more, most of the booklets point out (while skillfully underplaying) the dangers of investment, and that you can lose money as well as make it. There is, in addition, a lack of honesty in facing the motives which make a large segment of people play the stock market. Nowhere in the Stock Exchange literature is the fact revealed that a lot of people in a lot of places are out to make a fast buck without working for it.

Its publications also tend toward unrealistic assumptions.

Ostensibly, the Stock Exchange is trying to encourage investment on the part of lower-income groups, yet in one advertisement in the *Reader's Digest* it listed several case histories of "four successful shareowners and how they grew." One of them was Mrs. G., a 54-year-old widow who earns $75.00 a week, and managed to buy $15,000 worth of stocks out of her husband's insurance money. The stock has now grown in value to $20,000, and she received $855.56 in dividends from them. But how many people have $15,000 clear and free to invest in stocks? There are no exact figures available, but the number is small. Dr. M., a physician with an income of about $30,000 a year, is another case history offered by the Stock Exchange in its ad. He has been able to put $120,000 into common stocks, which is an uncommonly large and hefty savings figure, unmatched by thousands of eminently successful people.

Although the Stock Exchange reflects daily the volatile and somewhat chaotic urges of investors and speculators, there is little doubt about its being the height of respectability in most of its operations. A floor member's own special morality is impeccable when it comes to keeping his word on a deal. In few other places can hundreds and thousands of dollars change hands without so much as a handshake to seal the deal. A member might be shallow, narrow, confined, unthinking, opportunistic, and lacking in social conscience, but his word is as good as his bond, and he wouldn't stay in business another day if it weren't.

In addition, the regulations of the New York Stock Exchange are as stiff as or stiffer than those of any similar institution in the country. They far exceed the regulations of the SEC in severity, and the buyer of a listed stock can count on its being thoroughly checked out before it's allowed on the ticker tape. Member firms are regularly checked by surprise audits, and the specialist faces regular periodic examinations in his routine.

But wherever there are people involved in sensitive areas, there are anomalies. The literature of the New York Stock

Exchange would lead you to believe that the stock market is entirely and totally free of the previous dangers of the past. It isn't. It would have you believe that it is impossible to circumvent its elaborate rules and regulations for self-policing. It is possible. It would have you believe that the small stockholder is growing in such strength and numbers that a democratic capitalism is a growing reality. It isn't. It would have you believe that the speculation which had such a rapid growth in recent years is not gambling. It is. It would have you believe that there is no manipulation in the market any more. There is. It would have you believe that the New York Stock Exchange is a major force in helping the underwriter create new American industry. It isn't. It would have you believe that stock prices rely solely on the laws of supply and demand. They don't. It would have you believe that the Stock Exchange cordially helped the SEC usher in a new era in American finance. It didn't. It would have you believe that its Board of Governors, which represents the most important single force in the securities market, is totally above reproach. Yet on February 28, 1962, the Chairman of the Board of Governors of the New York Stock Exchange was indicted for major income tax fraud and evasion. And while this does not reflect directly on the operation of the Exchange itself, its implications are severe. When the top man of the top symbol of the financial world is so indicted, the question is bound to be asked, what kind of institution is this.

The position that the Stock Exchange finds itself in demands not only leadership, but vision and imagination. It demands a sharp understanding of the mass psychological pressures its machinery produces, and bold new thinking to create the spread of capitalism, instead of the narrowing of it. The meeting of this challenge is the most important single economic job the country faces. To date, the Stock Exchange has armed itself with little more than worn-out clichés to carry out the battle.

Bill Richards had arrived at that exciting point where he had his own company affairs in order. He was ready to branch out and put some money to work in other businesses.

Bill's "company" consisted of wife Grace, and three youngsters as personnel; a ranch house and all that goes with it (TV set, whole and busted bikes, jungle gym, well-used furniture) and a two-year old car. His financial resources included GI and other insurance, a couple of thousand dollars in the bank, a steady income as manager of a local super market. At the same time he had certain liabilities: A mortgage that was pretty well in hand, and about a hundred dollars due next month on department store charge accounts.

Bill was happy enough with his job, but just the same he had ideas about other things: Aircraft, chemistry, and business generally tracing back to his Dad's work at the bank.

Now was as good a time as any, Bill figured, to see if those interests couldn't be picked up again —maybe profitably—with some of his investable money.

—From the New York Stock Exchange booklet
THE RICHARDS' BIGGEST DAY

CHAPTER II

This little portrait, drawn by the New York Stock Exchange (Leaflet Division), is designed to whet the appetite of the Average Man on the Street for buying the listed securities of the Exchange, so that his life will be enriched, his future secure, and his family purring like contented kittens.

Assuming that such a family as Bill and Grace Richards ever did exist, the situation bears a little more scrutiny than the Stock Exchange gives it—busted bikes, jungle gym, and all.

In the atmosphere of today's inflated prices for goods and services, sometimes rigged in conspiratorial industry meetings, the premise that Bill and Grace have ever reached the stage suggested by the tract is highly questionable. A great many families of Bill's and Grace's stamp are skating on the thin edge of heavy debt, wondering where to dig up the next Sears, Roebuck monthly payment, and staggered by the fact that their 1952 Dodge is on its last legs. That well-used furniture so warmly referred to by the Stock Exchange copywriter is probably in similar shape to the copywriter's own: more obsolete than obsolescent. Two days before pay day, the Bills and the Graces have not infrequently wondered whether to charge some vitally needed wonder drugs and face the embarrassing suggestion from the local druggist that perhaps it might be better to pay up the three-month-old bill there first.

The Stock Exchange's glowing report might also have taken cognizance of the fact that just about 1½ per cent of the adult population in the country owns approximately 80 per cent of the corporate stock, as we'll see later, and that little leaflets painting a glowing picture of a nonexistent family can do practically nothing to allay this condition. The Richards family is lucky if it has a couple of hundred dollars left over at the end of the year, which, if invested in stock, might bring in enough on an investment basis to buy a carton or two of cigarettes. If invested in a speculative stock, it could very easily mean little more than pouring the money down the drain.

But most important is the fact that Bill Richards is contemplating putting too large a proportion of his money, small as it may be, into a piece of financial machinery which is at the mercy of unpredictable tides, often affected by perfectly legitimate maneuvers of insiders who know how to do exactly the opposite of what the public does—at the public's eventual expense. All of this, the pontifical works of the Stock Exchange fail to point out.

As a matter of fact, the Exchange often finds itself in the odd position of neutralizing its own words. In April of 1961 Keith Funston issued a sharp warning to the public about reckless investment, while his Leaflet Division continued to pour out its steady stream of booklets urging the small investor to get aboard the bandwagon.

"One night after the youngsters had left the TV for bed," the Bill and Grace fable of the Stock Exchange continues, "Bill talked it over with Grace. They agreed that, with careful management, they could maintain their insurance and a suitable savings account and still put $1,000 a year into common stock."

The leaflet does not explain how many families find themselves in this position, or look under the corner of the Richards' rug to see if this isn't stretching this idyllic picture a little too far.

As a manager of a local supermarket, Bill's income, according to one state's employment-office estimates, would run in the vicinity of $8,000 per year. For a large portion of the country, this figure would be high. But assuming that Bill has reached this point, a look into his theoretical budget reveals some interesting things.

In the geographical area where Bill might command as large a salary as $8,000, he's lucky if he can find a respectable home with carrying charges as low as $100 a month, but we're going to take the liberty of assuming that he's found one. Since he is subject to transfer to another area any time, we'll assume he's not going to have to sell the house at a loss, although this would remain a distinct possibility. We also won't question just how Bill was able to accumulate enough money to put a substantial down payment on the house he is living in, supposing that he has a G.I. loan or a benevolent father-in-law—two factors which not everybody can count on.

On the basis of a typical, actual family budget unearthed by Kiplinger's *Changing Times* (April, 1961), we could set up a rough hypothetical budget for Bill and Grace like this:

SHELTER	$1,200
FOOD	1,200
CLOTHES	500
MEDICAL	240
RECREATION	160
PERSONAL	240
HOUSEHOLD EQUIPMENT	560
CAR	1,000
INSURANCE	400
CONTRIBUTIONS	200
TAXES	1,200
EVERYTHING ELSE	800
	$7,700

According to these figures, there remains a balance of $300 which, if not dissipated in the innumerable crises which every family faces every year, could easily be (a) absorbed in increased insurance, (b) saved for education, (c) providing a slightly more restful vacation than $160 per year will allow, (d) put directly into a savings account against a future emergency. In fact, the chance that Bill and Grace could have any luck whatever in setting aside $1,000 a year for the "investment in America's industrial growth" looks very slim indeed. As a matter of fact, neither the Stock Exchange nor the most callous broker would recommend their taking a flyer at the stock market under these conditions. Two of the most important things in the world are ignored in the budget: books and education. The insurance is far from adequate. And $300 per year savings is not nearly enough protection.

Any way you figure it, you're likely to get the some sort of picture. A booklet called *Facts for Bargaining,* issued by one of the leading unions in March of 1961, shows how a family of four has a rough go making ends meet on a salary of $9,815.63. Reducing these estimates considerably, and rounding out the figures, the Richards family could come up with an alternative budget looking something like this:

FOOD	$2,300
BEVERAGES (ALCOHOLIC)	80
HOUSING	1,200
HOUSEHOLD OPERATIONS	300
FURNITURE	400
CLOTHING	700
TRANSPORTATION	1,000
MEDICAL	600
RECREATION	400
PERSONAL	150
CIGARETTES	100
BOOKS	50
EDUCATION	50
CONTRIBUTIONS	100
OTHER	50
	7,480
TAXES	1,200
	$8,680
DEFICIT	$680

While this budget is a little more liberal, it fails completely to provide anything whatever for insurance, which could easily carry the deficit to over $1,000 per year. In case the alcoholic beverage allowance should cause any fear that Bill and Grace are swinging every week in riotous living, or even sitting down before dinner every night for a quiet martini, it's important to remember that their $80 liquor allowance would allow them ¾ of an ounce each evening—provided they made sure to hide the bottle any time a guest arrived. Just how Bill and Grace could sit down among the busted bikes and jungle gym to take a plunge in the market —even a conservative one—under these conditions is a little hard to fathom. But the Stock Exchange cheerfully sets up the picture without bothering to explain it.

The tragic part of the alluring enticements the Stock

Exchange pours out is that there is serious question that enough people who make *double* what Bill and Grace are making can afford to invest in stocks and in that glowing, rosy picture of America's industrial growth which the Exchange literature paints for us in Technicolor.

For instance, the family which Kiplinger's *Changing Times* analyzes for us consists of the very real Marjorie and Walt Patterson, both of whom happen to be certified public accountants, and who know whereof they speak when it comes to budgets. They have made a hobby out of their family financial records, and have kept them religiously for thirteen full years.

"The net result," says the article, "is that in 13 years, $153,805 in cold cash was earned, and at the end of the period the Pattersons were exactly $1,082 *in the hole.*"

Although they have no big debts, they have no savings account whatever (a must, according to the Stock Exchange, before you invest), yet their income for 1960 was a whopping $18,510. Walt carries $60,000 insurance (another Stock Exchange must before buying securities), but he doesn't think this is nearly enough. The fact remains that there are millions of Walt and Marjorie Pattersons, millions more of Bill and Grace Richards, all facing the same problems, and all unable to invest in the future—even though they may have a strong desire to do so.

On another scale is the family with an even larger income, who must, by reason of position, keep up a front beyond its means in order to exist in the treadmill the high-earning job demands. They face the same problem their lower-income brothers do, and the possibilities of their buying a solid growth stock for future security remains just as remote.

A gentleman we shall call Richard Williams (Bill Richards, backwards) is forced by the nature of his job as a Madison Avenue account executive to keep up a fairly high front, even though he doesn't particularly want to. He has threatened several times to quit the rat race, but every time he thinks it over he finds his fixed commitments so high it's impossible for him to do so. He and his family (two of his kids are in college) do not live riotously, but they live well. They are forced to do considerable entertaining, both in and out of the home, and this runs as high as $50.00 a month. They do not go to night clubs, take long vacation trips, or drink much more than a couple of martinis before dinner. His budget, in the terms of the others we've looked at, runs something like this:

RENT	$3,600
FOOD	3,000
CLOTHES	1,000
MEDICAL	750
RECREATION	1,500
PERSONAL	1,000
HOUSEHOLD EQUIPMENT	750
CAR (TWO)	2,000
INSURANCE	600
CONTRIBUTIONS	1,500
TAXES	6,000
OTHER	1,200
	$22,900

But this isn't all. Because of the requirements of their position, they have added expenses which run like this:

ENTERTAINMENT	$ 600
MAID	1,000
THEATRE (12 SHOWS)	500
BOOKS	200
COMMUTING	600
STATE COLLEGE (2)	2,000
	$4,900

Adding this to the basic budget above, Richard Williams comes up with a total budget of $27,800. And the problem with this figure is that Williams makes exactly $25,000 a year. He has nothing in his savings account, and the checking account scrapes bottom periodically. He can no more sit down after the kids have turned off television and think about investing than the kids themselves can. And there are far more

Richard Williamses in the country than the Stock Exchange likes to admit. His salary is over three times that of Bill Richards.

It's of course economically desirable for stock ownership in the country to be broadened. In fact, it's almost an urgent necessity, to prevent the alarming concentration of the means of production which is taking place and increasing by logarithms. The Stock Exchange is proud to point out that one out of every eight adults is now a shareowner, and that nearly 13,000,000 Americans own shares of stock as of 1959. But it fails to register its comment on the fact that the principal concentration of corporate-stock ownership still remains in a fraction of the population. If 39 million households in the country owned one share of stock each, and one household owned 39 million shares, it could be argued statistically that 97 per cent of the homes in the country were shareowners— but it would present a distorted picture just as the current Stock Exchange survey does today. The problems of Bill and Grace Richards trying to break into the stock ownership picture are many.

According to the Stock Exchange flyers, which are issued like confetti on every conceivable aspect of the Exchange operation, adequate savings and insurance are so necessary before a common-stock investment can be considered that it is unthinkable for anyone to come into the market without this obligation being fulfilled.

Yet the Institute of Life Insurance and the National Association of Mutual Savings Banks are of the firm opinion that the average household in the country has neither adequate savings nor adequate insurance for ordinary day-to-day living.

The ideal figure for life insurance coverage has been set at four to five times the annual income of the family involved. At the present time, the average family carries enough for about a year and a half—or not even half of what the ideal figure should be. And while 94 per cent of families with incomes of $10,000 or over are insured, only 52 per cent of those with incomes under $3,000 carry insurance. Again, the problem remains of broadening the base of insurance ownership so that eventually stock ownership can be broadened. Otherwise there is no chance for a genuine democratic capitalism to grow. But this can't be achieved by writing pamphlets about Bill and Grace Richards. One government agency recommended that an ideal allocation for insurance premiums would be 10 per cent of the gross family income. Since the average disposable income for each family in 1961 totaled a little over $7,000 per year, insurance payments should, under this yardstick, come to $620. Institute of Life Insurance figures, however, show that the family in this average bracket is putting out only $165, or barely 25 per cent of the desirable amount. Bill and Grace Richards, on one of their hypothetical budgets, would be slightly better off: they would be carrying 50 per cent of the ideal amount of insurance—but still not eligible under the Stock Exchange recommendation of "adequate insurance." On the other budget, they would have none, and would ostensibly be booted out of a broker's office if they tried to buy stock.

The general savings picture throughout the country tells roughly the same story. Although it's highly debatable what the ideal reserve in a savings bank should be, many conservative estimates indicate that an average family should have enough in reserve to tide them over three or four months if an emergency should strike. In June of 1961, Department of Commerce figures show that personal savings ran about 24 billion dollars, but at the same time, consumer credit was running about 55 billion dollars—or nearly twice as high.

Under these conditions, it's a little difficult to discern to whom the Exchange is addressing its little booklet *The Richards' Biggest Day*.

But the booklet gets right down to specifics, as it carries its story along:

"You can buy as many shares as you can afford right now," Bill and Grace are told by a friendly Mr. Foster, who is the mythical broker conjured up by the Stock Exchange for this story, "or you can budget your purchases periodically through a Monthly Investment Plan—on a pay-as-you-go basis."

The friendly Mr. Foster then goes on to explain that Bill will be "dollar cost averaging" (his regular payments would buy more stock when the price of the stock is down; less when the stock is higher) through the Monthly Investment Plan.

If you should walk into a dozen different brokerage houses, all certified members of the New York Stock Exchange, and ask them about the MIP, you're likely to get at best a halfhearted shrug and the suggestion that you'd be better off waiting until you can put a big chunk down on stock. The reason: the brokerage fees are so much higher on the Monthly Investment Plan that the small investor who tries this is going to pay through the nose—and in some cases actually lose money. Again the Leaflet Division (our term) of the Exchange carefully dodges this question in all of its glowing literature. *We're Putting Part of Our Paycheck in Stock Every Month* is the title of one of its tracts, which goes on to say:

"We never knew it was so easy to own a share of American Business. Like many people we figured we had to have quite a bit of money to be able to own stock. Then we heard about the Monthly Investment Plan which is sponsored by member firms of the New York Stock Exchange. We found this plan a simple, convenient way to invest on a budget, and that maybe it might even help us send the children to college or retire some day. . . . The more the broker told us, the better we liked the idea."

But a sampling of brokers' comments about the MIP realistically ran like this when we approached them directly for information:

"Well, I'll tell you—I think you might as well forget that idea, and try to get enough together before you take the plunge. Sure—you get a little advantage on dollar cost averaging, but we've got to charge pretty much to handle your money, and you're going to lose out in the end."

Or: "Look—forget about dividends and return on your money. Forget about this MIP crap. Buy yourself a good growth stock and stick with it—but buy it outright."

Or: "You see, sir, the cost of handling MIP accounts runs very high, and I'd rather see you avoid it it you can."

Or: "Tell you what we'll do. Send your money in regularly, and we'll keep it for you until you accumulate enough to buy a decent amount of stock. In that way, you'll duck some of these high charges."

While the Stock Exchange suggests that you can invest as little as $40 a month, a quick look at one of their own tables tells the bitter story. For $40 you are credited with $37.74 worth of stock, and stuck with a fat 6 per cent commission of $2.26. The same commission applies all the way up to $100, where you receive $94.34 worth of stock for your $5.66 commission. Compare this to the commission on a $1,000 purchase: 1.5 per cent. In other words, the small, struggling investor—the one who needs the biggest break possible in order to participate in the capitalistic structure—gets stuck for the biggest chunk of his hard-earned dollars, paying exactly four times as much for the privilege.

Martin Mayer, in his book *Wall Street: Men and Money*, points out that if a small investor put $100 a month for 12 months into the Monthly Investment Plan, he would pay a brokers commission of $67.92.

If he bought the stock in one lump, he would merely pay $14.85. In other words, Bill and Grace and anyone else would put out $53.07 the first year for the questionable privilege of joining the MIP. What's more, Mayer points out, even if the stock went up 15 per cent at the end of the first year, Bill and Grace would own stock worth less than the cash they put in! And if, by some miracle, they found a stock which paid a 6 per cent dividend, they would have to be in the plan for two and a half years before the dividends caught up with the commissions.

If the MIP is the Stock Exchange's answer to the challenge of helping more Americans become part of the great democratic process which made it strong, it would seem that the Exchange is in need of an agonizing reappraisal.

The problem of dividends catching up with commissions becomes even more startling when you examine the list of the "50 Stocks Most Popular with Investors Using the MIP."

If Bill and Grace went into the MIP on the 12th of September, 1961, and bought Minnesota Mining, RCA, Brunswick, or Minneapolis Honeywell they would have been faced with yields of 0.8, 1.7, 0.6, and 1.4 per cent respectively. On the basis of these yields it would take years before their dividends caught up with their commissions. Since then, a sharp adjustment has taken place in yields because of the 1962 market break. But the change has been made at the expense of the investor's equity.

On the other hand, if Bill and Grace decided to put their entire $1,000 into Minneapolis Honeywell in a lump, avoiding the expensive and creaky machinery of the MIP, they would receive as a reward for their money a little less than 7 shares at $146 per share, and a handsome yield of 1.4, or about $14.00 for their risk and trouble. This would buy them about two bottles of medium quality Scotch, which they could sip and wonder why they can't get ahead in today's economy, where prosperity is supposed to be ringing everywhere. These are admittedly "growth" stocks, but the earnings needed to bring a decent return in some cases might not be forthcoming until another generation. And the possibility of forced selling at a loss in the case of some emergency creates the question whether the return is worth the risk in Bill's and Grace's position.

In spite of the crashing popularity of the stock market in recent years, the yields on the bluest of the blue chips have been slim, as they have been even on the yeasty, more speculative stocks. From the point of view of straight return on your money, the savings bank returns of anywhere from $3\frac{1}{2}$ per cent to $4\frac{1}{4}$ per cent are far superior, and your money is safe. This of course doesn't take into consideration the "growth" factor, which is what everybody had been buying with a kind of obsessional passion. This ungentlemanly passion, of course, is what forces up the prices of stock to the point where the yields diminish, and dividends become almost meaningless.

To the trader, stocks with low yields mean something, because he makes money on fluctuations, short selling, and in-and-out speculation. To the long-term owner who has held these stocks for many years, over-priced stocks represent excellent profits, because he has bought them low, and his yields are far in excess of the current yields, to say nothing of the paper profits he has made by holding on to the stocks for a long time. But to the newcomers with small budgets (if indeed there is any surplus at all) like Bill and Grace Richards, it means they are buying into an extremely expensive market, often too late to get a decent return, and too early to count on immediate growth.

There are many stocks, of course, which offer higher yields. But the growth possibilities are usually low, or the risk of loss is greater, especially to a family with this kind of budget.

The "disposable personal income" in the country is supposed to be that which is left over after taxes, or in other words, the amount which the families and individuals in the country have left to live on. In June of 1961, the personal income totaled $413.2 billion, and after taxes there remained $361.8 billion to spend. Personal saving throughout the country on the same date totaled $25.2 billion, and it is from this amount that future stock owners can become integral parts of the American industrial scene. In addition to being sharply offset by consumer debt figures, there are other hurdles which prevent the genuinely adequate spread of a sound people's capitalism.

Dr. Simon Kuznets, of the National Bureau of Economic Research, in his report *Capital in the American Economy* in late 1961, indicates that it is the limited availability of savings in the country which is preventing capital growth. He sees no shortage of investment opportunity.

He insists that "unless in the next few years the private sector can generate savings and capital formation in a greater proportion to a rising private produce," inflation is bound to continue.

Dr. Kuznets, a conservative economist, finds that the supply of voluntary savings is not adequate for the job, and that inflation is chopping down the savings needed for capital formation. "This is a specter of intolerable consequences," he says.

The total amount of personal saving in the country means little toward extending stock ownership, if these savings are concentrated in a small number of households. From another report of the National Bureau of Economic Research by Raymond W. Goldsmith (*Savings in the U.S., III*), we find that 50 per cent of those saving $2,000 or more in 1949 were held by spending units whose total assets were $60,000 and over. Another 22 per cent of the savings was accounted for by spending units with assets of $25,000 to $60,000. In other words, very few families in the country are able to boast of savings of $2,000 or more, and very few families can afford to buy any significant amount of stock unless they have at least this much on hand for protection. None of these figures come from any irresponsible or left-wing sources. The National Bureau of Economic Research is supported by leading executives and representatives of such companies as Nationwide Insurance, Eastman Kodak, du Pont, Manufacturers Hanover Trust, Ford Motor, and others, who sit on the Bureau's Board of Directors.

Another significant figure is the total amount of wages and salaries earned in the country. It is the wage- and salary-earners who make up the broadest consumer market in the country, and whose consumer spending makes it possible for corporations to declare dividends and produce at a profit. The eventual success of the investor depends on this wide market group and its ability to match mass production with mass spending power. It is in this group that the velocity of spend-

ing rests and, as every economist knows, velocity is as important as the volume of money. It is also in this group that stock
ownership should increase in order to broaden the base of
ownership. Yet there are so many straws in the wind which
point to the fact that the member of this group is unable to
participate, much as he would like to—and, as a matter of
fact, as much as the Stock Exchange would like him to.

Compared to total personal income, wages and salaries
account for about 67 per cent, or $280 billion against the
$400 billion-plus figure. But the wage and salaried worker is
also burdened most by the nearly $55 billion consumer credit
figure, which neutralizes the savings available for stock investment. And when you match the $55 billion debt figure
against the $25 billion personal saving figure, the circuits
seem overloaded as far as encouraging more new stock ownership on a sound basis.

Capitalism and democracy are facing a world today
which is hostile and unsympathetic. Capitalism must grow,
or, like anything else, it will die. But the trend must be
toward wider distribution of the ownership of capital goods,
where a greater number of people become realistic owners,
rather than token owners. Mortimer Adler, in his book *The
New Capitalists,* points out that all but a small fraction of
the capital instruments are owned by 5 per cent of the
households of the economy. He points out that the great
corporations of America think nothing of adding 50 or 100
million dollars to their productive capital in a manner that
will not create a single new capital-owning household. They
do this by building up huge surpluses and financing their
own expansion so that, as their stock increases in value, it
becomes further out from the reach of the average man in
any kind of realistic terms.

The stock market today presents a picture of a strange
paradox. On the one hand, the sober, average American cannot afford to buy stock. On the other hand, there has been
wild and growing speculation on the part of the public who
can least afford it. The result of the former condition is the

increase of an unhealthy concentration of power. The result of the latter is a market full of emotional steam and frenetic illusion. Neither condition is good for the individual, the country, or the Stock Exchange itself.

Bill and Grace Richards would be in a better position and a better mood to invest if they could see more evidence of the ability of the securities market to explore the core instead of the surface of its problems—and if the profit motive were extended more liberally down to Bill's level so he would have more recognition of what the free enterprise system is all about.

*"Democracy is the hope of the free world today—
and democracy's greatest ally is capitalism . . ."*

*"The answer to who owns American business is a
key—and perhaps the best there is—to understanding the United States economic system. In one way
or another, almost every American owns American
business . . ."*
—STATEMENTS BY THE NEW YORK STOCK EXCHANGE

CHAPTER III

It was seven o'clock on a typical weekday morning
at the home of the mythical Bill and Grace Richards, the
favorite family of the New York Stock Exchange.

Bill yawned, reached over and shut off the electric alarm
clock (General Electric).

"Don't forget, darling," said Grace, "to phone (AT&T)
that dealer about the Chevrolet (GM) he has for sale. It
sounds like a good buy."

"I won't," said Bill, groping for his slippers. "I'll do it
when I take the toaster (Westinghouse) to get fixed."

"Don't worry about that," said Grace, "I took it yester-
day when I went shopping (Sears, Roebuck). I also got gas
and oil (Standard Oil Co. of N.J.) and got the television set
(RCA) fixed. Wasn't that bright of me?"

"Sure was, honey," said Bill. "Don't tell me you picked
up the prescription (Charles Pfizer & Co.), too?"

"You'll never believe it, Bill," said Grace. "But I remembered that, too. Along with turning down the thermostat (Minneapolis-Honeywell) last night. You forgot it."

"Ouch," said Bill. "I also forgot to pick up the films (Eastman Kodak) from the drugstore."

"Don't worry, darling," said Grace. "I'll do that today—after I cook (Aluminum Co. of America) you some breakfast (General Foods)."

And so begins another typical day under the roof of the Richards' home. Like most of our own homes, its whole routine is dominated by the able and efficient companies who make up the blue chip corps of the New York Stock Exchange.

Each of the 1200 or so stocks listed on the Exchange has been carefully screened to reduce the extent of risk to the investor. Many of them have a sound record of growth and dividend reliability. The standards of the New York Stock Exchange are high, and its soil is most receptive to industrial aristocrats. In general, they must maintain their record of exemplary behavior or they will find themselves on the outside looking in.

Nearly all of them have grown up in America's great industrial expansion, nurtured by the free enterprise system and fostered by the democratic processes, which encourage initiative, vitality, and self-respect. They are living proof that democracy's greatest ally is capitalism—and that capitalism has been able to provide a standard of living unequaled anywhere in the world, or in history. And if capitalism and free enterprise continue to grow, there seems to be little question that democracy can compete successfully with any other political system in the world, bar none.

As the Stock Exchange claims in its statement, "The answer to who owns American business is a key—and perhaps the best there is—to understanding the United States economic system . . ." It is the key, and yet the Stock Exchange fails to take full enough recognition of the growth of the concentration not only in individual stock ownership, but in corporate ownership as well. Concentration increases power, and power increases the danger to the consumer of inflated prices. As a result, the average consumer can buy less and less stock in the over-all picture, and the industrial corporations in basic industries continue their concentration of power by financing future expansion out of the profits made by high consumer prices. As a result, both democracy and capitalism become more confined rather than expanded. There is little question that the factors which are creating this situation are unconscious as far as the Stock Exchange or any of its listed corporations is concerned. Such a throttling of free enterprise is actually the last thing that they desire. But their blindness to the danger is just as damaging as if it were a conscious desire on their part to lose the very elements that helped to make them great.

The very stark fact is that capitalism is not spreading today; it is narrowing. Americans as a whole do not "own American business"; they support it. The Stock Exchange does not encourage the broadening of the base of capitalism; it is unconsciously confining it by providing the best possible market in the country for the securities of those companies which need it least.

The forces which are moving the economy in this direction are complex and subtle—but the very structure of the modern industrial scene makes them inevitable. The problem becomes not one of trying to stop companies from growing large—this is impossible and not even desirable. The problem is to keep the giants in a genuinely competitive position so that they will serve the consumer well, and not grow at his expense.

With modern efficiency almost demanding this concentration of industry, it's easy to see how it came about. A local bakery, for instance, is producing well and profitably, and quite naturally wants to expand its operations. A smaller, competing bakery is operating in the area, producing inefficiently, but making a considerable dent in the sales of the profitable bakery. The idea of a merger is brought up, through which a great many economies can be effected, in addition to expanding the market for the profitable company. As a result of the merger, the customer is at first unaffected, but the withdrawal of competition in the market leaves him at the mercy of the single, dominant corporation as far as price is concerned. Since bread is a necessity, the newly merged company can, if it desires, charge almost anything it wants.

The same situation could apply if the two local bakeries remained apart but got together and decided to jack up the price of bread. The consumer would still be helpless, and would have to pay the price which had been set arbitrarily. Even if the bakeries commanding the market decided not to raise prices exorbitantly—and for the most part most companies do not do this capriciously, even if they are in a position to—the *power* to do so is still there.

The bakery in control of the market might, for instance, decide that it wanted to expand and modernize its plant. Previously, it would sell additional stock to do this, and the new stockholders who bought it would gain a fair equity and share in the improved earnings brought about by the modern plant and expansion. Now, however, with the market at its command, the bakery might decide to raise prices to such an extent that it would not need to sell additional stock. It would finance the expansion out of the price increase. Later, when the new production facilities began to pay off, it would split its stock and give its original stockholders a generous bonus. Meanwhile, however, no one else in the community would be increasing his share of ownership, even though he had helped pay for the expansion by higher prices. Classically, a new bakery could come in and provide enough competition to bring prices down. But in large, basic industries this is seldom possible.

Such a process does nothing to increase and broaden the base of ownership in American industry. Yet this has been happening in some industry groups represented on the New York Stock Exchange, and brought dramatically into focus by the greatest price conspiracy in history, among the electrical equipment manufacturers. Headed by General Electric and Westinghouse, two of the Stock Exchange's leading lights, the government and public was criminally bilked of millions of dollars, and leading executives of the corporations went to jail.

Of particular significance is the fact that those corporations in which the greatest concentration of power lies have been able to increase prices heavily—even though the demand for their product has declined during a recession period. Such a phenomenon, operating against all natural law, has created considerable admiration among brokers and investment houses, and prompted one of them to record in its newsletter: "The ability of leading companies to generate substantial earnings even in periods of greatly reduced demand has been amply demonstrated during the recession in 1954 and again more dramatically during the severe setback in 1958."

There is little question that those companies in which power is concentrated are able to do this. Angus McDonald, an official of the National Farmers' Union, reveals that his organization's studies show that the Continental Baking Company increased its profits from $4,882,000 in 1952 to $7,762,-000 in 1957. The other top five baking corporations had similar increases. Yet the prices paid to farmers tumbled at the same time as the bakers raised or maintained their prices.

"Unhappily," Mr. McDonald says wryly, "farmers are not able to practice this kind of competition. We have to lower our prices to meet competition, not raise them."

The Senate Subcommittee on Antitrust and Monopoly reveals that in some cases in many of the concentrated industries, as few as four companies control more than 50 per cent of the total output in that industry. In industry after industry it is actually an exception if eight companies fail to control upwards of 70 per cent of the output of their industry.

The unsought effect of all this is to reduce the profit incentive for the mass consumers and small businessmen and confine it to increasingly narrow areas. With the profit incentive removed from so great a percentage of the population, the great impetus which free enterprise used to furnish for America becomes greatly diminished. If the trend were toward the spreading of the "People's Capitalism" which the Exchange's president Keith Funston is promoting, nothing could be healthier. It would increasingly furnish a reasonable profit incentive among a growing number of Americans and replace part of the urge for individualism that every American wants through his heritage. The trend toward concentration has the tendency to create in the modern corporation an atmosphere of Civil Service which is often stultifying to the average employee, and the refreshing vitality of genuine free enterprise is manifestly lacking.

Colton Warne, president of the Consumer's Union, told the Senate Subcommittee on Antitrust and Monopoly that his organization was appalled at the practice, on the part of major United States corporations, of announcing price increases in the face of falling demand during a recession. He upbraids both U.S. Steel and the United Steelworkers for opposing legislation which would make a public hearing mandatory before a price increase could be effected in a heavily concentrated industry. Warne's statement was made in 1959. In 1962, his words took on a magnified significance as U.S. Steel raised its prices in the face of moderate union demands and intense foreign competition.

What the Subcommittee hearings eventually boiled down to was the committee's arrival at the conclusion that a handful of dominant corporations have control over the production, distribution, and the price of basic commodities. Without the exercise of high industrial statesmanship, they become a serious threat not only to the consumer but to free enterprise as well.

The objectives of the Stock Exchange in spreading the base ownership in American Industry are urgent and obligatory. But the objectives cannot be gained by whistling in the dark and issuing rosy-cheeked reports which simply are not true when all the facts are assembled. Instead of taking note of the growing concentration of ownership of American capital, the Exchange headlines its survey *Share Ownership in America: 1959* with the sentence: "American capitalism is strong—and growing stronger."

The Exchange publication goes on to read: "The report mirrors a remarkable growth in shareownership—a quiet economic revolution which is reshaping America . . . And it justifies the confidence of those who believe that America can be a society composed of many millions of private capitalists."

Mr. Funston, who wrote these glowing words, is an able and intelligent man. His failure to probe, to inquire, to dig at the roots of the problem, can probably be attributed to the fact that he must, by the nature of his job, present an overly optimistic picture.

But there are two very important trends which he fails to make note of and which, if not corrected, can damage his dreams severely. Beyond that, these trends can do more harm to industry itself than it seems to be able to realize.

First, as noted before, concentration is increasing across the entire industrial spectrum. The thirty leading corporations increased their sales by over 160 per cent in the decade between 1947 and 1957, while over 100,000 other manufacturing corporations showed an increase of slightly over 100 per cent. The 30 giants also increased their profits before taxes by 181 per cent, while the other manufacturing corporations managed an increase of about 45 per cent. The fact that they have been able to produce profitably is good. It is in those industries which increase profits by cartels and conspiracy that the damage lies. But this is only part of the picture.

Not only has concentration been closing in swiftly on the industrial scene, but the concentration of stock ownership within these corporations has been increasing markedly.

In its survey of share ownership of America, the Stock Exchange makes a considerable fuss over the fact that one out of every eight adults is now a shareowner, and that ap-

proximately 12½ million Americans now own shares in public corporations. (Labor figures show gains, but they are
not highly significant.)

But it does not point out that the wealthiest 1.6 per cent
of American adults held 80 per cent of all this corporate stock
in 1953, as Robert Lampman does in his book *The Share of
Top Wealth Holders in National Wealth*. Published in 1962
by the conservative National Bureau of Economic Research,
the book goes on to say that the amount of concentration in
stock ownership has jumped over 11 percentage points since
1949.

"Presumably," Robert Lampman writes, "since wealth
is a good thing to have, it would be good for all families to
have some. Also, it would seem that the wider the distribution of wealth, the broader the political base for capitalism."

The Exchange survey points with pride to the fact that
almost half the shareholders in the country are in the $5,000
to $10,000 range, but it fails to indicate that just about 85
per cent of those in this income class do *not* own any stock.
The Exchange survey will tell you that the number of shareowners is growing, but it will not mention the fact that a
survey by the Federal Reserve Board in 1957 pointed up the
fact that the great majority of families in the country—about
nine out of ten, to be exact—owned no stock at all. The Exchange survey will indicate that California is second to New
York in total shareowners, but it studiously avoids mention-
ing the fact that the 1957 Federal Reserve survey showed that
nearly half of the meager 3 per cent of the population in
the *highest income groups* owned no common stock whatever. These are families who take in $15,000 a year and more.
And of those families which are in the $10,000 to $15,000 a
year class, nearly two out of three hold no common stock.
The Stock Exchange survey will give you everything but the
color of the shareholder's eyes in its survey, but it won't point
out, as Mortimer Adler does in his book *The New Capitalists*,
these illuminating facts:

(1) Conventional methods of financing corporate en-

terprises are bound to lead eventually to socialized ownership.

(2)   Not over 1 per cent of the households in America can qualify as capitalists, if the latter phrase can be defined as a household deriving at least half its income from capital sources.

(3)   The sale of newly issued corporate stock has all but ceased to be an important source of corporate funds. (About 75 per cent of new capital comes from earnings, and most of the rest from borrowing. This does not create a single new capital-owning household.)

(4)   Every major increase in new capital formation that is not accompanied by an increase in the number of *new* capitalists is a leap in the direction of socialism.

The ideas in this small but important book of Adler's could be profitably memorized verbatim by all those who deplore government interference and who would want to stem intelligently the trend toward government control. The recognition of these simple, straightforward facts of life could be the road to the liberation of industry from this threat. Yet, for the most part, they are being ignored today by those who champion free enterprise most.

The New York Stock Exchange is one of the most stubborn in ignoring these facts. In spite of its hopeful utterances championing the importance of investment, it urges people who have little means to invest their savings, those who by doing so will withdraw from consumer spending much of the money in circulation which the corporations depend on to maintain or increase their gross sales. As Adler again points out, the only purpose of share ownership is to *increase* consumption. If hoards of consumer dollars were placed suddenly into common stock, a recession and "over-production" would be bound to hit with the force of a sledge hammer. Methods must be found to increase public investment without destroying too much purchasing power.

There are few other studies on stock concentration. The Federal Reserve System has available no other figures than those of the Stock Exchange Surveys. The Brookings Institution study made in 1952 carries very little information on this point. They show that less than 4 per cent of common stock issues account for almost 35 per cent of shareholdings of record, but this merely reflects the concentration of stockholders in the biggest corporations. The Brookings field investigators found they had a considerable difficulty in getting their respondents to report how many shares or issues they owned. Nearly all those who refused, not unnaturally of course, to offer this information, fell into the class of those who had substantial holdings. About all the Brookings survey is able to report is that 62 per cent of all shareowners own two issues or less. Families with three or more members show a declining rate of share ownership, the Brookings study tells us, indicating that some kind of choice might unconsciously be forced on people to decide between General Motors and an obstetrician, either of which can be expensive. But most significant is the fact that over 97 per cent of the shareholdings represent holdings of 1 to 999 shares, while only 2.1 per cent of the shareholdings total over 1,000 shares.

A. A. Berle's reaction to the over-all picture of stock and corporation concentration caused him to stop and wonder, especially about the fact that 500 domestic corporations dominate over 66 per cent of our industrial wealth. He said, in *Economic Power and the Free Society:*

"This is, I think, the highest concentration of economic power in recorded history. Since the United States carries on not quite half of the manufacturing production of the entire world today, these 500 groupings—each with its own little pyramid within it—represent a concentration of power over economics which makes the medieval feudal system look like a Sunday School picnic. In sheer economic power this has gone far beyond anything we have yet seen."

Don Villarejo, in the publication *New University Thought,* produces a battery of tables, statistics, and data to demonstrate that the bulk of individuals have small holdings while a small minority of owners have moderate or very large holdings. He points out that, in addition to the concentration of individual stockholders, the shield of secrecy around nominee holdings in various trusts makes information regarding these virtually impossible to penetrate. Even government regulatory agencies can't make the breakthrough.

All of this creates a major problem, not only for the mass consumer, but for the corporations who understandably want to remain free of government control. The solution of it cries for imaginative thinking and a high degree of industrial leadership rather than government directive. There is no pat or easy solution. Big Government, Big Business, and Big Labor squeeze the consumer on all sides. Somehow, an escape valve must be found which will make it possible to bring the profit motive and incentive back to a growing percentage of Americans rather than a narrowing percentage of them. Heavy government spending does nothing to reward the efficient company and worker, and can never be a solution to the problem in a free economy. But unless the business community comes up with its own ideas—new, fresh, creative ideas—the trend toward government concentration is likely to increase more rapidly than the present trend toward industrial concentration.

But the dangers of government concentration are open and obvious. State control is abhorrent to the philosophy of most Americans, and there are many safeguards against it. Industrial concentration is quiet and subtle, and the penalties against antitrust-law violators have been so light that the laws have been consistently disregarded by some of the most reputable of the large corporations.

The generous but restricted stock option plans offered to executives by the leading companies of the Stock Exchange —and by many others—do little to check the trend toward concentration, and in fact sometimes encourage it. The offering of ownership incentive to management, if not abused, can be a beneficial lift to a company. It provides a stimulus for the management to operate the company at top efficiency, and enables them to share in the profits they are heavily responsible for creating.

However, the extremes to which management has often carried the bonus stock plans do little to deter the concentration picture.

Chief exponent of the fight to keep management from going haywire in making exorbitant profits from its stock options is Wilma Soss, the colorful and energetic president of the Federation of Women's Shareholders in American Business. You can find her at almost any major stockholder meeting, complete with ship-to-shore megaphone to override the tendency of impatient management officers to turn off the microphone. She feels there is a squeeze play between big management and big labor which is raising hob with the consumer and small stockholder. When asked how many stockholders she represents, she is likely to reply as she did once to an inquiring senator: "Fewer than I would like and more than you would think!"

Her battle with U.S. Steel is sharp and testy. She feels that Steel's management in demanding extra incentive at the time of labor negotiations is disastrous and inflationary, and that Steel management has been getting away with murder with pensions running as high as $90,000 without any contribution on the part of the executives involved. She would put a $25,000 ceiling on non-contributory executive pensions.

She has been trying to push through a ruling for U.S. Steel and other big companies to require an executive who gets stock options to hold his stock three years before he dumps it at a profit.

A look at Roger Blough's activity in this area, as chairman of the board of U.S. Steel, points up what a handy device top executive privileges can be. As David McDonald, president of the United Steelworkers of America, relates it, Blough purchased 4,000 shares of Steel in 1954 at an option price of $18.50. This transaction cost Blough $74,000, but the value has blossomed to about $360,000. He bought another 4,000 the same year at $20.50, putting out $82,000 in return for $362,000 in value. In 1955 he bought 8,000 shares at his special option price of $20.50, at a cost of $164,000. They reached a value of over $700,000. With more purchases in 1956 of a similar order, Mr. Blough has put out a total of $542,000 in return for a $2,520,000 value. Even in the 1962 bear market, the equity remains high.

"He stands to make a tidy profit at no risk whatever," says David McDonald. "The shareholders have no choice," he adds. "The Board of Directors says: 'How about it, Roger. Would you like us to put a block of 28,000 shares of stock aside for you, which you can pick up at these prices—$18.50 and $20.50?' The stock is lying there. He could sell them at $90 a share. This is absolutely for free."

Although McDonald fails to take account of the fact that the value of the shares can go down, his barb is not without validity.

Wilma Soss, no great friend of the union, agrees with him. At one time she felt so strongly about the antiquated customs of U.S. Steel management that she appeared at a stockholder's meeting dressed in a 1902 costume. She takes grave exception to the stock option calisthenics of Benjamin Fairless, a former chairman of the board of U.S. Steel.

"In 1955," she says, "after he testified before Congress on the importance of stock options as an incentive, it was discovered that Mr. Fairless sold 46 per cent of the stock he had acquired through stock options, somewhere around 20,000 shares. He had 43,000 shares, and he had about 23,000 left . . . It is said that it was believed he needed the money to pay off loans to acquire the optioned stock. When I asked about this at the annual meeting of Big Steel, Mr. Fairless was very angry with me, especially when I said he was setting a poor example for his young executives who had optioned stock. And he said, well, he had to sell his. He was in debt.

"To poor Mr. Fairless, the private enterprise system hardly seems to be very rewarding."

She goes on to point out that, out of 800 companies, over half are issuing new stock for options, so they dilute the stockholder's equity in doing so.

She feels that options have contributed to speculation

because they encourage the executives to speculate instead of investing in the long-range future of the company. She also feels that the concentrated power within the concentrated industries has prevented any constructive action on the part of the small stockholder.

"I have been at stockholder meetings," she says, "where I thought I was in Russia."

In spite of the abuses of stock options, they remain a valuable tool toward maintaining a profit incentive for greater productivity. The problem remains to broaden the practice to include more than management and to keep the abuses down.

The answer to "who owns American business" is nowhere more pungently demonstrated than in the proxy system of stock voting. The battlefield is another favorite of Wilma Soss's.

It must be remembered, parenthetically, that Mrs. Soss is not anti-management.

"We do not wish to deprive our executives of anything," she says. "I have the greatest feeling for their problems. They work hard, many of them. In fact, in some cases we even asked that they be sent on vacations where we find them a little too pale for the investment we have in them. We think we should safeguard them, and we even took 20 pounds off Mr. Fairless because we thought he was getting too fat—and I must say, he did diet at our request."

But when it comes to the proxy system practiced by many corporations, Mrs. Soss wears a different hat.

"We have only begun to modernize our proxy mechanism," she says, "which still creaks from feudalism, and, as we public stockholders see, is shadowed with robber baronism. The new stockholders must not be disillusioned, as members of the Federation of Women Shareholders have been, by outmoded, unilateral, cynical, arrogant, shameless procedures under a veneer of corporate democracy. They might not be as patient as we have been."

Mrs. Soss is drumming for a free, uninstructed secret ballot, on the basis of the theory that stockholders are corporate citizens. "The time has got to come," she says, "when we realize we have ownership, and ownership and control cannot keep on being divorced in the United States. It's not American. It belongs to the old feudal days."

Although Mrs. Soss fails to give enough credit to the SEC for its partial proxy protection and although her enthusiasm is sometimes as over-generated as her ship-to-shore megaphone, her view is backed up soberly on many sides. Adolph Berle and Gardner Means have pointed up the fact that the direct manifestation of the shareholder's power is his right to vote, but that this right begins to weaken with the right to to vote by proxy. In their book *The Modern Corporation and Private Property* they go on to explain that the proxy was designed as a convenience to the absent shareholder. Later, it evolved into a process of delegating the voting power to a patsy for management or a group seeking to establish control.

"The proxy machinery," they conclude, "has thus become one of the principal instruments not by which a stockholder exercises power over the management of the enterprise, but by which his power is separated from him."

Proxy fights have been increasingly giving the small stockholder a bout with uncertainty lately, and the entire process is under the scrutiny of the SEC and the Senate Subcommittee on Banking and Currency. The issues in the late Robert Young–New York Central fight were complex and often hazy, but the end result was that the expense of the battle was shouldered by the stockholders to the tune of $1,308,733, which Young spent for them in gaining control.

Robert Young, who was referred to as "the smallest man ever to come out of Texas," was a two-fisted fighter who took over the New York Central from the traditionally entrenched Morgan-Vanderbilt back-court defenders and cleared a neat $2 million in the process. As a result, Central stock went up from 21⅞ to 43½, and he felt justified to ask his new stockholders to reimburse him for his fight.

Regardless of the merits of the joust, it did emphasize another glaring area of concentration of power. Young, who was no mean power-player himself, spotlighted the fact that J. P. Morgan, First National, Chase, and Mellon banks furnished a fantastically tangled web of interlocking directors and officers in and among the corporations which represent some of the most highly concentrated businesses in the country. Young pointed out that the presidents of these four banks, holding 450 shares of stock, dominated the $2 billion New York Central, and that the directors and officers of these banks are directors and officers in several scores of companies with assets totaling $107,933,337,000.

A. C. Nagle, for instance, of the First National Bank, served simultaneously as a member of the board of directors of the New York Central, Prudential Insurance Company, American Radiator and Standard, National Biscuit Company, American Sugar Refining Company, and United States Steel Company.

And, as great a concentrator as he was himself, Young feared the growing over-all tendency toward concentration as much as anybody. "Why should the Metropolitan Life," he said, "that would make anyone tremble with the power it possesses, interlock all over the place with about $107 billion, or $200 billion or $300 billion of assets as they do? It is wrong, it has got to be stopped, or our whole economy, political as well as business, is going to fall within their power. And we can lose our freedom to others than the Communists."

A small thumb in the dike to stem the tide toward concentration is offered by the Small Business Investment Company program, which Congress created in 1958 to provide a new source of equity capital for the small businessman. The purpose is to provide large sums of private capital, which had previously been far out of reach, for the smaller company. The struggle is a tough one and the process is slow. None of the investments of a Small Business Investment Company can be in the outstanding securities of the small business concern; it must be acquired directly from the issuer. This is a hopeful note, and it is in sharp contrast to the big investment trusts and holding companies which make little if any original contribution of capital to industry, since they hold only securities which are already issued and outstanding. This is also true of practically all of the investments handled on the Stock Exchange. New capital is not being created; it is, at most, being maintained. But more will be examined about this later on.

Small business, unable to be listed on the Stock Exchange and facing an offensive line of giants, from tackle to tackle, is fighting hard to participate in the huge government procurement buying program, and making equally small progress. The trend here, in spite of some efforts by government procurement agencies, is to concentrate buying in and among a handful of giant corporations, while the orders to small but competent businesses are on the decline. As Senator Proxmire has pointed out, small business received 25.3 per cent of the prime military contracts in 1954. In 1961—seven years later—the percentage had shrunk to 14.8 per cent.

But even more alarming than this is the fact that in 1960 20 companies—a mere handful—received 49 per cent of the net value of the contracts.

Naturally, much needed equipment cannot be furnished by smaller companies. This is the age of giants in more ways than one. But when the concentration reaches this point, the situation needs a sharp reappraisal. Even the share of subcontracts small business has been getting has not been enough to reverse the trend.

Joseph Noonan, Executive Secretary of the New England Smaller Business Association, who calls on 15 or more businessmen a week, says: "They are pretty sore, they are pretty frustrated, and mighty disgusted with this whole business and the way they get pushed around when it comes to getting government contracts."

Small business itself is not in itself small. About half the labor force is in it—nearly 29 million people, in 4½ million companies. The average size of the small firms is 6½ people. But like buffaloes and Indians, they are diminishing in both numbers and strength, and in doing so, contribute to a more stagnant economy with increased unemployment.

Alvin Hansen, Professor Emeritus of Political Economy at Harvard, writes in *The New York Times* that the economy must grow or sink. He is concerned about the recent rate of unemployment, which represents a total of 12 million people, counting the families of the unemployed. This is "more than the entire population of all the six New England states," he writes. "A free society should do better than that.

"Higher business profits will help," he continues, "but rising sales volume is also needed."

The rising sales volume can basically come from only one place, and that is the mass consumer market. If enough purchasing power is not placed into its hands the entire economy stagnates, and unemployment rises. Concentration hurts this purchasing power, and can hurt it badly. On the other hand, the removal of investment incentive by over-taxation dulls the edge of enterprise and encourages a handout form of government. The profit-making company, including employees, should not be penalized for the drag which a non profit-making company creates. The intelligent investor should not be penalized for the folly of the foolish investor. The goal must be to reward not only the profit-making investor and management, but the profit-making employee as well. Only in this way can the stockholder and management be secure in anticipating enough purchasing power to increase profits and grow. And through an increased share in profits the employee can participate in a genuine trend toward the idea of ". . . almost every American owning American business."

"It is easy to see that if there were no national market place where people could voluntarily invest in their country's future, or sell their securities for cash, the financing of new industrial growth would be curtailed sharply . . ."
— STATEMENT BY THE NEW YORK STOCK EXCHANGE

CHAPTER IV

In the Year of Our Lord 1959 there were approximately 990 thousand corporations in the country, just a little less than a million. Of these, only a little over 1100 were represented on the New York Stock Exchange, or about .001 per cent of active corporations doing business. Yet, by official figures of the New York Stock Exchange, these companies pay out nearly 60 per cent of all the dividends disbursed in the country. By the same figures, the listed Stock Exchange companies produce nearly all the automobiles and trucks made in the country, more than 90 per cent of all the steel, nearly 90 per cent of all the electric power, and over 96 per cent of all the aluminum, and handle 95 per cent of our railroad traffic. This leaves the remaining 988,900 corporations with fairly slim pickings. The chances that any of them will join their bigger brothers on the littered floor of the Exchange are extremely dim.

Those firms which are willing and able to take a crack at joining the club are likely to find themselves in a vaulted office at 11 Wall Street, seated on leather chairs across the room from a few staff members from a section of the Exchange known as the Department of the Stock List. This department has never been known to win any blue ribbons for cordiality. It is inclined to suggest a series of informal chats before any formal application is made, on the basis that if a company is turned down the embarrassment might not be felt in public quarters. This has proved to be a rather sound policy, because nine out of every ten companies who do apply informally are given a polite brush-off. Those who do receive a curt nod to proceed further find themselves filling out an application which requires of the aspiring corporation everything but a certificate of vaccination and a Rorschach test.

The basic minimum requirements are not calculated to broaden the base of corporate brotherhood. The company has got to show that it has a record of annual earnings exceeding $1 million and that its net tangible assets are worth at least $10 million. This automatically limits the number of eligible corporations to a little less than 4000 out of the sea of almost a million. And, of course, a new and unseasoned corporation has no chance whatever of being listed.

All of this puts the Stock Exchange into the role of providing the machinery for stock trading, and little else. It contributes nothing to venture capital. In its role as a stock exchange it contributes little to the floating of new issues. It takes no risks whatever. As far as the financing of new industrial growth is concerned, it leaves that pioneering job to the investment banker, the underwriter, and the venture capitalist, all of whom carry the load of the creative process which fosters new industrial ideas. Many are members of the Exchange, however. During World War I, when the Stock Exchange was closed for several months, the economy proceeded at an accelerated rate, and no visible scars were left on it as a result of the closing.

The Exchange is not averse to letting the public believe

that it is the keystone of the entire security market operation, and its literature carefully smothers any grudging mention it might make of the National Association of Security Dealers, even though most of its member firms belong to it. The NASD, as it is known, is the basic over-the-counter organization in the country.

This enormous market, while not as exclusive, literally dwarfs not only the Stock Exchange, but all the stock exchanges in the country put together. It is so large in its total volume that accurate figures are altogether lacking. As the Securities and Exchange Commission points out, the annual over-the-counter transactions of as much as $200 billion in United States government bonds are alone about five times the total bond- and stock-volumes on all the combined stock exchanges and make the over-the-counter market the world's largest securities market.

The New York Stock Exchange handles practically no volume of State and Municipal bonds. The over-the-counter market handles $50 billion worth. The government bonds handled on the Stock Exchange represent .00005 per cent of those handled over the counter. Corporate bond sales taking place on the Exchange come to $1.5 billion, a fraction of those sold over the counter.

Only about 20 banks remained on any stock exchange on June 30, 1959. The rest were handled over the counter, their market value being 60 times that of the bank stocks on the exchanges.

The aggregate market value of insurance stocks sold over the counter is nearly ten times that on all combined stock exchanges. Compared to the 1100 corporations on the New York Stock Exchange, almost 50,000 security issues are traded at one time or another on the over-the-counter market. The total day-to-day dollar value of securities traded is higher than on all the stock exchanges combined.

Even in those securities listed on the Stock Exchange, the over-the-counter market will sometimes have a larger volume of transactions than the Exchange itself. Eighty per cent of the trading in corporate bonds, nearly all the trading in high-grade preferred stocks, and practically all of the raising of new capital is done over the counter. It handles penny stocks on up to Christiana's, the du Pont holding company, which once sold as high as $17,000 a share.

Yet nine out of ten people you might stop in the street have never heard of the National Association of Security Dealers—or the NASD, as it is more often referred to.

Its executive director is Wallace H. Fulton, a fiery, intense man, who directs the organization's activities from his modest Washington office and who carries little enthusiasm for the dominance of the New York Stock Exchange in the public eye.

There are plenty of high-grade, blue-chip stocks handled over the counter, including Anheuser-Busch, Dun & Bradstreet, Plymouth Cordage, and Chase Manhattan Bank in this market, which could better be called the over-the-telephone market since that is the way most of the sales are made by its broker-dealers.

Instead of trading by auction, as is done on the exchanges, over-the-counter deals are handled by negotiation. In a large percentage of cases, members of the NASD buy the stock outright and sell it at a profit, rather than arranging for a buyer and seller getting together and charging a commission. In place of the daily Stock Exchange quotations, the National Daily Quotation Service furnishes the bid-and-asked prices of a sampling of the over-the-counter issues. Most member firms of the New York Stock Exchange of course handle over-the-counter business as well.

Wallace Fulton has his hands full policing this sprawling market, whose annual volume runs several times the total trading amount on the exchanges. Nearly 100,000 salesmen roam the country selling over-the-counter securities. Many have not been subjected to the pre-screening job which the Stock Exchange carries out, and the buyer has to be as much *caveat* as he is *emptor*.

On the other hand, there are a lot more bargains available over the counter by virtue of the fact that the market is less known, and sometimes not so overrated as many of the Stock Exchange favorites. But to find bargains, the buyer has to combine the wisdom of Solomon with a Ouija board. What's more, it's the only place in the country where a vigorous young company can get started, and the only place where capital serves in the really creative capacity it must have in order to keep the economy dynamic. Comparing it to the Stock Exchange is like comparing the Union League to Madison Square Garden.

Because it is so sprawling and less concentrated, the chances of hanky-panky are much greater than on the New York Stock Exchange, in spite of the conscientious efforts made by the NASD to keep things in line. The NASD is empowered with considerable authority, and it doesn't hesitate to use it if the occasion warrants. In 1960 alone, the NASD expelled 23 members and revoked the registration of 36 representatives. It suspended 16 members and fined 189. It co-operates with the SEC, as does the Stock Exchange, in tracking down offenders in its efforts to promote self-discipline among its members.

The relationship between the NASD and the New York Stock Exchange is not exactly cordial. The Stock Exchange likes to have it known that its regulations are far more strict and often exceed the minimum requirements laid down by the SEC. It feels, and with some justification, that the free-swinging issues handled in the over-the-counter market are not burdened by many regulations demanded of securities listed on the New York Stock Exchange. These include the separation of customer's fully paid securities from those which are put up for collateral by a broker, the stiffer margin requirements, and other safeguards which listed securities are saddled with.

What's more, the Stock Exchange is not at all happy about the new "hot issues" which were breaking out like a rash in the over-the-counter market, and which has prompted the full-dress Congressional investigation of the security market as a whole. Anything which gives the over-all securities business a black eye shows up markedly in the reaction on the Stock Exchange, even though it has nothing to do with the operation.

But the NASD is not happy about the hot issues, either. Nor is the SEC.

These issues are sometimes referred to as "Tronic" stocks, since they often include a garbled version of the word "electronics" somewhere in the company title, or if not that, something to do with the Space Age. Kiplinger's *Changing Times* unearthed a company, for instance, which previously had been known as a music company, but at the flick of a fountain pen had been changed to a fancy electronic name. The company peddled a phonograph and records from door to door, and that was the extent of its business. Its shares went on the market at two and were up to 14 some weeks later.

Issues like these flooded the 1961 bull market in a surge, some of them holding up and creating paper profits, others diving down into limbo within a short period of time. A number of them doubled in price on the day of issue.

Manipulation had been evident in some of the issues, and the SEC had indicated that often parties issuing the hot securities held off a substantial amount from the market, making it so thin at the start that the price would move up rapidly after the day of issue. Another manipulative trick is giving the stock to a broker-dealer on the condition that he begin trading it at rising prices. The investor is told that he can have some if he will buy more in the market after the stock is issued, which jacks up the demand more.

The issues, of course, can be perfectly good issues, and still be subject to trading maneuvers which benefit the insider while the outsider takes it on the chin. Complaints have been piling up with the SEC of underwriters withholding large portions of a hot stock for the benefit of insiders, and the SEC has tightened up its regulations on this "free-riding" practice.

There is no question about the fact that some "hot issues" have been really hot—at least for a while. They are not of the "Tronic" classification, and they will inevitably rise when placed on the market. The NASD and SEC are attempting to throttle the over-all hot issue practice with undermanned staffs in an enormous market area.

The SEC has run into several different types of gambits in this sort of situation. In one offering, a hot issue almost doubled in price on the first day of trading. Over 13 per cent of the entire offering was sold by the underwriters at the public offering price to four broker-dealers, and one of the broker-dealers sold his entire allotment within a few weeks at a substantially higher price. Another underwriter sold an issue which was supposed to reach the public at $3 to several broker-dealers at that price. On the first day, six of the broker-dealers quoted the price at anywhere from $2 to $4 higher.

The SEC also reports the increasing practice, on the part of underwriters or selling group dealers, of allotting a large portion of hot issues to insiders—partners, officers, relatives—and also broker-dealers who might return such a favor. One selling group allotted over 28 per cent of its participation in a new issue to insiders, another 87 per cent, another 47 per cent, and so on. But the offering circular leads the public to believe that they may be able to purchase the stock at the price these insiders are getting the issue for. When the public finds it has to pay out double that amount, it's in for a rude shock. Considerable headway has been made in reducing this practice.

The amount of manipulation and double-dealing which can go on behind the scenes is illustrated by hundreds of cases, some of them involving hot issues, others involving straight, ordinary issues which are pushed out onto an unsuspecting public.

In 1955, a chain of stores with the unlikely name of Gob Shops decided to sell nearly 300,000 shares of its common stock at $1 a share. A substantial Wall Street house, Bruns, Nordeman & Company, members of both the New York Stock Exchange and American, took over the job of floating the stock, under the wing of its partners, Harold Coleman and Lawrence Lubin. Gob Shops was engaged in retailing such items as sporting goods, camping equipment, men's work clothing, and other items of similar ilk, under the guidance of Ernest Nathan, its president. By March of 1956 the public was in possession of some 200,000 shares, while the two Bruns, Nordeman's partners held about 50,-000. The executives of Gob Shops held nearly 500,000 shares, but they could not sell these without the Bruns, Nordeman team's approval for a specified period. With the deal went warrants to partners Coleman and Lubin for nearly 90,000 shares at 97 cents a share.

A few months after the first wave of stock had been assimilated by the public, in June, 1956, the Bruns, Nordeman underwriters entered a bid of $1 on the National Quotation Bureau "sheets." From July to October of that year the underwriter was the only bidder, and the price had dropped to $\frac{5}{8}$. By this time, underwriters Coleman and Lubin had received the questionable honor of being elected to the Board of Directors, and decided that a cash dividend must be declared, "in order to increase the confidence of the stockholders." President Ernest Nathan strenuously objected, on the simple grounds that the corporation had lost over $19,-000 in a previous nine-month selling period, and a cash dividend was impossible. Undisturbed, Coleman and Lubin pushed for, and got, a 3 per cent stock dividend declared.

At just about this time—September, 1956—the underwriters began a steady campaign to paint a bright picture for the stock. For the next 80 out of 82 trading days, they began pushing up the bids on Gob Shops stock, making it yeasty enough to rise from $\frac{5}{8}$ to $1\frac{3}{16}$, a practice which the SEC clearly found to be ". . . designed to stimulate buyer interest and thereby create market activity which would induce the purchase of Gob Shops by others at rising prices."

The announcement of the unearned stock dividend which was so generously provided by the persuasion of Coleman and Lubin was timed so that it would hit just two days after the underwriter began jacking up the price of the stock by incestuous bidding. This was accompanied by glowing sales literature which managed to overlook the basic fact that the company was losing money. Stockholders were informed by letter that the stock dividend was the result of increased sales, and the underwriters' salesmen were given a hearty sales pitch to raise their adrenalin level, in spite of the fact that the company was running in the red.

The unsuspecting buyers of Gob Shops at that time were victims of a thoroughly convincing snow job. They were told that the corporation was enjoying a remarkable success, that it was making money hand over fist and plowing it back into the company. They were told that not only was the stock a safe and sound investment, but they were practically guaranteed to make money. Other frills thrown in for prospective shareholders' ears were such daydreams as that Gob Shops stock was going to rise appreciably in the future, that it would probably be listed on a national exchange, and that a large chain store was thinking seriously about buying the company. That all these inducements came out of an opium pipe was never mentioned.

What's more, the unfortunate new investor in the firm was told that the underwriter was holding on to its stock for dear life, and that the supply was short, while in reality it was being unloaded.

After the underwriters ran afoul of the SEC on these field maneuvers, repentence set in fast. They offered to repurchase all shares sold during the forced-rise period of the stock at the price the customer paid for them, and if the customer had gotten rid of the shares, to compensate him for any loss he might have suffered. What's more, they claimed before the SEC that they had never handled any of this type of stock distribution, known as "Regulation A" since most of their activity has been acting as brokers for conventional New York Stock Exchange transactions on a straight commission basis. Up to this time, their activity had produced no SEC action against them. They also swore off any future business of this sort.

Taking this into account, the SEC suspended the firm, and partners Coleman and Lubin, for 60 days from both the

NASD and the stock exchanges, adding another 30 days for Coleman as far as his exchange activity was concerned. Although one commissioner vigorously dissented, stating that the underwriter's offer of restitution came only after discovery of the activity, the milder form of punishment was imposed.

This is just one of hundreds of cases which the NASD and the SEC face every year. With the general public developing an unholy passion for the get-rich-quick dollar, the smallest bait has often been snapped at almost before it hits the water. Without the public passion, the manipulators wouldn't stand a chance. With it, anything can happen—and it does.

In spite of the fact that the over-the-counter market swings from ultraconservative reliability to wild and manic hot-shot operations, its variegated convolutions provide the genuine ignition for American enterprise. Without it, local enterprises would come to a standstill. New businesses would be unable to get off the ground. New issues of old businesses would have considerable trouble in launching. None of these essentials is handled by the large stock exchanges. While the New York Stock Exchange acts in the capacity of an exclusive club, the NASD is a more democratic organization, bringing with it both the vigor and the headaches always found in the democratic form of operation.

Unless a broker or dealer has a spotted record or has been expelled from a securities association or a registered exchange, the doors of the NASD are open to him almost without exception. Banks are not admitted, since they are not brokers or dealers. If he hasn't had at least one year of experience, the applicant must pass a qualification examination. He must subscribe to the fundamental philosophy of the organization, in which he ". . . shall serve high standards of commercial honor and just and equitable principles of trade." This, of course, is designed to preclude such things as fraudulent and manipulative acts and practices, and unreasonable profits and commission rates. The extent to which this code is lived up to, however, leaves a lot to be desired. Registered representatives of the member firms are of course under the same obligations as the firms themselves. The membership fee is only $50, compared to the recent price of over $200,000 paid for a seat on the New York Stock Exchange. Members of the NASD board of governors, both regional and national, volunteer their services without pay. Members are spot-checked by examiners on the problems of overcharging customers, misusing funds, lending securities which shouldn't be lent, and keeping proper records. (One violator, for instance, was discovered to have all his records stuffed into two suitcases.)

Because of the magnitude of the policing job, the NASD attempted to check its members by questionnaire, but this obviously failed to do the proper job. One little habit of the unscrupulous broker is to "churn" his accounts—constantly shifting his customers from issue to issue without real motivation, for the sake of building up commissions and profits. Obviously, a questionnaire could do little to stop this, or other habits resulting from a salesman's enthusiasm for commissions.

As on the Stock Exchange, a man's word is all that he has to trade with, and a broker or dealer knows that he won't be in business another day if his word isn't as good as his bond. A lot of money hinges on the proper understanding of the spoken word, and since so much volume on the over-the-counter market is done over the telephone, phonetics play an important part in the day-to-day routine of the business. An over-the-counter man is likely to find himself treated like a leper if he shops around for a new bid after accepting a trial offer. If he fails to report back to another broker on an accepted bid or offering, leaving the other broker in suspense, he is not going to enhance his popularity. Or if he employs another person as a decoy to make it appear that there's a big demand for an issue, he'll probably run into trouble with his fellow brokers. Most important, clear reporting of a bid or offer is absolutely essential to avoid an explosion on the other end of the wire. The NASD takes great pains to point out to its members that if a bid or offer is only tentative, the inquiring party must be told clearly that this is the case. The organization lists several ways of doing this:

"It is *quoted* 35–36 . . ." (Meaning 35 bid, 36 asked.)

"It is 35–36, subject . . ."

"I am not firm, but it looks like 35–36 . . ."

"Last I saw was 35–36 . . ."

"It is 35–36, CTM . . ." (Meaning "Coming to me— from another source.")

When a sale is definite, the simple words "We buy from you . . ." are all that are needed to make the contract firm.

With the over-the-counter market handling practically all the new issues of securities, plus 99 per cent of all the bank and trust company shares, all railroad-equipment trust certificates, most real-estate bonds, many railroad, industrial, and public utility securities, all the securities of states, cities, and towns, and all the United States government bonds, the New York Stock Exchange's attitude toward it is often cavalier. Except for a stiff and chilly nod to "the investment banking industry," the Exchange's booklet *Understanding the New York Stock Exchange* gives the reader the impression that the Exchange is the *sine qua non* of the entire securities business. It fails to emphasize the static and unproductive function it plays in the real growth of the country's industry, relegating to a secondary role the NASD, which, with all its faults and problems, represents the nearest thing we have today to democratic capitalism.

Attempting to stand up against the Goliath of the exchanges is the former Curb Exchange, now known as the American Stock Exchange, or Amex in its briefer form. Like the NASD, the American Exchange is more free-wheeling, more volatile, less exclusive, and generous to a fault in its support of the industrial underdog. The annual market value of its traded securities (some $26 billion at the end of 1959) is a slingshot compared to the $307 billion traded on the New York Stock Exchange. Its volume of bonds, amounting to a little over $882 million, is a fly speck compared to the New York Stock Exchange's $150 billion for the same period. Amex handles roughly 900 stocks, as opposed to the 1500 plus of its bigger brother. Its per cent of dollar volume traded on all exchanges is 9½ compared to NYSE's 83 per cent. Amex has an inferiority complex, dating back to its days when it actually performed its trading on the curb of Wall Street, using wild and cryptic hand signals to signify various stages of its dealings.

One result of the more free-for-all atmosphere on the Amex floor has been a considerable amount of hanky-panky which will be taken up in a later chapter. In the light of its recent inner explosions, it is fortunate for Amex that its literature and statements have not taken on the pontifical coloring of the New York Stock Exchange's pronouncements.

Although the New York Stock Exchange would never go out of its way to relieve you of the opinion, Amex is not a second-class exchange. What's more, nearly 90 per cent of its regular and associate member organizations are also members of the New York Stock Exchange. It is over a hundred years old. Representatives of some of the most outstanding firms and individuals in Wall Street are on its board of governors. And in spite of its recent violent misdemeanors, it is willing to accept the smaller corporation and give it a chance to get off the ground before it becomes squashed by the concentrated power of the giants. Over 40 per cent of the corporations on the Big Board got their start on Amex, when it was known as The Curb. Among them were Armour & Company, Swift & Company, nearly all the airlines, Aluminum Company of America, Cities Service, Eversharp, Gulf Oil, Quaker Oats, Singer, and others.

In giving the smaller company a break, it provides the advantages of an exchange market which the New York Stock Exchange allows only to the giants. In doing so, however, the risks increase by the very nature of the fact that a smaller, new company does open up more temptation for illicit maneuvering, characterized by some portions of the over-the-counter market.

It is too early yet to tell just what place, if any, the new National Stock Exchange will take on the financial stage. Opening up early in 1962 with the popping of Marcel 1955 champagne corks, the infant exchange began with eight listed stocks and the hope of gaining a score or so more by the end of the year. As a splinter of the New York Mercantile Exchange, which deals mostly in potato futures, its main objective is to provide the smaller company with the advantages of a national listing.

Lawrence H. Taylor, its chairman, is young, energetic, and dedicated, but he faces a lot of problems.

"We're not exactly competing with the Big Board yet," he says, "but we're going to help a lot of smaller companies to go national, who will be able to supply popular-priced stocks for popular-priced pocketbooks."

Of the eight charter listings, Ansonia Wire opened at $3.60; National Electronics, $1.70; Camp Chemical, $4.00; and Goconda Lead, $1.80. Interesting is the fact that the National Exchange will be traded in five-and-ten cent price tags, rather than the fractional quotes of the Big Board. Its two trading posts are supplemented by completely automatic bookkeeping procedures, but it hasn't yet had the chance to give them a complete workout. Its requirements for listing are softer than those of any national exchange. They include a minimum of 500 shareholders, a net worth of half a million, and 100,000 shares publicly owned.

The potential investor is faced with navigating through many shoals in his investment program. On the one hand, he is tempted by the glitter and fascination of the Big Board, whose fluctuations can be as dangerous as the risks of the more free-swinging tactics of Amex. On the other hand, if he takes the channel in both the over-the-counter and Amex directions, he must pick and choose more carefully in order to avoid risks inherent in the less seasoned timber.

Neither Amex nor the NASD includes in its literature the pretensions of the New York Stock Exchange. For the most part, they are more frankly buckeye in their approach, more content to let the buyer beware, and to do the job in shirt sleeves. There is no comparison, in the contribution to original industrial growth and vigor, between the combined efforts of Amex and the NASD and those of the New York Stock Exchange. In effect, the Big Board becomes something of a parasite, sitting back and waiting for their more imaginative and less inhibited brothers to be bled and bruised in the battle for early industrial survival.

Where imagination, vitality, and creativity are at work—in this case, in the American Exchange and in the NASD —there is bound to be a certain amount of confusion, chaos, and a tendency at times to disregard the rules of the road. Only an informed public can protect itself against these problems—a public skeptical enough to realize that there is no such thing as getting something for nothing, any time, anywhere.

"Day to day fluctuations are generally caused by the needs, plans, hopes, and problems of thousands of individuals . . ."
— STATEMENT BY THE NEW YORK STOCK EXCHANGE

CHAPTER V

In February of 1959, a gentleman whom we'll call Harvey—and this is not his real name, although he is a very real person—went up to Manchester, Vermont, to enjoy a week end of skiing. As a bachelor in his thirties, he enjoyed both the exhilaration of the mountain air and the congenial company of the post-skiing fireside.

His story—which starts with this week end—is neither a tragedy nor a comedy. In a sense, it has neither a beginning nor a middle nor an end. But it is a typical story, a story which in graphic detail shows what goes on in the mind of an average investor as he tries to steer himself through the shoals of the modern investment scene. Every detail in it is authentic, factual, and documented.

Harvey worked five hard days a week as a sales-promotion manager of a medium-sized food packager, and skiing was one of the few luxuries he allowed himself. He had grown up in a somewhat shabby section of Cleveland, Ohio, and resented the fact that he had had to work so long and arduously for every cent he ever saved. But he had few responsibilities, and he had been able to put aside nearly $14,000 in a savings bank, which reflected the instinctive caution he had about money. During his four years as a sergeant in the Marine Corps, he had been able to allow his overseas pay to accumulate at home, and from the time he had worked on a newspaper route in Cleveland, through his early days in the shipping room of an advertising agency, he had put aside nearly 20 per cent of his pay, sometimes more, with an almost obsessional desire to build something to fall back on. He had never really known the feeling of security, and he was determined to find a measure of it at almost any cost.

On the week end in Vermont, he noted that the fireside chatter again seemed to turn away from the usual talk about klister and powder snow and centered on the stock market.

"It was a growing trend," Harvey recalls. "The guys who went up to the slopes with me couldn't seem to talk about anything else. Some of them were doing damn well. The girls we met used to get bored to death with the talk. Nothing but stocks, margins, puts and calls, and Wall Street. But I was pretty well insulated, with my money in the savings bank, and besides I figured that if I weakened and went into the market at that late stage of the game, it would be sure to go down. I used to kid them about it, and said they could keep the market, I'd stick with the bank."

But as the stories of his friends' successes grew, they began to gnaw at Harvey. He wondered if he might just possibly be missing out on something good. He found himself some nights lying awake wondering whether, if he made just one or two killings in the market—as a couple of his friends had claimed to have done—he might double his savings and then jump off the band wagon and go back to the bank and government bonds. And then there was the hi-fi set. For years, Harvey had had in the back of his mind the desire for a lavish set, which he postponed buying. He might just get this quickly with windfall money—money he might make through a plunge in the market.

His unrest wasn't soothed any on this particular week end when he met a very attractive girl who seemed to know a lot about the stock market. Her brother, it turned out, was a heavy investor who was constantly getting inside information, and she just by chance happened to know of one tip which looked as if it couldn't miss. For the first time, Harvey was tempted to take a flier. It seemed that there were rumors going around that Noma Lights of the American Stock Exchange was going to be bought up by another company, and the prospects for a good rise were definitely in view.

Driving back to New York at the end of the long holiday week end, he talked the tip over with his friends, who felt that it sounded like a good bet. As a matter of fact, they agreed among themselves that when they got back to New York they'd take advantage of the tip and go in for a couple of hundred shares themselves. But Harvey's caution got the better of him again, and he decided to hold back, in spite of their urging him to join them.

Within a short time, Harvey found that his friends had jumped in and out of the stock to take a few hundred dollars in profits, while he sat on the sidelines. He was a little irked at himself and at his customary caution, and he decided that if he ever got hold of another tip of any consequence, he was going to take the plunge.

It wasn't until a few months later—in April of 1959—that another tip came his way from the same girl. This time it was another Amex stock—United Aircraft Products. The story was vague as to why it was supposed to be a good buy at this particular time, but there were rumblings that the company was expecting a rise in earnings and that several big government contracts were almost certain to be awarded.

Whatever the story was, Harvey decided to ride with it. By temperament, any kind of risk with his long-time savings affected him sharply. The mere thought of taking a chance bothered him at the time, and he recalls a couple of restless nights trying to make up his mind. He decided that before he did anything, he would get a professional view of what proportion of his savings it would be appropriate to invest, just how much insurance he should have, and all the other basics which are customary in an investor's first step. The net result was that he decided to start with $1000, well within the prescribed amount for his means. He was convinced this was a safe amount, win, lose, or draw. He promptly found a broker recommended by a business associate.

"The night before I took my money to the broker, I got apprehensive," he says. "I wish I could take this sort of thing in my stride, but it's impossible. For some reason, I seem to swing between a wild desire to make a big pile on a quick speculation, and a complete pulling in of my horns. There's nothing in between. A lot of my friends seem to take it or leave it, or shrug off their losses. I'm just not built that way."

Regardless of his ambivalence, Harvey made his way to a broker on April 21, 1959, and bought 100 shares of United Aircraft Products at an even $10 per share. He paid a broker's commission of $17.00, and went back to his office, still shaky. He tried to tell himself that if he lost his money, he could absorb the loss and forget about the whole thing. But this persuasion didn't work too well. His Greenwich Village apartment began to show signs of neglect. Late editions of evening papers with Wall Street closings began piling up to create quite a clutter. The visions of that grand hi-fi set continually danced in his head.

Almost immediately United Aircraft Products started to go down. Not drastically, or even dramatically. The drop varied between 1/2 and 1/4 or 1/8. He tried to condition his thinking to accept what he felt was the inevitable: he had made a bad mistake. He felt most disturbed by the fact that he had thrown his usual caution to the winds, that he had upset his traditional pattern and was suffering for it. He was constantly torn between selling the stock at a small loss, and holding on to it in the hope that it would go up. For several months he was content to follow *The New York Times,* sip his black coffee, and try to persuade himself that he could charge the whole thing off to experience. As far as unloading the stock was concerned, he couldn't quite bring himself to that point. It would be a total admission of defeat and he wasn't ready to admit that. What bothered him most during the spring and summer months was his frozen immobility. He couldn't bring himself to buy more stock, to sell his one investment, or to make a clear decision on any long-term basis.

It took until September of 1959 for him to bring himself into action again. Through an associate in a sales-promotion club he belonged to, he learned that two other stocks seemed to have very interesting prospects. The associate was close to the management of both concerns, and felt confident that they would do very well. One stock was Barnes Engineering, which at that time was riding on Amex at 21⅝; the other was Acoustica Associates, with a price of 29 asked on the over-the-counter market. United Aircraft Products was now selling at 6⅝, down from the 10 at which he bought it.

"I figured," Harvey says, "that I had made a bad choice with United Aircraft Products, but that I would just swallow that one and take advantage of the new tips because I respected the source of them very much. I was still green, still wide-eyed and innocent about the market, but still intrigued. I took a deep breath, and made my second stab at the market."

On September 8, 1959, Harvey bought a cautious ten shares of Barnes Engineering for a total cost of $222.25, including a $6.00 broker commission, along with 15 shares of Acoustica for a gross amount of $444.35, including a $9.35 broker charge.

Belatedly, Harvey then began to find out a little more about the market. For the first time, he learned about price-earnings ratios, and discovered to his horror that Barnes Engineering was selling at 60 to 70 times earnings, which on the normal scale of things would make it a very questionable buy. For five days he worried about what he had done, and finally became resolute. On the fifth day he sold his shares of Barnes

Engineering for a net loss of $18.75, including the payment of $6.49 for taxes and broker's commission.

"I felt lucky to get out of it," he says. "Why I had never explored price-earnings ratios before, I don't know. But let me tell you what happened later. Barnes went wild. Crazy. In 1960, it went up to 57⅝, and as a matter of fact it started going up very shortly after I had sold it at my $18.75 loss. I called myself the biggest jerk in the market." He switched brokers out of annoyance when his first one laughed at Harvey's request for a sample $5000 portfolio of selected stocks. The broker told him that "portfolios" were only for big investors.

He remained in his state of indecision for several more months. He bought or borrowed every book he could lay his hands on about the stock market, and read them. He took out a subscription to *Barron's*, and finally enrolled in a class in investments conducted by the New York Stock Exchange. He was resigned to his position for the next several months. In examining his own actions, he decided that he must either rid himself of his obsession with the stock market or contend with his tendency to panic. On the few occasions he bought stock he became nervous and liverish, and the clash between his conservatism and his gambling instinct churned in him constantly. In spite of the warnings against tips, he felt that sometime, somewhere, he would get that one big tip he was waiting for.

In February of 1960 he had lunch with a friend who told him that there couldn't be a better over-all investment than RCA. There seemed to be a lot of big things in the wind for the company, and the friend knew of several people close to the firm who were buying in considerable quantities. Harvey was intrigued, and he asked the friend bluntly whether he was buying stock or not. The friend was. This was enough to convince Harvey, and he took another breath and went to his broker again, for the first time in almost five months.

"There is one minor annoyance," says Harvey, "which I'll never get over. Every time I go to a broker with an idea, he seems to say only one thing: 'That's an interesting speculation.' He never tells me *not* to buy, and he actually never tells me *to* buy the stock. He just makes some sort of comment like that, and I guess what I want is some kind of father image who will do a lot of my thinking for me. Anyway, this is the kind of reaction I got from my broker when I came to him with the RCA idea, and I suppose there was little else that he could say."

Harvey decided that with a blue chip like RCA he could afford to plunge deeper than he had in the past, and his speculating blood was beginning to surge up in him again after the long months of inactivity. He placed an order for 100 shares of RCA at 60⅝, which cost him a total of $6,107.56, including the broker's charge of $45.06.

This time his nerves were really raw. The money represented the bulk of his net worth, and what worried him most was his tendency to panic. He found himself going through constant changes in mood after each investment, with high feelings of elation and then deep, rumbling feelings of despair. He was comforted by a rash of stories in the financial press about RCA's plans for building computers, and other stories indicating the company's robust financial position. What's more, RCA began to rise, and rise steadily. Harvey's mood became more confident as February wore on and RCA kept climbing. He felt that he had now covered his losses on United Aircraft Products, and as a result he treated himself to another week end in Vermont.

He wasn't at all surprised when he found the same conversation about the stock market replacing all the usual ski talk. He felt more buoyant than any of them because of his RCA purchase, and now felt more like one of the boys.

On this week end he met a pilot with one of the airlines, who made a strenuous hobby of stock, especially aviation stocks. He was more or less an informal specialist in one of them—Lockheed Aircraft—and he had information on everything which was ever said or done about Lockheed. Harvey was impressed. The pilot could answer just about every question Harvey had, and his questions were more sophisticated as a result of his reading and courses. Lockheed was then selling for around $22.00, and every indication which Harvey got seemed to point to its being a good buy at the time. But he checked his enthusiasm for a few more weeks, and finally on April 18, 1960, he bought 100 Lockheed at $22.75 for a total investment of $2,304.75, including the usual broker's charges of $29.75.

By now he was gaining in confidence. Not only was RCA going up, but also Acoustica. He felt that his judgment was being corroborated, that his increasing sophistication about the market was paying off. What's more, he picked up another tip from another friend who claimed to have some inside information on American Motors. The information seemed so valid and persuasive that, for the first time since he had begun investing, Harvey felt that at last he would be able to make a real quick killing. The thought of this made him strangely excited, but again exercising caution, he waited until May 31 of 1960 to buy 100 American Motors at $23.00 a share. His total cost was $2,330, with $30 going to the broker.

For the next two days, he did practically nothing but watch American Motors on the Big Board. And it went up, suddenly hitting 24⅝. But the action of the stock in those few days gave him the intuitive feeling that there would be no killing here. Two days later, Harvey put in a sell order. He sold the stock for a net of $2,426.14, making himself a profit of $96.14 in two days' time.

The amount of money Harvey made was in no way related to his elation. To him, it proved that he could move in and out of the market at a profit, and it began to justify in his mind all the time he had spent studying it. For the first time since he had begun investing, he was happy.

He was happier yet in noting that RCA was continuing its climb. In the first part of June it had gone up from the 60⅝ price he had paid to hit an amazing high of 78. His confidence was near the bursting point. He called his broker, and told him to sell the stock when it reached 80. This, he felt, would be his crowning achievement, since he had over $6,000 invested in the stock, and a sale would return $8,000.

Meanwhile, he began sweeping the horizon for more tips with a confidence he had never had before. On June 3, 1960, he learned from one of his skiing friends that Sonotone on Amex was going to be involved in some kind of merger, and that the stock looked very interesting. At the crest of his confidence, he lost no time in buying 100 shares of Sonotone at 127⁄8 for a total price of $1,307.38, including the $19.88 broker's charge.

At this point, over a year since he had first begun to play the market, he had involved over half of his savings in several transactions which were neither tragic nor brilliantly successful. Aside from the RCA transaction, which would give him a $2,000 profit if his sell order at 80 were carried out, he was more or less marking time. What bothered him most was his constant preoccupation with the stock quotations and his sometimes imaginary fears, which kept cropping up. The RCA stock, however, remained the one bright spot in his portfolio and gave him enough euphoria to overcome his fears. The hi-fi set seemed nearer than ever.

But the crash of a Lockheed Electra at this time brought back his feeling of panic quickly. News that Lockheed would have to redesign a portion of the plane discouraged him deeply.

"I can only say frankly that once again I panicked," Harvey says. "I just couldn't see the possible loss of a couple of thousand dollars if the stock should take a sharp drop as a result of all this. On June 15, 1960, I sold my Lockheed at 197⁄8, after having paid 223⁄4 for it, and took my first real big loss of nearly $350. I don't need to tell you what happened right after I sold it. It more than doubled the price I paid for it right now. The only comfort I have is that most of my friends sold out the stock at the same time I did. Misery likes company."

However, on the same day he sold Lockheed his broker called to tell him that Lionel appeared to be a strong winner, and was worth taking a plunge in. Since his broker rarely made any out-and-out recommendations, Harvey bought 100 Lionel on the same day he sold the Lockheed stock, putting out $2,203.75, including all charges.

By now he was in daily contact with his broker, if only to chat about the market in general. Toward the latter part of June, he began noticing that RCA, his prize holding, was beginning to slip. He dropped his 80 sell order in the hope of catching a profit in the high 70's. But his sell orders were always a point or two above the market. His broker chided him a little about this, saying that the only thing to do was to sell at the market, that you had little luck with sell orders above the market at any given time. But Harvey kept pressing for that extra point, even though the stock was obviously slipping. Since his broker agreed that RCA was a good long-term investment in any case, Harvey was content to watch it slip down gradually without selling at the market. There didn't seem to be any good reason why RCA was slipping, and he felt confident that the stock was bound to take an upturn so that he could pick up his 20-point profit. There was no particular reason why he had set his goal at 20 points; it was merely that psychologically this seemed to be a nice, round figure for a profit on his first big gain.

On April 18, 1960, RCA had reached its high: 78⅜.

On June 13, it ticked down to 77⅝.

On June 24, it had thumped to 65⅜.

On June 30, it hit 66, having dropped as low as 64 on that day.

It was on this day that RCA called its convertible debentures with a face value of $100,000,000, an action which was perfectly legal and which had been disclosed publicly as a future possibility at the time the debentures were issued in 1955. The action had the effect of reducing the equity of the current RCA stock, by giving the bondholders an option to buy authorized but as yet unissued shares of the company. By July 25, the stock was down to 58. By the following October, it reached the low for the year of 46½. After a slow climb back, it again reached the area of the price Harvey paid for it.

"My faith in the market was completely shaken," Harvey says. "Not that a lot of it wasn't my own fault. I had wanted to get out, but there was always that one or two points above the market that I felt I had to get. I was furious—both at myself and at the entire securities market. I felt that the insiders knew about the debenture recall, that the little investor was at the mercy of whatever whim management wanted to exercise. I had no proof of anything like this, of course. There was no evidence whatever in the SEC insider reports which came out later to indicate that RCA officials were selling in large quantities. But to watch my dreams of both the glorious profit and the hi-fi set go down the drain overnight was too much for me."

On the day the RCA news story broke, Harvey's reaction was violent. He examined his portfolio with a jaundiced eye, and, spurred by his previous lack of action and prompt decision, he moved swiftly and boldly. The first to go was United Aircraft Products, which he sold at $522.90, for a major net loss of $494.10. It was a bitter loss for him but he felt ruthless. He decided that Sonotone and Acoustica were going nowhere, that they were dogs, that he wasn't going to ride with them any longer. In spite of this he made a small profit, netting $55.65 on the sale of Sonotone in the brief few weeks he had held it, and $32.47 on Acoustica, his only long-term gain. On the strength of another inside tip about Lionel, he decided he would increase his shares in that company and he bought a hundred more shares at 26, bringing his total holdings in Lionel to 200 shares.

Still smarting from his failure to sell his RCA stock when he could have made a major killing, he summarized his fourteen-month excursion into the investment field to see just where he stood. He had lost nearly five hundred dollars on his United Aircraft Products, and nearly $350 on Lockheed for a total loss of nearly $850. On the other hand, he had taken a profit on both American Motors and Sonotone for a total gain of about $150. His net loss to date, then, was roughly $700, with the RCA paper loss of paper profits still nagging at him.

During the summer months he decided to take a breather. He continued studying various books on the market, and determined to become an investor rather than a speculator. But by the time September had rolled around he saw a chance for his first big profit, aside from the RCA one he had missed. Lionel had jumped to 32, and he unloaded his stock in it, selling his 200 shares for a grand total of $6,319.31, and gaining a net profit of $1,483.56.

"I wasn't feeling too bad that day," he says. "I had more than offset my losses, even though the government was going to take a 35 per cent tax bite out of my short-term profits. What's more, my new philosophy of investment instead of speculating made me feel better. The panic wasn't there. RCA taught me a bitter lesson. I felt that I didn't really know how to read a company's financial position from its annual report, in spite of all the time I had spent studying. I tried to analyze my own motives. I had to admit to myself that what I wanted to do was to get rich quick without putting the sweat behind it. And then along about November of 1960, I got another tip. My friend the airline pilot called me to say that he had heard that Diner's Club and American Express were going to merge, and that I really couldn't miss by buying into Diner's Club. Everybody was doing it, he said, and I ought to get on the band wagon. So I went ahead and bought 100 Diner's Club at 18⅝, for a total of $1,888.13. Then I began thinking about American Motors again. I had made a little money on it before, why shouldn't I do it now? I felt really loaded now that I had taken my Lionel profit. I felt there ought to be some kind of quickie profit on American Motors, so I bought 100 shares for the same amount the Diner's Club cost me. This was on December 8, of 1960. I still have the stock today, and at this stage of the game it is wobbling around at about 16. I bought it at over 18. That's some quick profit. I'd lose a couple of hundred bucks if I sold it today. What it'll be in the future is anybody's guess."

But on the basis of an inside tip from a friend of a friend, who was close to Diner's Club, Harvey heard that the merger was not going through, and he decided to get out. On January 6, 1961, he took a $525.61 profit, selling the stock at 24½ in contrast to the 18⅝ he had bought it for several weeks previously. He was beginning to feel more satisfied with himself, although he continued to be fitful whenever he stopped to think about the market.

After his January profit in Diner's Club, he held himself in check.

"Although I didn't like to admit it," he says, "in my role as an investor instead of a speculator, I was really waiting for another tip. The Big One. The real one. Along about that time, I got talking to a friend of mine who had a very modest job in the jewelry business. He was making about $125 a week, but he liked the market, and he often had good luck with it. He told me he had a hot tip about Tishman Realty on the Big Board. I wanted to know where he heard it, and he told me that he had a very sound, inside source, whom he had a great deal of confidence in. I asked him the question I always ask in this sort of situation: Was he buying the stock himself? He told me he was, and I went along with it."

On May 31, 1961, Harvey bought 100 Tishman at 25⅞, which turned out to be close to the high water mark of the stock up to this writing. It has also drifted as low as 15½ since that time.

Harvey notes that his personality during all this time had been going through a slow change—from a person of overcaution to one of impatience and occasional impetuousness. Right after he bought Tishman he noted that nothing in particular was happening to the stock, and he made a point of calling his friend who had given him the tip to find out what the trouble was.

"I found myself demanding to know what had happened; why the stock went down instead of up—as if I had practically been guaranteed a definite rise," Harvey says. "I told him I wasn't going to sit with it, and I wanted to check the source who had given him the tip to find out the the reasons for the tip in the first place."

But his friend felt reluctant to check at this point, and the matter was dropped.

Through the next year, Harvey repeated his constant pattern. He would wait for a tip, dart in, dart out, pray, and hope for a killing. His high aspirations to be a quiet investor rather than a speculator never came to fruition. Instead of decreasing in volume, the tips increased. None of them were particularly rewarding.

"Tips were flying around like confetti," Harvey said in the spring of 1962. "I've got a wallet full of them. Some of them are over a year old, and I don't know why I carry them around. There are dozens of stocks I *almost* went into. Then I'd change my mind."

The figures in the early spring of 1962 were anything but inspiring. After three years of tremors and doubts, they stood like this:

LOSSES		GAINS	
United Aircraft		American Motors	$96.14
Products	$494.10	Acoustica	320.47
RCA	883.07	Sonotone	55.65
Barnes Engineering	18.74	Lionel	1,483.56
Lockheed	347.97	Diners Club	525.61
		Outboard Marine	424.98
TOTAL LOSSES	$1,743.88	TOTAL GAINS	$2,618.41

On the surface, it looked as if Harvey made a profit of $874.53 on his three years of stock market activity. Actually, the amount was much less, of course. Approximately $330 was paid off for federal and state taxes, since none of his transactions were long-term capital gains, not having been held for over six months. His holdings at the time of his review were not exactly robust on the basis of the price he paid for them. They stood:

100 Tishman	(A $300 paper loss)
100 American Motors	(A $250 paper loss)
100 Lionel	(A $250 paper loss)
100 Libby-Owens-Ford	(A $150 paper gain)

His paper status stood at a net loss of $650, which brought down his total standing from three years of transactions to a loss of approximately $105. He estimates he spent a total of roughly 700 hours in reading, study, telephoning his broker, and actively carrying out his transactions, which would indicate a minus rate for his labor: not a labor of love, but one of a love-hate syndrome.

"It's not just the time I put into all this," says Harvey, "it's the blood. Three lousy years of gray hair, panic, fear, a queasy stomach and a few rare happy moments, all for a loss of $105. Instead of meeting attractive girls on a week end, I'd sit around and talk about stocks. I'm going to try to cut all this out. No more talking—unless maybe it's a real good tip. I have to admit I'm still looking for that killing, but I'm afraid it's going to kill me first. I keep feeling that if I go big, if I go heavy, I'll make it. But I also know that if I make this killing, I'll go in deeper, I'll be more daring, and I'll push my luck, and I'll go even heavier, and I'll be stuck. I'll be stuck for good. This is the prognosis for my type of investing—I don't know whether I'm typical or not. I haven't taken enough losses yet to be really bitter. But I've had days and days on end of bitterness. And I have said a dozen times if I've said it once: I only want to break even. But I'm even now—and I'm still looking for good ones. So what's the conclusion? I'm a bloody gambler. That's all I am. You read stories about guys like Getty who probably know good stocks, because they buy good ones, good quality. But good quality stocks are expensive. For a hundred shares of 60-dollar stock —you could buy 600 shares of a ten-dollar stock. You get a couple of points on a ten-dollar stock, you go some place.

"So—you're still looking for that ten-dollar sleeper—or five bucks—somewhere in there where you're going to make it—*because* every one of us has a friend. I have a friend who invested two thousand dollars in uranium stock back in 1950. Less than six months later, he had forty thousand dollars. He does not have one dollar in the market now. When he started getting tips several years later—the elevator men and the barbers used to give him tips, you see—he said: 'Now's the time to get out.' He said, 'Everybody's in it now.'

"And he's a bright guy. Very bright. So he put his money in mutual funds, and now he's happier. I might do the same. I always remember that I've got a partner in the game—and that's the U.S. government. Because for every dollar that I make, I've got to give up more than 35 cents. Because with my kind of temperament, I'm not a long termer, even though I am cautious. I'll never wait out that six months. Because if a stock is making money, my temperament now is to sell it. So therefore I'm not an investor, and I'll always have the government for a 35 per cent partner.

"Am I going to make any killings? I don't know. I have a feeling that the days of killings are over. There are these isolated cases. How to get hold of one, I don't know, but believe me, I'm still looking at every turn—for a friendly face—who's got an inside track on a good stock. Who's going to give me the sleeper that I'm waiting for where I'm going to make my killing. To buy my hi-fi set. The hi-fi set I never bought with my $2,000 paper profit I had with RCA. So I'm still listening to my scratchy record-player. I won't buy a hi-fi with my own money. Now it's a matter of principle, I've got to buy it with their money.

"So right now, I'm losing a hundred bucks if I liquidate. I don't want to do that just yet. Not right now anyway. I'll keep going for just a while longer."

Later, after the May 28th debacle of 1962, Harvey commented: "They tell me my stocks were all overvalued—but they never said that when I bought them."

That is the story of Harvey. It's a simple story, with no great climax, triumph, or defeat. It is typical, because it reflects what a vast army of investors do who churn endlessly in their tracks, get nowhere, yet cling to the hope that the Big Killing in the Sky will come along someday when they least expect it. Harvey is one of the thousands whose ". . . needs, plans, hopes and problems" make the market what it is.

The stock market is more human nature than economic nature. The hot tip resulting in the hot issue is basically the fault of the public itself. If there were no one to buy it, the hot issue would be worthless. The frenzy generated by tips can begin with the issuer, is fanned by clever publicity, fostered by a broker, and sustained by quotations. But the chain can be broken at any time by the public if it refuses to buy, if it buys with genuine knowledgeability and with some nature of restraint on an investment basis.

The SEC emphasizes that the first law of investing is to investigate the security thoroughly. But this alone is not enough. The investor must know his company, know the broker he deals with, avoid fast-talking telephone salesmen, and make sure he can afford to lose whatever money he is putting into the stock.

Harvey eventually learned to do all this, but he has one final thing to lick: himself.

This is the thing neither the SEC nor the stock market can do anything about. There are a great many Harveys in the country who wish they could.

The plans and hopes and problems of people sometimes carry them far beyond the limits, and they are swept on their own emotional tides to endanger not only their own lives and limbs, but those of others with them. One such planner and hoper was Cecil Rhodes, Jr., Brown University, Class of 1943, who made the acquaintance of Marshall Feld (not to be confused with the late civic leader, Marshall Field) in 1950, at which time they began a long friendship dedicated to the art of making money in the financial markets. Rhodes had an impressive background. After Brown, he had gone on to Harvard Business School, and further, took his LL.B. from Harvard Law School in 1948. Feld's background is elusive, but he was the son of a garment manufacturer, and shrewd and adept in the complexities of the market. He would often visit with Rhodes and his wife in their Cranford, New Jersey, home, which became the center of their informal business alliance.

Rhodes liked the market and he liked to invest. He also took a turn as a trainee with the brokerage firm of Dominick & Dominick from the spring of 1950 to the fall of the same year. During this time he made it a point to get to know the senior members of the firm as well as possible, at one time enjoying the privilege of having a social dinner with one of the partners. As later events were to prove, he also made it a point of familiarizing himself with the larger accounts of the firm, in addition to picking up significant details about his associates at the office.

He had no further significant contact with Dominick & Dominick until 1956, when he returned, this time as a client, to place an order for 3,000 shares of a stock on the Toronto exchange. He later phoned and increased the order to a total of 5,000 shares at a cost of $25,151.57. When payment was not forthcoming, the firm called Rhodes, who denied ever placing such an order at all. All he wanted, he claimed, was general market advice about the stock, and at the most in a quantity of 500 shares. At this time, the stock had fallen in value, from as high as a $4.95 level down to $4.00. In liquidating the order Dominick & Dominick took a loss of $5,000, which they have never been able to collect.

A few years later, in 1959, Rhodes met a broker by the name of Eugene Szemzo, a Hungarian who had been in this country since 1957. He met him through the secretary of a well-known book publisher, who happened to know that Rhodes was interested in investing and that Szemzo was interested in starting a venture of some sort.

By September of 1960 Szemzo had become Rhodes's broker, in the firm of Walston & Company. Rhodes's first transaction through Szemzo was to buy 2,500 shares of Lionel at 30, at a total cost of $79,618. According to Rhodes, Szemzo was able to arrange a factoring operation with Chatham Securities, who put up $65,875 of the money for him. Factors are money lenders not subject to Federal Reserve restrictions. Szemzo denies Rhodes's story. But within ten days Lionel dropped considerably in price, and Rhodes was forced to put up $7,500 more. As the stock went down still further, Rhodes was called on for more and more money but was unable to produce it. Within a month the stock was sold out from under him, and he was left with a debit of $2,600.

Meanwhile he ordered 200 shares of IBM at a cost of $101,350. He entered an order to sell the stock within a few days, but allegedly payment was neither demanded nor made for the whole transaction. Since this was strictly against the policy of Walston & Company, the firm did not comply with his instructions to sell, and a 90-day restriction was placed against his account.

But Rhodes was undaunted. At almost the same time he was going through these transactions, he opened an account at Goodbody & Company, and on October 26, 1960, he sold short 600 shares of IBM and 1,400 shares of Polaroid. With Polaroid selling at over $200 a share, and IBM at over $500, he was now in up to his neck with over a half a million dollars worth of stock which he would have to replace at a future date because he was selling stock which was borrowed for him. He made an initial payment of $114,781.92. But the margin requirements of both the New York Stock Exchange and the Federal Reserve Board required additional funds immediately, and Goodbody & Co. pressed him hard for a further payment of $266,700.

Phone calls were useless. The Goodbody firm received nothing but empty promises from Rhodes, and finally a special delivery letter went out from them stating that if the $266,700 was not delivered on Monday, November 14, the firm would buy in IBM and Polaroid to cover Rhodes's under-margined short position, charging him for whatever loss was incurred by the transaction. Rhodes responded this time by promising that he would send a check in immediately, and the firm extended the deadline to 2:30 P.M. on Tuesday, November 15.

Rhodes was now desperate. From November 7 up through November 11, Polaroid had skyrocketed in price, from 216 to 231⅜. IBM had leaped from 526 to 542. The short seller has only one hope in mind: that the stock will go down in price. Every share he has borrowed must be replaced, and the only way to replace it is to buy it from the market. For every share of IBM he had borrowed and sold in the 500-point range, he would now have to pay 542. And there were 1,400 shares to be replaced, each one which would now bring him a loss approximating $40. For every share of Polaroid he had borrowed and sold in the 200-range, he would now have to pay $231. What's more, the buying pressure he would exert in trying to buy back the stocks might raise the market even more.

From November 7 on, when both IBM and Polaroid began their meteoric rise, Rhodes could not help but be aware of the horrendous trouble he was in. And along about this time, a strange series of events began taking place in several Wall Street firms.

On November 7, 1960, some time between the hours of 2:00 and 3:00 P.M., the manager of the Grand Central office of Merrill, Lynch, Pierce, Fenner & Smith picked up his phone to be greeted by a caller who said he was William Bateman, a vice-president of the Chase Manhattan Bank. The caller went on to say that he would like to know the name of an account executive to whom he could refer the bank's customers. On being told that the manager would have to check and call back, the caller said he could be reached at the 60 E. 42nd Street office of the bank, and hung up. Later, the Merrill, Lynch manager tried the office, found there was no Bateman there, but there was a Bateman employed by the bank, a vice-president, at the downtown office. On reaching the real Bateman later, the Merrill, Lynch manager found he had never made such a call.

On November 9, 1960, two days later, a Sutro representative by the name of Ruth Dwyer received a call from Cecil Rhodes, Jr., whom she had had dealings with, telling her that he wanted her to meet with Marshall Feld, a friend of his who had some important stock market business to transact, but that he was quite temperamental, and wanted only to deal with someone he could be introduced to. Feld met her the next day and discussed an impressive portfolio with her, centering his attention on 1,000 shares of Polaroid he said he wanted to sell. He left references with her, including a man named Chappell at Irving Trust. On investigating, Miss Dwyer found that there was no such person at the bank.

On November 11, 1960, John Morgan of Dominick & Dominick picked up his phone at 9:52 A.M. to take a call from a man who represented himself as a "Mr. Freund." Freund said he was a close friend of one of the firm's large clients, and he talked engagingly and at length about the various partners at the firm, with whom he seemed to be on intimate terms. Freund indicated that he had several banks holding some of his stock as collateral, and that he would like to liquidate some of it to clear the loans up. He indicated that he would drop by the next day at noon. Mr. Freund never showed up.

As these and other scattered incidents were taking place, Polaroid and IBM were continuing to climb. The deadline for Rhodes's payment to the Goodbody firm was getting closer. On November 14, one day before Rhodes's extended deadline, the firm of Bache & Company received a call at 11:52 A.M., alleging to be from William Bateman. This time the voice said he was concerned with the effect of a possible announcement that Eastman Kodak would make on Polaroid stock. The rumor had it that Kodak was about to come out with a new color process, which would produce color pictures instantly. The Bache representative checked and found that

Chase Manhattan's William Bateman had made no call whatever. By this time, the real Bateman had put the Protection Division of his bank to work on trying to solve the mystery.

At almost the same time on that morning, at 11:30 A.M. an almost identical drama was being enacted at a mid-town office at Walston & Company. The same routine was followed, ending up with the discovery by the office manager that the real William Bateman had never phoned the office.

More mysterious calls were taking place on that same day. In the middle of the morning, a top executive at Dominick & Dominick, Cecil Rhodes's former employer, received a call from a man purporting to be Ivan Obolensky, the publisher whose secretary had brought Szemzo and Rhodes together. He chatted amiably with the Dominick representative and then asked if the firm had heard the rumor about Eastman Kodak's forthcoming announcement of a new instantaneous color camera. The Dominick executive checked, and reported that he could find no truth at all in the story.

But by noon the voice which claimed to be Obolensky was back on the phone again, this time being referred to another Dominick executive, since his original contact there had gone out to lunch. By the time the call was switched, the line was dead. Calling back to Ivan Obolensky's office, the Dominick representative found that the real Obolensky had made no call, and it was suggested that the caller might be another member of his family.

But just after 3 P.M., another partner in the firm received a call from the voice which said it was Obolensky. This partner had known Obolensky slightly in the past, and knew that Obolensky was on familiar terms with a retired partner of the firm and with another partner who had been transferred to London. For five minutes, the chatter was about these men —how the London man planned to return to the United States soon; how his wife preferred to live in New York; how the retired partner had ventured into a successful candy business in Mexico, selling out at over three times the original investment, and so forth. Obolensky had often consulted with

Dominick in the past, and it was not strange that he should do so at this time.

After the social chatter wore thin, the caller then asked if the new Kodak color process had been formally announced yet. He went on to say that he was topheavy in Polaroid stock, owning 6,700 shares of it. He would appreciate it if Dominick would sell 1,000 shares for him because of his heavy long position. The Dominick partner was glad to accommodate such a distinguished client, entered the order, and tried to find out more about the alleged Kodak story. Before he got far in this, the voice claiming to be Obolensky called back again. The Kodak story was definitely confirmed, the caller said. Because of it, he would like to sell 4,000 more shares immediately and urgently. The Exchange would be closing at 3:30—only minutes away. He would, of course, be in the first thing in the morning to deliver the actual shares. Although the time was short before the Stock Exchange closed —there were just 12 minutes left—the Dominick partner said he would do his best.

And he did. Two hundred shares went at 222; 100 at 221¼; 200 more at 221; 200 at 220½; and finally, a giant 2,300 at 220.

When the caller phoned back, he said he was delighted with the job Dominick had done. He inquired what time the partner would be in the office in the morning, and arranged to come in with the physical shares of the stock at 9:45 A.M.

At almost exactly the same time that "Obolensky's" orders to sell were put into action by the Dominick firm, Cecil Rhodes, Jr., called his broker at Goodbody & Company and placed an order to buy 1,400 shares of Polaroid to cover the shares he was short. He protected his price by setting a limit order of 700 shares at $220 and 700 at $219. The first half of the shares were bought for him, but the price never dropped low enough for him to pick up the balance.

As the frenetic activity was going on between the voice which said it was that of Ivan Obolensky and the firm of Dominick & Dominick, another voice was going through simi-

lar gymnastics at Walston & Company. This time it was purporting to be the voice of Eugene Szemzo, who called the
chief order clerk about selling 500 shares of Polaroid. This
date happened to be Mr. Szemzo's last day with the firm as an
employee, and the request was turned down. Later, Mr.
Szemzo denied making this and other calls.

But on that same afternoon of November 14, Eugene
Szemzo did drop by the office of Muriel Bailey, manager of
the Plaza Hotel branch of Walston & Company, just for a
friendly chat. He had struck up a mild acquaintance with her
only a day or so before, and on this day he asked if he could
borrow the phone to call the downtown office.

"Life is funny," he told Miss Bailey. "Here I have been
sitting around Walston all these months without doing much
business, and now that I am leaving them tonight, suddenly
my business is starting to come in. I just gave them a very
nice order and also one to my new firm." This was the last
time Miss Bailey laid eyes on Szemzo.

Rhodes, meanwhile, had received one more final extension on the money he owed Goodbody & Company, a twenty-
four-hour extension which would carry him over until November 16, at 2:30 P.M. And on that morning Miss Bailey
received a call from a voice she believed to be Szemzo's, telling her that Carl Walston had asked him to have her handle
an order through a nearby Chase Manhattan Bank branch.
Miss Bailey was not suspicious, but she felt that any such
order should come from Carl Walston direct.

"All right," she said. "Have Carl Walston call me if he
wants to do anything."

Around noon her telephone rang. The Walston switch-
board announced that Carl Walston was calling from Houston, Texas. The voice on the other end said "Hello," and
then was disconnected. In a few moments, the call came
through again, and Miss Bailey checked her operator to make
sure she had heard right that this was Carl Walston on the
phone.

It was a bad connection, but after a few clicks, the voice

came through loud and clear. "Hullo, Muriel," the voice said. "This is Carl Walston."

It sounded exactly like him; there was no question in Muriel Bailey's mind. He announced himself just as he always did, giving his first and last name. His voice and mannerisms were the same. Although Miss Bailey had not been aware that Walston was in Texas at the time, she found out later that he was.

"Will you be good enough to help us out today?" the voice continued. "A Mr. Szemzo will call you from downtown. He has an order which *has to be executed today*. It will be handled through Chase Manhattan and the simplest thing will be for you to take the order from Mr. Szemzo and handle the securities through the Plaza office."

"Okay, Carl," Miss Bailey said. "Mr. Szemzo has already called me but I was waiting for your go-ahead. However, you boys sure get around fast. I didn't know I was going to hear from you from Texas." She was a little surprised, because she had seen him in her office the day before, and he hadn't mentioned his trip. Then she added: "Carl, before you hang up—Mr. Szemzo said something about my knowing them at Chase 57th. Well, I don't."

"That's all right," the voice replied. "Just help us out, please. It's all right. This is something which has to be done today. Just take the order—a sell order—and receive the securities in at the Plaza. Mr. Szemzo will phone you and give you the details."

A short while later, the voice which Miss Bailey believed to be Szemzo's called. The caller indicated that he was "going up town to the bank" and hoped that Miss Bailey would help him later, that he had to "find out something in the loan department."

Feeling completely secure, now that she had spoken to a voice which she was convinced was Carl Walston's, she agreed to stand by to handle the order.

The details came through around two in the afternoon. The voice which claimed to be Mr. Szemzo seemed to be consulting at the other end of the line with someone at the bank. In the pauses, the Szemzo voice gave the name of the account as "Chase Manhattan—account of Frederic (no *k*) Weiss"— plus an exact code identification of a Walston office system of numbers. But, the voice said, he would have to call back.

He did, at 2:45 P.M. "All right, we have our 'figurations' now," the voice claiming to be Szemzo said. "And we have to sell some IBM. Can you quote it, please?"

The quote was slightly over 550 per share.

There was more mumbling at the other end of the line. A Mr. Weber of Chase Manhattan was supposed to be the man with whom the caller was consulting. Several minutes went by as Miss Bailey held the phone. Then the voice which claimed to be Szemzo came back on the line.

"Sell 1,500 IBM at the market," the voice said.

Miss Bailey literally gasped.

"That's an awful order to give me so late in the day," she said. "You'll murder the stock!"

"Can't be helped," the Hungarian voice replied. "It's a liquidation of a loan."

"Put Mr. Weber on the phone," Miss Bailey said.

Another voice came on, this time with an American accent. "Don't worry about it," the American voice said. "This man bought the stock very low."

Time was getting short. Miss Bailey had direct orders from the man she was sure was her boss, telling her that the order must be executed that day. She turned to an assistant and gave her the order.

"Two hundred shares sold at 550 before your order hit," the assistant told her.

Miss Bailey repeated this advice to the Szemzo voice. "Can't be helped," was the response.

While she held the line open, Miss Bailey literally ran to the quote phone, where last-minute prices are available. She was now in a tight press. If the order was not completed, she would be derelict in her duty to her boss. If the order pushed through too fast and sent the stock tumbling out of sight, it would be a stigma against herself and her firm. She ran back to her desk, where she found a message from her order room saying that other sellers were coming into the "crowd" on the Exchange floor, and that even the Governors of the Exchange were coming in to investigate. The order room also left a message that they would hold up the order until Miss Bailey was able to give them a limit, beyond which they would not execute the order. When 1,500 shares of a high-priced stock hit the market in one concentrated lump, there is a sharp reaction. Especially when it is selling in the 550 range. Here were over three-quarters of a million dollars worth of stock hitting the floor just before closing time.

Miss Bailey was immensely relieved when she got the word that the order room was holding up for limit order. She picked up her own phone and told the Hungarian voice on the other end that the order was held up until a limit was set on the price. Even a drop of two or three points could be serious.

"Let me call you right back," she said. "What is the number there?"

Suddenly, inexplicably, they were disconnected.

She tried to get Vern Walston, another senior partner, whom she had unsuccessfully tried to contact during the earlier part of the pressurized deal. She was still not suspicious of the deal itself, because of Carl Walston's apparent insistence that it be carried out. An assistant was immediately assigned to call Mr. Szemzo and Mr. Weber back.

Vern Walston had not heard about the deal, but reassured her that it would be Carl's responsibility and not hers, since he had obviously been anxious that it be put through on that day. He indicated that he would contact Carl in Texas immediately and get the whole situation clarified. Miss Bailey now felt completely relieved. The order would be held up for a limit order; and Vern Walston would clarify the whole situation with Carl.

The call to Chase Manhattan had now come through, and she took it on her phone.

There was no Mr. Weber. There was no Frederic Weiss account.

Miss Bailey was stunned. And in the brief moments it took to get this information, she was looking at the tape. 1,500 shares of IBM went by, sold at 540, over ten points down from the time she had first quoted on it. She didn't need to inquire to know it was her order.

As this whole, fantastically complex operation was going on, Cecil Rhodes, Jr., placed an order to purchase 600 shares of IBM to cover his short position in the stock. The time was 3:15 P.M., again just a few minutes before the close of the market. In addition, he tried to sell short 600 shares of IBM through Sutro Brothers, just prior to Muriel Bailey's order to sell 1,500 shares, but was thwarted because he couldn't produce a $25,000 deposit in time for the deal to go through. If it had, Rhodes would have stood to pick up approximately $7,000 in immediate profiit.

In the wake of all this activity, in which IBM dropped ten points with a single offering and Polaroid slipped from a recent high of 231 to as low as 219¼, the New York Stock Exchange governors moved in fast, investigated, and notified the SEC.

Under the direction of William Moran, SEC's Associate Regional Administrator, attorney Arnold Weinberg was assigned to the case, along with investigators John McNichol and Joseph Jedlowski. They knew nothing of Rhodes or Feld or Szemzo—only that some mysterious activity had taken place suddenly and without explanation on the Big Board. They began putting the pieces together meticulously, working backward from the 4,000-share sell order of Polaroid and the 1,500-share sell order of IBM.

The path eventually led to Rhodes and Feld and Szemzo. Evidence painstakingly collected by the SEC staff showed that calls from Rhodes's New Jersey phone coincided exactly with the long series of calls which had accompanied the elaborate machinations. Calls from Rhodes's phone to Dominick & Dominick showed nine conversations on the day of November

14, from 10:21 A.M. through 3:38 P.M., ranging anywhere in length from two minutes to fourteen minutes. Every broker and individual involved was called from this phone at one time or another between the days of November 7 and November 16. On the day that Muriel Bailey was swept off her feet by the skillful imposters, she talked seven times to the voice which claimed to be that of Eugene Szemzo. The telephone toll charges for the Rhodes number showed that exactly seven calls were made that day to Muriel Bailey's phone. The SEC investigators also discovered that Carl Walston's secretary received two calls during the day from an unknown person attempting to find out Walston's whereabouts. On one of these calls, the caller was informed that he was in Houston, Texas. Records showed that two calls were made from Rhodes's number to this number, at 11:23 A.M. and 12:00 noon. In almost every instance, the calls from this number jibed with the records and recollections of all the individuals involved.

Rhodes was grilled for several days, as was Szemzo. There are many conflicts in their stories. Szemzo denies that he ever made the calls to Muriel Bailey; he claims that he was being impersonated. Rhodes claims that on the critical days when the manipulations were taking place, Marshall Feld was staying at his apartment and was making many phone calls—to whom, Rhodes claimed not to know. Feld was nowhere to be found, even though a round-the-clock vigil was put on his home and the home of his parents, who have since been said to have disowned him. Szemzo says that he never met Feld, yet on January 2, 1961, several weeks after the SEC investigation began, Feld is alleged to have made a call to him in Paris, France, offering him $5,000 to stay in Europe, with more to follow if he would advise the SEC that Rhodes had nothing to do with the securities bought and sold on those fateful days of November 14 and November 16.

Rhodes claims that Szemzo arranged for the "clearance" transaction with Chatham on his early IBM deal; Szemzo denies this. Rhodes claims that Szemzo advised him to sell IBM and Polaroid short, because there was supposed to be a large

European account that was going to liquidate these stocks, thus bringing the market for them down. Szemzo denies this. Szemzo claims that Rhodes offered to find him a job on leaving Walston; Rhodes denies this. Rhodes claims Szemzo wanted to charge him $2,000 for advice; Szemzo denies this.

The violations of the Securities Exchange Act involved in the manipulations were enough to riddle the Act as if it were Swiss cheese. The result: a stiff injunction against both Feld and Rhodes, and a dismissal of the complaint against Szemzo on the grounds of insufficient evidence.

If ever there was a lesson in knowing the persons with whom you deal in the securities market, this is it. But more than that, it shows how the market yields to pressure which is likely to rise up any time, either legitimately or illegitimately.

"Over the years, the Exchange, largely through experience, has evolved a complex system of rules for self control. Regulations for trading on the floor repeatedly stress that secret deals are impossible ..."
—Statement by the New York Stock Exchange

CHAPTER VI

There is no question whatever that the New York Stock Exchange, the American Stock Exchange, the NASD, and every other organization connected with the business make every effort to keep their slates clean, their morals up, and their sins down. Most people, oddly enough, are honest most of the time. The morality of the stock market is in most aspects no different from the morality of any other part of the American scene. But the critical areas in which the stock market is concerned make those small percentages of lapsing morals of far greater impact than almost anywhere else. All the regulations in the world cannot make "secret deals" or anything else "impossible." Thanks to the alertness of the Stock Exchange and the SEC, the Rhodes fiasco was exposed. But the situation is not always so happy.

Throughout the history of the stock market, a great many

impossible things have happened—and it is not unlikely that they will continue to happen.

On one frosty day in the middle of January, 1938, a specialist on the New York Stock Exchange by the name of John Shethar was going about his business on a routine day. As a conscientious man, he kept a sharp eye on the stocks he specialized in: Greyhound Corporation, common and preferred. The usual tips and rumors were buzzing about the floor, as they might on any day. But one particular rumor caught Shethar's ear. Someone, it was said, was going in for a lot of distress selling in Greyhound stock. As the guardian of the stock, Shethar got busy and explored the rumors immediately. And what he found out seemed almost unbelievable. The venerable firm of Richard Whitney & Company was supposed to be the source of the distress selling, so the rumors said, and they were unloading the stock with ungentlemanly haste.

Shethar was inclined to discount the stories. Everybody on the floor knew Richard Whitney, and why wouldn't they? He had been President of the Stock Exchange for five complete years, from the spring of 1930 to the spring of 1935. He had been the anchor to windward for the Stock Exchange all during the stormy months after the Crash, when the SEC was steaming into the harbors of free enterprise and churning up a lot of flotsam and jetsam in its wake. Dick Whitney was the first to put on his chain mail and gauntlets to defend the Stock Exchange in the face of the fury of investors who had plunged to unbelievable depths in the Crash. At 41, he had been the youngest president the Stock Exchange ever countenanced, but more than that, no one could ever forget the day he became a legend on the Street. It was October 4, 1929, better known as "Black Thursday." With the ticker tape running 100 minutes behind time, and with stock prices cascading to out-of-sight levels, Dick Whitney had made his way through a roaring, groaning crowd on the floor, described by *The New York Times* as sounding like a primitive requiem, to push into the Steel crowd at Post 2. Here the crowd was literally swaying in the melee as shareowners plunged waves of stock on to the market, pulverizing previous lows. With the President of the Exchange in Europe, Whitney was at that time Vice-president, and he assumed charge.

"Ten thousand shares of Steel at 205!" he called, in Horatio Alger tradition.

But he was hardly heard. Either the noise was too great, or no one could believe him. Steel at that moment was down near 100. The harassed specialist put him down for 200 shares at 104, although Whitney left the rest of his order for the 10,000 shares at a hundred-plus points higher, and went on to a score of other stock trading posts to some $30 million worth of bids, to stem the incredible tide of falling prices.

He failed, of course. Not even the Morgan interest he represented at that moment could stop the falling tons of paper values. But, for his heroism, he became the white-plumed knight of the Street, commanding almost reverential respect from that time on. No single broker had ever in history placed such a mountain of orders, even though the cause was hopeless.

Later, as President of the Exchange, Whitney turned his attention to putting the house at 11 Wall Street in order. Speaking before the Philadelphia Chamber of Commerce in April of 1931, the florid, distinguished Harvard graduate said:

"Security frauds are as rampant today as they have been at any time in the past, and the loss they are costing to the people of the United States annually aggregates hundreds and millions of dollars."

Then he added: "I hope that in calling your attention to the extent of this evil I may be able to induce a large number of you to take an active part in the war which the Exchange and all honorable security dealers are waging against security criminals. Let us all support and co-operate in every possible way with our earnest and hard-working public officials."

This was Richard Whitney—the soul of propriety, wearing his Harvard-crimson ribbons on his shield and his J. P.

Morgan pledge pin on his lapel. How, specialist John Shethar might reason, could he be involved in anything so minuscule and tawdry as dumping shares of Greyhound on the market?

But the rumors on that January day in 1938, more than a decade after Whitney's thumb-in-the-dike maneuver during the Crash, were persistent. So persistent that specialist Shethar was moved to report the story to an officer of the Exchange. The officer lost no time in informing Howland Davis, chairman of the Committee on Business Conduct.

The Committee went to work. But nothing was found out of order in connection with Greyhound stock. No blocks of Greyhound were being shoveled out the door of Richard Whitney & Company, either on its own behalf or on the behalf of its customers—mainly other brokers of significant size and stature. Whitney did practically no business with the Great Unwashed Public. He was mainly a brokers' broker, although he did handle a few private estates, including his wife's trust fund. He was also treasurer of the New York Yacht Club and broker and trustee for the New York Stock Exchange Gratuity Fund.

Cleared of the Greyhound scuttlebutt, Whitney was relieved of the charges, and went back to business. There were, however, a few unanswered questions in the minds of the Exchange's Committee on Business Conduct. In looking over Whitney's books, they had noticed what seemed to be a few irregularities which might require further study. In addition, Dick Whitney had been taking out quite a few loans recently, some of which were of rather staggering proportions. But since Whitney was feared almost as much as he was revered, he seemed to have little trouble picking up whatever loan he needed. The fact that he was the brother of George Whitney, a bulwark at J. P. Morgan, didn't seem to hurt this capacity any. He had been able, on forty-two different occasions, to borrow without any security a total of over six million dollars from 16 members of the Stock Exchange, and over three-quarters of a million dollars worth of

securities from six other firms on the Exchange. He had bad
luck, though, on 21 other occasions in which he tried to borrow a near $3 million.

Whenever Dick Whitney approached another member
of the Exchange for a touch, he seemed to be treated not
only with respect, but with awe. It was not unusual for one
of Whitney's benevolent lenders to keep the whole transaction quiet, perhaps feeling a little sheepish that he had ac-
ceded to such an unbusinesslike loan.

On the surface, everything went well for Richard Whitney & Company through the rest of January and February
1938.

Then on March 8, 1938, the sky fell.

Richard Whitney, five times President of the New York
Stock Exchange, was suspended for insolvency. The Curb
Exchange took the same action. The business conduct committee charged the firm with "conduct apparently contrary
to just and equitable principles of trade." Most ironically, it
had nothing whatever to do with the unloading of Greyhound Stock.

It was Grand Larceny.

At the time, however, it simply seemed that the firm
was unable to meet its obligations and was filing a routine
petition for bankruptcy. The governing committee of the
Exchange, of which Whitney was a member, preferred
charges, and sent its then-president, Charles Gay, down to
Washington to bring the bitter news to the SEC. The State
Attorney General's office was notified, and at the opening of
the market on March 8, President Gay, back from his quick
trip to Washington, climbed the rostrum and gave out the
news. For a moment, it seemed as if the entire floor of the
Exchange were bowed down in silent prayer. Within minutes, the accountants of the New York State Securities Bureau were swarming down on the Whitney offices at 15 Broad
Street. Here they found some of Whitney's attorneys and
the hapless cashier of the firm, Robert Rosenthal. Later
Henry Mygatt, a partner of Whitney's, arrived and, when

pressed by a *New York Times* reporter for a statement, he turned to one of the lawyers and said:

"Have I anything to say?"

"No," snapped the lawyer.

The Corn Exchange Bank Trust Company immediately accepted Whitney's resignation as a director, pointing out that a loan to Whitney for $145,000 was adequately covered by securities "having a market value in excess of the indebtedness."

Mr. Whitney's other interests included a grab-bag of varied enterprises. He was treasurer and director of Colloidial Products of America, Inc., president of the Florida Humus Company, vice-president of the Florida Insectide Company, vice-president and director of the State Bank of Apopka, Florida, and director of the Distilled Liquor Corporation, which planned to produce applejack, better known as Jersey Lightning. Reports had it that Whitney was attempting to corner this stock.

Three days after the news broke about the Stock Exchange suspension, the headlines in *The New York Times* blared: WHITNEY INDICTED FOR THEFT OF $105,-000 IN SECURITIES IN SURPRISE MOVE BY DEWEY. And the story went on to reveal that he was indicted for stealing that amount from the trust fund of his father-in-law, George R. Sheldon. Not the least interesting of the revelations was the fact that the beneficiaries of the trust included his wife, his sister-in-law, and his alma mater. He used the securities of the trust as collateral for three loans, including one for $100,000 in 1932, the year after he had made his noble and flowery speech to the Philadelphia Chamber of Commerce. The final loan of some $400,000 was made in January of 1938, *after* the Greyhound stock rumors had been investigated.

Whitney's business affairs were so chaotic that District Attorney Dewey was unable to tell what other indictments might follow. Cashier Rosenthal made a clean breast of things by admitting that Whitney had asked him to hand over securities from Whitney's "safe-keeping" accounts, so that they could be used for collateral on loans. One of Whitney's partners, Edward Morgan, Jr., testified that Whitney had kept him and the other partners in the dark about the fact that he had attempted to corner the stock of Distilled Liquors, leaving the Whitney firm with practically all the stock of a practically worthless company. The federal government was standing by, ready to close in on Whitney.

The securities of the Sheldon trust were left in the physical custody of Whitney, as co-trustee with the Central Hanover Bank and Trust Company. George Sheldon had been a banker, president of the Union League, an associate of J. P. Morgan, and treasurer of the Republican National Committee. And Whitney had quite a list. It included 43 shares of the Corporation Trust Company of New Jersey, worth $750 a share; 200 shares of the Corporation Trust Company of New York, at $250 a share; ten $1,000 bonds of the Louisville and Nashville Railroad; ten $1,000 bonds of the Pacific Gas and Electric Company, and others. In order to raise the funds needed for his company, Whitney transferred the certificates to his own name, using names of two innocent employees as dummies for endorsement. The single lonely security left in the trust fund was a share of Bethlehem Steel, worth 54⅝ at the time.

Wearing a dark-blue suit and a somber face, Whitney stood at the bar as General Sessions Judge William Allen fixed a $10,000 bail, provided by the Fidelity and Deposit Company of Maryland. Then, at 6:22 P.M., he put on his dark overcoat with a velvet collar, and a pearl grey fedora hat, and went with two detectives to the Elizabeth Street Police Station. Here, according to *The New York Times,* he faced a police lieutenant who had to clear the room of a group of Bowery derelicts before he could turn his attention to the former President of the Stock Exchange. It was the beginning of the end for Whitney, who later quietly and with dignity accepted his jail sentence for Grand Larceny.

When all the figures were in, the SEC reported that

Whitney had negotiated a total of 111 loans for nearly 30 million dollars in a desperate effort to stave off bankruptcy. For at least three and a half years, the firm had been carrying on its business even though it had been insolvent. From 1936 to his apprehension in 1938, the misappropriation of funds became a regular, day-to-day practice.

The total value of securities illegally pledged for loans came to nearly half a million, including over a hundred thousand from the estate of his father-in-law, a similar amount from the New York Yacht Club, and over $250,000 from two other estates he handled. In addition, he put to his own use $600,000 worth of securities in his custody from the gratuity fund of the Stock Exchange itself. These, however, had been returned before his indictment. One Exchange official, explaining Whitney's uncanny ability to borrow money in extremely unbusinesslike conditions, said: "I always had in mind that Richard Whitney would be able to borrow money from his brother, George Whitney, and as a last resort, if worse came to worst, he would swallow his pride and go to his brother."

The Whitney case was significant in many ways. It came at a time when the Exchange was fighting tooth and nail against SEC regulations and it muffled the effectiveness of the SEC critics on the Exchange forever. It represented the end of the Old Guard. It also indicated that secret deals are always possible—and that they were likely to come from places where you might least expect them.

1938 was a bad year all around for the Stock Exchange. No sooner had the smoke cleared from the Whitney case than another bomb was exploded at 11 Wall Street, this time under one of the Big Board bigger listings.

It all started when Julian Thompson, Treasurer and Director of the century-old drug firm of McKesson & Robbins, was making a routine check of the insurance status of the company. Conferring with the president, F. Donald Coster, an expert in the crude-drug aspects of the firm. Treasurer Thompson was a little startled to discover that the in-

ventories of the enormous quantities of crude drugs McKesson used were not covered by any insurance policies. Coster
quickly explained that the insurance for this was carried by
W. W. Smith & Company, a 75-year-old English trading
concern, with which McKesson had a contract for the purchase of crude drugs. The W. W. Smith Company was something of a mystery, even to the directors of McKesson. It was
supposed to have very large assets, and its operators came
directly under the supervision of President Coster, who exclusively handled all the crude drug buying and billing for
the concern.

Under the contract, W. W. Smith made all the purchases of crude drugs for McKesson & Robbins, storing them
in four Montreal warehouses. Another Montreal firm handled all the accounts receivable for this end of the business,
a concern by the name of Manning & Company. This outfit
rendered monthly statements to McKesson, showing exactly
what bills had been paid and how much cash there was on
hand. Only President Coster himself knew the details of this
operation, which seemed to have grown up out of his extensive experience in the crude-drug business. The whole situation reflected by the activities of W. W. Smith & Company
and Manning & Company, both operated up in Montreal,
seemed very robust at the time. Inventories and accounts receivable were high, and the monthly statments from the
Canadian firms showed in the smallest detail all the transactions.

But the insurance situation in connection with the four
warehouses full of crude drugs in Canada was confused.
Treasurer Thompson pressed Coster for more details.

"As I told you," said Coster, "W. W. Smith & Company
insure everything. They guarantee the accounts and they
handle all this business. The insurance runs to them."

But Thompson was not satisfied. He pressed further.
Coster got angry and upset. He refused to discuss the situation further.

By this time, Thompson had decided that the situation

ought to be looked into. He immediately got in touch with Price, Waterhouse, the McKesson auditors, and discovered that they had annual reports on W. W. Smith & Company through Dun and Bradstreet.

Thompson quickly had photostatic copies made and sat down to study them. He was immensely relieved to find that the reports showed that the Smith trading company was doing business over the whole world; that it was founded three-quarters of a century before; that it had offices in London and Liverpool, and branches from Bombay to Greenland. Its assets included several ships, and its net worth was reported to be between $6 and $7 million.

But Thompson was still not completely satisfied. He wanted to find more exact information, so he went directly to Dun & Bradstreet to get more of the latest details of the firm.

Dun and Bradstreet followed up with another special check, talking with their Bridgeport office, where McKesson & Robbins had its offices, and with Montreal. And then came the crushing blow.

The Dun & Bradstreet reports were complete forgeries.

And they were skillful forgeries. They read exactly as if they had been prepared by the firm—followed the exact style, the exact form, the exact language. Even Dun & Bradstreet itself was fooled, until they double-checked their files.

Thompson rushed to Coster and confronted him.

"Why," said Coster, "there is something wrong here. W. W. Smith is an old firm, and this report is right. There is something wrong in Dun & Bradstreet's."

There was something wrong, but it wasn't at Dun & Bradstreet's. Flaring up, Thompson said to Coster:

"I have got to be satisfied now on this whole thing, and I want the whole details concerning this operation. I want to know who Manning & Company are. I want the privilege of talking to them. I want to go into the warehouses and check the inventories personally."

Coster tried to calm Thompson down. He told him that

there were no irregularities, that everything was in proper order. The inventories were all there. There was nothing to worry about.

But for Thompson there was plenty to worry about. He checked up on W. W. Smith & Company's New York address, found it had moved from Wall Street to an address in Brooklyn. Arriving at the Brooklyn office, he encountered a man by the name of Bernard, who seemed to know little or nothing about the operation. He told Thompson that everything was handled out of McKesson & Robbins's main office in Bridgeport, and that Coster was the only one who knew what went on and who had all the records.

Thompson then tried to find out more about Manning & Company. He discovered that they had a small New York bank account, but no New York office. He went back to Bridgeport and told Coster that he wanted a complete explanation of the entire operation. He found that the crude drug department, about which only Coster knew the details, claimed about $9 million in inventories, and something like $7 million in accounts receivable.

But Thompson checked the four Montreal warehouses. One of them was the address of a public stenographer. Another was a mimeograph operator. The other two were mailing addresses.

The next major news was a statement by a $10,000-a-year assistant under Coster, who admitted that the crude drug department, whose books had been separated from the main operation, was $10 million short.

On December 8, 1938, the Department of Stock List on the Stock Exchange suspended the stock from trading. Later, F. Donald Coster put a bullet through his head. His real identity: Phillip Musica, ex-convict.

Secret deals might be unlikely; they are never impossible.

Even in the present day, with the sharp but fatigued SEC staff checking the scene, a secret deal can hit the outsider and benefit the insider to the detriment of both the Stock Exchange and the investing public.

In November of 1959, Curtiss-Wright announced to the press and the world the development of an entirely new internal combustion engine, which would have a radical effect on the aviation field, and would make investors sit up and take notice correspondingly. On November 23, 2,000 press representatives were invited to the unveiling, with the news breaking in papers across the country on the following day.

The response on the New York Stock Exchange was immediate. The price of Curtiss-Wright zoomed up from $32\frac{1}{4}$ to $35\frac{1}{2}$ as 88,700 shares changed hands. All through November, Robert Gintel, a partner in the New York firm of Cady, Roberts & Co. had been buying Curtiss-Wright shares for his discretionary accounts, collecting a total of 11,000 shares by the time the news broke about the new engine. On the day the newspapers carried the story, he began unloading. On November 24 he sold 2,200 shares, and when the price climbed to a new high of $40\frac{3}{4}$ on the following day, he sold 4,300 more shares before the trading on the Exchange was barely an hour old.

As Gintel was carrying out these transactions, the Board of Directors of Curtiss-Wright was preparing for its meeting to decide just what kind of dividend would be declared for the quarter. During the first three quarters of 1959, the company had paid $62\frac{1}{2}$ cents per share, and President Roy Hurley was intent on keeping the dividend at this rate. Over his objections, the board insisted on cutting the dividend rate to nearly half of what it was before, down to $37\frac{1}{2}$ cents. The meeting began at 11 A.M. on the morning of November 25, and at 11:12 A.M. the secretary of the corporation made his way out of the board room to make the arrangements for notifying the New York Stock Exchange of the drop in dividends.

Sitting on the Board of Directors was the late J. Cheever Cowdin, who was also a registered representative of the same brokerage house as Gintel. The moment the decision to cut the dividend was made, Cowdin made a call to Gintel's office and left a message to Gintel to that effect. Meanwhile, there was some delay because of a typing problem, and the public message about the situation did not reach the floor of the Stock Exchange until 12:29 P.M. The Dow-Jones tape got the news at 11:45 A.M. and printed it on its tape at 11:48 A.M.

But Gintel, privy to the news over a half an hour before this, lost no time in getting to work. He sold some stock for Cowdin at 11:45 A.M. at 40¼, and another lot at 11:18 for 40⅜. He sold other stock for ten of his accounts totaling 2,000 shares, and sold short 5,000 shares for 11 other accounts, including three of Cowdin's. Immediately after his 11:18 sale, Gintel also sold 2,000 shares for a mutual fund which owned a considerable chunk of shares in the company. An analyst for the fund happened to be in Gintel's office at around 11 o'clock that morning, and telephoned from Gintel's desk to his office to advise the manager to unload Curtiss-Wright. Both claim that the dividend action didn't come up in their conversation. But the fund sold 9,000 more shares at that time, plus the 2,000 Gintel sold for them, although Gintel had never handled any transactions for the fund at any other time. All of this activity took place before the first public announcement of the dividend cut was made on the Dow-Jones ticker tape.

When the news did flash at 11:48, the Big Board was swamped with so many sell orders that trading had to be suspended, and it remained that way until 1:59 P.M., when the stock reopened at 36½. At the end of the day, the stock closed at 34⅞, a sharp drop from its previous high.

In its decision, the SEC found that Gintel had willfully violated the antifraud provisions of its regulations. There was no evidence, however, that Cowdin had not acted in good faith.

"It is obvious," said the SEC release, "that the reduction of the quarterly dividend was a material fact which could be expected to have an adverse impact on the market price of the company's stock. The rapidity with which Gintel acted on receipt of the information confirms his own recognition of that conclusion."

The report goes on to say: "Intimacy demands restraint lest the uninformed be exploited."

The number of times in which the insider gets the benefit

of inside information at the expense of the public is uncounted and probably uncountable, in spite of the SEC and Stock Exchange efforts to keep it under control. The Gintel-Cady case was a landmark, being the first time that the SEC has clamped down on the use of inside information by brokers. Both the New York Stock Exchange and Amex have hefty regulations to keep secret deals and manipulation down to a minimum. Both are nervous and sensitive about the possibility of fraud, and they are usually quick to take action when anything goes amiss. They are charged by the lynx-eyed SEC to maintain their own policing and discipline, and the New York Stock Exchange is credited with stiffer regulations and penalties than its more footloose and frenetic younger brother.

What happens on Amex can affect the equilibrium of the New York Stock Exchange, as has just recently been demonstrated. The new stiff look of several Congressional committees has been brought to a head by the swift and sudden proceedings by the SEC against two specialists on Amex who violated their privileges as specialists in order to issue false and misleading information about some of the companies they were involved with, and to engage in illegal short selling and illegal purchases during a distribution of stock. In their specialist's function as broker's brokers they had rigged prices on several stocks, and cleaned up more than half a million dollars in over half a decade of perilous hidden-ball plays.

Jerry Re and his son Gerard were the key figures, as specialists for the firm of Re, Re & Sagarese. As specialists they were real insiders on the more than fifteen stocks they handled on the floor of Amex. With all the exclusive information that a specialist gets coming his way, they were able to manipulate and massage the prices of these stocks in direct violation of all the rules and bylaws of the Exchange and of the SEC. Their sleight of hand was magnificently profitable for an amazing number of years. With such stocks as Silver Creek, Swan-Finch, Thompson-Starret, Skiatron, Rokeach, Trans Continental Highway Trailer, United Pacific, and Servo Corporation they were able to sell stock worth $6,000,000 in a way which profited only themselves as insiders. In the Thompson-Starret case they used threats and coercion to get their ends. The companies themselves were not charged with any of the misdeeds of the Res.

Like all the specialists on an exchange, the Res were obliged to maintain a fair and orderly market. Instead, the father and son team set up dummy accounts, acted as broker and dealer in the same deal, and created false activity in the stocks. Among many other violations, they were charged with having engineered themselves to the point where they had effective control of I. Rokeach & Sons, a kosher foods firm. With control of the company in hand, they saw to it that Rokeach acquired a company known as Seamless Girdle Industries, Inc., from another firm, Exquisite Form Brassiere, Inc. As if this exotic and voluptuous atmosphere were not enough, they latched on to a roving horse trainer who happened to live in New York's 10 Downing Street (reminiscent of, but not the same as, the renowned address of the British Prime Minister in London). Charles Grande, as he was known, was one of the "fronts" for the Res, to the tune of two and a half million dollars worth of phony transactions. In addition, a Cuban by the name of Jose Miranda acted as another front. The proceeds on the dealings with Miranda, who is a confidant of the deposed Cuban leader Batista, were also up in the millions of dollars. What's more, Mr. Miranda lives in Switzerland, keeps his accounts in a Zurich bank where the SEC can't touch them.

The upshot of the whole Re, Re & Sagarese situation was to stimulate the widespread Congressional investigation, which will include the New York Stock Exchange as well as Amex and the over-the-counter market. And while the regulations of the New York Stock Exchange are more strict than those of the American, the unusually ticklish position that any specialist holds on an exchange could give the lie at any time to any pontifical pronouncements by its Ministry of Optimistic Information.

The Re case brought thudding repercussions down, not

only on Amex, but on the entire securities market. Edward McCormick, president of Amex at the time of the scandal, was forced to resign, even though many informed financial men feel that he has been made a scapegoat. He was severely stung with criticisms for having had personal stock transactions with the Res, even though they took place six years prior to the suspension and involved three transactions over the counter, totaling $2,500. When one of the stocks he bought was later listed on Amex, McCormick immediately sold it at a loss of $32. He owned no stock whatever, traded on his own exchange. But this and other indiscretions didn't help him when the crisis arrived.

Most interesting is the fact that the Re case took place in the face of a "complex system of rules for self-control," which, while said to be more lax than the system used on the New York Stock Exchange, was still systematic and still complex.

Surveillance on Amex at the time was carried out by 12 members of the floor committee and eight alternate governors. The 20 trading posts of Amex are broken down, according to activity, into ten sections. The chairman of the floor committee has assigned a member to each section, and it is up to that governor to supervise and enforce the rules and regulations at the trading post under his charge. He keeps a check on the activities of the specialists and keeps a weather eye out on the Trans-Lux machines at the north and south ends of the trading floor, where all transactions are flashed shortly after their completion. It's up to him to watch the course of the prices, whether the specialist is doing his job, and any unusual activity.

In addition to this corps of sleuths, Amex has 56 reporters in what is called a "reporting division." It's up to them to see that all sales are properly recorded. In addition to the floor officials, there is a staff division of floor transactions. The vice-president in charge of this division gets all the data from the chairman of the floor committee about any possible violations taking place on the floor.

The rules these men must enforce are extensive, but their enforcement obviously left something to be desired. Before an Amex member can become a specialist, he must qualify before the floor committee, according to both his financial responsibility and his knowledge of the specialist's rules. He is supposed to have proper and extensive personnel working for him, and a clearing agent on tap to compare trades and deliver or receive stock as a result of his transactions. The stocks he specializes in can be snatched away at any time by the board of governors if he doesn't maintain a fair and orderly market. He must adjust prices as far as the public is concerned if he fails to maintain proper price continuity. He must time-stamp his orders, file according to stock and price, and give public orders priority based on the time they are entered. His "specialist's book" is built up in this way, and he cannot operate for his own account if it is in competition with public bids and offers in his book. Regardless of the trend of the market, he must buy or sell against the trend. He is not allowed to divulge any information as to orders in his book, not allowed excessive trading beyond his means, and must keep a record of all orders, modifications, executions, and cancellations. He cannot reopen a contract, be a director or officer of any company in whose stocks he specializes, solicit proxies, vote his interest, purchase over the counter, or deal in the stocks of other specialists in his vicinity. He has to subscribe to practically every regulation there is except the Boy Scout oath, and there's talk around the Street which indicated that it wouldn't be a bad idea if he did just that.

Yet with all these restrictions the two Re specialists neatly turned their transactions into transgressions, and the question asked by Joseph Reilly, himself a former chairman of the board of governors of Amex, is: "Did the governors of the American Stock Exchange govern?"

Reilly reveals that vice-chairman Charles Bocklet of Amex brought to his attention data which was collected by the floor committee (before Reilly was on the board of governors) that the common stock of Swan-Finch Oil Company, handled by the Res as specialists, began taking a series of unusual flips. The floor committee rolled up its sleeves and checked the price range, volume over a period of time, and any unusual trades that took place. Among the unusual sellers was one by the name of Charles Grande, who happened to sell 256,200 shares.

The minutes of a meeting of the committee on floor transactions back in February of 1957—four years before the case broke wide open—showed that the committee immediately voted to forward a comprehensive report to the SEC. The SEC then filed an action against Swan-Finch and the Res, in which the defendants consented to a permanent injunction against any further sales of unregistered stock.

The recent SEC staff report on Amex suggests in fairly strenuous terms that, when it comes to such things as handling the public's money for investment, self-regulation, in spite of a vast network of noble phrases, is strictly for the birds.

On Amex, for instance, a new member buying a seat could walk in and be in business with the qualifications of a hod carrier or mattress picker. He doesn't need to bother to prove his qualifications, either by examination or any other way, as long as he can put up the $75,000 required for buying a vacant seat during 1961. Nepotism can be found in and around a lot of nooks and trading posts on the Amex floor, with fathers and fathers-in-law begetting sons and sons-in-law to carry on the traditions, such as they are. Ex-President McCormick admits that he spent most of his time digging up new listings, and seemed successfully to look the other way when wayward specialists and floor traders were having a heyday on the floor. McCormick admits that Alexander Guterma, the famous convicted stock swindler, in attempting to get a company known as Shawano Development Corporation listed, picked up a neat $5,000 gambling tab for him in Havana, although the stock never made the grade. McCormick also went along with several dubious transactions of Gilligan, Will & Company, the firm of specialists who threw their weight and influence around the floor with ungentlemanly force, and who have been charged by the SEC for violations of the Securities Act of 1933. With McCormick owing tribute in several quarters the impartiality of his administration was hard to keep in balance.

The professional staff of Amex has been acting as a group of puppets, and little else. Although a staff member attends the meetings of the committee of floor transactions, he has been keeping his mouth quiet and his pen moving merely for the recording of the minutes of the meetings. The vice-president in charge of the division of floor supervision has admitted that his functions were those of little more than a technical clerk, and that the floor governors maintained the real control. He says that no member of the exchange staff has authority to tell any member how to conduct himself or run his business. The director of the Department of Floor Transactions says that without instructions from the chairman of the committee, he can't even follow up on reported violations or customer complaints, even though he has broken that custom at times, at his own peril.

The SEC staff report makes it clear that specialists tumbled all over each other in dragging in new listings so that they could reap the commissions gained by handling such accounts. One specialist says: "I took down as many as ten, fifteen companies a week that I would write down . . . companies that would meet with the requirements of listing on the American Exchange. My week ends practically were devoted to nothing but correspondence, sending out letters trying to induce listings . . . my files at one time I would assume contained almost 600 or 700 companies that I had contacted."

Another specialist working in the scramble for getting new listings says: "I would crisscross around the country and on some occasions I would run into McCormick. . . ."

Adding to the Amex specialist's problem was the New York Stock Exchange picking up for its own listing extremely active issues, which would leave the bereft Amex specialist smarting.

In December 1961 the entrance requirements for listing

on Amex became stiffer, which put even more pressure on the specialist looking for a bigger volume of commissions. The ease with which previous listings were accommodated is indicated by this colloquy between the SEC and Adolph Woolner, chairman of the committee of securities:

Question: You said, Martin Keena (vice-president in charge of the division of securities) gives verbal discussion? Answer: Yes, he reads it off very rapidly.

Question: Do you read the form off?

Answer: We try to.

Question: Sometimes you don't get a chance to read all the form?

Answer: We glance through them. I was trying to tell you about the amount of work. He would say, on page 4 of this prospectus, you will find the last earnings, on page 3 you will find the net worth. He will call the things by telling you where to look for the important point.

But the SEC goes on to observe that only two objections were voiced in recent years to questionable entrants.

While flexible listing qualifications can certainly help the new and growing company in the economy, such laxity as is reflected above can be considered in the too-much-of-a-good-thing department.

The specialist, who of course on any exchange commands the most sensitive position in the securities market, has been dominating the government of Amex, shaping such policies as to give the specialist even more advantages over the public than he already has.

The specialist firm of Gilligan, Will & Company on the Amex floor accounted for as high as 10 per cent of the entire Exchange volume during 1959, and, in addition, it financed through loans a considerable number of other brokers in its activities. In the latter function, Gilligan & Will was in a position where it could put the thumbscrews on those specialists who depended on it for financing. But the position of power this firm held has made it almost immune from disciplinary action on the part of the Amex government. Its activities have widely exploited advantages over the general public, some of which will be examined later.

In July of 1959, partner James Patrick Gilligan was hauled up before the Committee of Floor Transactions to explain why he had violated Rule 174 of Amex, which is designed to keep specialists confined to the specific business of maintaining a fair and orderly market. The SEC had nudged the Committee with a reminder that Gilligan and his associates had bought 56,000 shares of Guild Films on July 10, which happened to be just about half of the volume of trading in that stock on that day. Oddly enough, the price of the stock had risen about 25 per cent during this day, and Gilligan explained to the Committee that he had bought so much of the stock to "cover a short position," and that he had information that a merger of Guild with another company was in the wind. And while the SEC points out that this was hardly an adequate explanation for the gambit, the Amex committee voted unanimously that Gilligan had not violated its rule. The SEC also reminds us that of the eight members of the Committee present, five were specialists and one was an ex-specialist.

One Amex member puts it: "My own personal feeling was that somewhere along the road Gilligan & Will had an interest in too many situations relating to the Exchange; that is the individual members, not the management of the Exchange. That in having an interest, say, in having financed seats, which I thought they had been doing . . . they were quite powerful over there. Having learned the nature of the man later, which I did not know when I had this feeling over there, I decided in my own mind that he would be the fellow to use whatever power he had."

The general rule of thumb with specialists is that they have little or no traffic with the general public. Gilligan & Will, however, did a land-office business with friends, relatives, business associates, and corporation insiders, as the SEC discovered. While they are not alone in this practice, it leaves the way open for further abuses of the specialists' privileges.

The friends, the hangers-on, the relatives can all enjoy a distinct advantage over the general public, getting preferential treatment of their orders.

It's supposed to be the job of the specialist to hold on to stock, mainly in order to supply the needs of the market. Any time he gets himself into a position where he is an investor in one of the stocks he handles, he becomes prejudiced in favor of that stock and can hardly be in a position to maintain a fair and orderly market on it.

A lot of Amex specialists put aside chunks of the stocks they represented to realize long-term capital gains on them. Not only the ubiquitous Gilligan & Will but up to half of the Amex specialists engaged in this practice where they bought stock, not for their main function, but for their own capital gains profit. Such activity removes a lot of the supply from the market and results inevitably in a rising price for the stock, which is convenient and pleasant for the specialist and uncomfortable for the general public. This long-term investment stock has been put aside by the specialist and is no longer available for him to use in providing a fair and orderly market.

Gilligan & Will's rich-uncle assistance to the other specialists on Amex practically made them the bankers of the Amex floor. Gilligan himself admits that any of the specialists who borrowed money from him had to check with him about what kind of purchases they might make, and that he wouldn't hesitate to make them unload a stock if he thought it would make his loan more secure. Under this pressure, the specialists under obligation to Gilligan were hardly free agents.

Another specialist firm on Amex, by the name of James F. Rafferty & Co., became the only incorporated specialist on the floor, according to the SEC. This working unit of five gentlemen got together, with only one member holding voting stock, who alone was subject to the Amex rules and regulations. Furthermore, none of the principals had any experience either in the securities business or on the floor.

But they went to work with a vigorous enthusiasm for their own accounts, their wives', investment clubs where they had particular interests, family trusts and foundations, and corporations which they controlled.

The SEC is quick to point out the dangers of this sort of operation, where the co-stockholders of a specialist sell and hold blocks of stocks in which the specialist is registered. The co-stockholders are exempt from the exchange rules. The old-fashioned "pool" operations of the 1920's were fashioned along a pattern like this. As a stockholder, the specialist might be inclined to show to his colleagues his confidential "book" of the stocks he specializes in, giving them a complete picture of the market unavailable either to the public or to other members of the exchange, ostensibly. What's more, it's bound to be that the specialist would be considered a thoroughgoing heel if he didn't favor his partners in any kind of an inside deal he got wind of. Just how the specialist could impartially maintain an orderly and fair market under these circumstances is hard to fathom.

In commenting on the role of the specialist as far as self-discipline on Amex is concerned, the SEC said:

"Specialists are at the heart of the problems of organization, management, and disciplinary procedures of the Exchange. Their dominance of the administration of the Exchange, their overriding concern for expansion of business through new listings, the misuse of their fundamental role in the operation of a fair and orderly auction market, and the breakdown of regulatory and disciplinary controls over them—all are part of a complex pattern of interlocking causes and effects. It is for this reason that any program of reform must concentrate heavily on the dominant role of the specialist."

Speaking about his proclivity for letting his special underwriter friends in on the inside track in partial return for the introduction of new listings on Amex, James Patrick Gilligan told the SEC in rather cryptic terms:

"Well, and because lots of times they may not care if it sells down an eighth or a quarter, but they don't want to see the stock break a half a dollar, you know, because it might upset the whole market in the thing, so they have a right to— after all, they have got a lot of customers in it. They have a right to know what is going to happen just as well as I have."

This statement, such as it is, seems to reflect the confused yet strangely profitable philosophy of Mr. Gilligan, the champion of the insider, and kingpin specialist on Amex. Gilligan & Will habitually made it their business to see to it that prior to the listing of any of the corporations they represented, their partners, wives, and others whom Gilligan would designate could purchase the stock at prices below the current market price. Then, with the securities fully listed, the Gilligan crowd would keep in close touch with the principals of the newly listed corporation, who made it a point to tip off Gilligan on any major development in the company before the public got wind of it. Gilligan's attitude is neatly summed up in his testimony to the SEC:

Question: Do you think a specialist is entitled to inside information about occurrences that are about to happen in a corporation?

Answer: Yes, I think he should be kept fully informed, because he has a duty to maintain a market.

Question: This being fully informed would be prior to informing the general public?

Answer: Yes.

Another group of privileged characters on Amex, and for that matter on any exchange, is the floor trader. His access to inside information—even though some of it might be unreliable—and his facility to take advantage of it have put him in a position where his activities are going to be spotlighted during the forthcoming investigations of the stock market authorized by Congress.

Only 30 members of the American Stock Exchange bear the title of floor trader, a group of yeomanry defined as follows in a publication known as *The Segregation Report*:

THE MONEY CHANGERS 133

"The floor trader has no contact with the public, extends no credit, and usually does not maintain an independent office. He is a professional speculator who deals in securities for quick profits. He constantly seeks opportunities for rapid turnover and he prefers to liquidate a position swiftly . . . Unlike the specialist, he professes no responsibility for the maintenance of a fair and orderly market. He does not solicit brokerage business and his brokerage function is distinctly of minor importance. He has few personal customers but occasionally is entrusted with the execution of large orders by members or firms who desire to conceal their presence in the market . . . He is not restrained in his trading by the forces of competition for brokerage business or the necessity for retaining the good will of customers."

The floor trader is, in effect, the barfly of the trading posts, flitting about with the basic purpose of nabbing a fast buck.

Yet, from his position, the floor trader enjoys a measurable advantage over the general public. The only regulation he has to worry about is one which says that floor traders "shall not congregate in a particular stock" or "individually or as a group, intentionally or unintentionally, dominate the market" or be "conspicuous" in the general market or in the market in a particular stock. But the Division of Trading and Exchanges of the SEC has discovered and reported that (1) floor traders of Amex concentrated their activity almost exclusively in the more active stocks; (2) floor traders dominated the market by frequently purchasing relatively large blocks of stock in a single transaction, often in a concerted manner and (3) the most active floor trader, Louis Alter, concentrated his activities at the Gilligan & Will post. At the time, Alter was also doubling as a specialist.

From January through March in 1961, the SEC studied the reports which five floor traders on Amex filed with both the Commission and the Exchange to see just how effective the regulations covering their activities were. To a man, the five traders' reports showed major differences between their reports and what actually happened on the floor.

According to the SEC, a trader by the name of William J. Halpern reported 3700 shares bought and 500 shares sold. His account showed 74,000 shares bought and the same amount sold. He admitted that he had forgotten to file many of the required reports.

Three other traders, Stephen W. Denman, Eugene F. Dunn, and W. T. Wuestehube, told the SEC that the wide differences between their reports and their actual accounts results from "off-floor" transactions, made from the Exchange restaurants and nearby drugstores.

Here was a neat dodge to get around regulations, like crossing your fingers behind your back, or other infantile gimmicks designed to mask the truth. It seems that Amex had ruled that orders originating "off the floor" were exempt from exchange regulations, and in 1960 had further designated that the "floor" included only the floor itself, plus the entrances and lobbies of the Exchange building. All the intrepid floor trader needed to do was to pick up a hot inside tip on the floor, make a fifty-yard dash to the nearest drugstore, phone a $2 broker on the floor, and climb in on a deal long before the public had a chance. Amex has since corrected the rule to prevent this track meet gambit.

The famous Gilligan & Will post was again featured in the actions of floor traders, the two most persistent of whom were Louis Alter and George De Martini. Alter's enthusiasm for Gilligan & Will stocks was such that about 90 per cent of his transactions in 1959 were confined to this choice. De Martini held in his enthusiasm to the extent that only 83 per cent of his total business was confined to the same post. The regulations against acting in concert, dominating a stock, and concentrating on particular stocks simply were ignored, even though Amex persuaded Alter to terminate his trading at that post. For his activity, Alter was finally fined $250 and his trading privileges were suspended for 60 days. Their relationship with the Gilligan & Will post was so chummy that they turned their orders in on green slips of paper, which would automatically set them aside from the run-of-the-mill, public order.

De Martini had a strong liking for Consolidated New Pacific stock. On July 28, the day before the registration became effective, he took part in 30 per cent of all the transactions in the stock. Over a million and a quarter shares of the stock were offered the following day to the public, the prices to be based on Amex quotations. At the beginning of July, the SEC reports, the price was $1\frac{3}{16}$. It moved to $1\frac{5}{16}$ by July 27. When July 28 came to a close the stock stood at $1\frac{11}{16}$, with De Martini's hard work and energy contributing to the price when the issue opened on the Exchange.

It is the SEC's opinion that the enforcement of the floor trading rules by Amex has been shoddy and unkempt. The public governors of the Exchange, the SEC notes, have been outspoken in their statement that a national securities exchange has a heavy responsibility to the public and in keeping the public informed. "A National Securities Exchange is a quasi-public institution," a 1941 statement by the public governors of the Exchange said. "If it is to continue to act in that capacity, it must render a full account of its stewardship to the public at all times."

But with all the high-toned pronouncements and elaborate regulations by both national exchanges, the fact still remains that self-regulation alone in such a critical field is obviously not enough. No such detailed study of the New York Stock Exchange as that of Amex has been completed by the SEC. What the new investigation will turn up in this regard remains to be seen. But President Funston still holds on tenaciously to the premise that the national exchanges can be left on their own. "The Exchange believes," Mr. Funston says, "that tough self-regulation and rigid enforcement provide the most practical means for policing all segments of the securities industry."

He further commented that ". . . there is nothing in what the Exchange has learned from disclosures made regarding practices elsewhere in the securities industry that lessens in any way its faith in the integrity of the auction market, or its confidence that this market place is operating efficiently, fairly, and effectively in the public interest."

The results of the SEC's Amex study had obviously not alarmed him.

Recent cases of more-than-secret deals have included companies listed on the New York Stock Exchange such as F. L. Jacobs Company, which underwent a reorganization under the Bankruptcy Act, after pleading *nolo contendere* to a conspiracy charge. This landmark case, know as *United States vs. Alexander Guterma, et al.*, represents the first criminal prosecution of corporate insiders for their failure to file stock-ownership reports, and for obstructing the filing of an annual report on a listed company. The motives behind the action of Guterma were clearly revealed as an effort to cover up an extensive and hearty manipulating program and the looting of the company for personal benefit. For his efforts in this direction, Mr. Guterma was handed down a jail sentence of four years and eleven months, plus a fine of $160,000. As if this weren't enough, Guterma was also indicted in a case involving United Dye and Chemical, in which he not only short-circuited the proxy rules of the SEC, but also jacked up the prices of the company stock on the Exchange and romped through a skillful defrauding scheme to lighten the wallets of United Dye and Chemical stock purchasers.

In the wake of all this, the Congressional and SEC investigations seem to point inevitably toward better enforcement and more stringent regulations.

Self-control is a great thing, but it's more effective when there's a referee around to blow the whistle.

"Stock prices change because of the law of supply and demand . . ."
"If more people want to buy than sell, the price of a stock goes up . . ."
"In the long run, the price of a stock tends to reflect the value of a company . . ."
—STATEMENTS OF THE NEW YORK STOCK EXCHANGE

CHAPTER VII

April in New York, when the air at times becomes winelike and gentle lovers sometimes brave a lunch or two on the terrace of the cafeteria at the Central Park zoo, is an intoxicating time. During the heady days of April in 1961, the stock market took a cue from the first robins of spring to swoop up to a new high—the highest peak in the history of the world. The sacred Dow-Jones industrial average soared to 694.11, a dizzy altitude which made the previous peak, in January 1960, of 685.47 somewhat unimpressive. The ministers and priests of the oracles noted this with mixed emotions. Some were gloomy, some were neutral, and some felt that this was only the beginning of a climb which would end they knew not where. Volume on the New York Stock Exchange was clicking over regularly at the rate of some 18,000 shares per minute, or over five million shares a day. Hardly a listed stock was neglected, and it wasn't uncommon for

137

85 per cent of the issues on the Exchange to see some kind of action during the day. Figures on the tote boards in the funeral parlors whirred with the velocity of a TV computer on election night. It all signified the start of the wildest, roaringest bull market the financial world had ever embraced. *Newsweek* reported that $65 billion had been added to the value of shares on the New York Stock Exchange in just five months—more than the value of all Big Board stocks at the end of 1929. It further pointed out that investors were grabbing new issues like unleashed puppies in a meat market. Morton Foods, of Dallas, went public with an underwriting price tag of $12.50 per share. By the time the first share was sold over the counter, the tag had gone up to $17, and before you could blink at the blackboard it was selling for $22.

By May the Dow-Jones industrial whisked through the 700 mark, a climb of 500 points in less than ten years. The Re, Re & Sagarese case had broken, and President Keith Funston of the Stock Exchange issued a sharp warning for buyers to beware. Congressional committees rolled up their sleeves and got set to turn a microscope on the whole securities market. Market loans were up to their highest peak since the dismal thirties.

The Great Unwashed Public was plunging into the market on an unheard-of scale. Tips and rumors were everywhere. The more sober Wall Street men were shaking their heads and hoping that the public's carbonated euphoria would go flat. The volume of trading on the Stock Exchange was 60 per cent above the daily average of 1960. The pace was ominously similar, and in fact above the early 1929 levels which led to its suicidal plunge.

Values of stock had little to do with the frenzied buying. *Forbes* reported that Polaroid was selling at 83 times its 1960 earnings. On Amex, Cubric Corporation sold at 100 times earnings. A company sold over the counter, Control Data, sold at 244 times earnings. In more conservative days, the figure of 10 times earnings was supposed to be the rule of thumb for a good buy.

For the non-stockbuyer, these figures may seem puzzling, but a look at what they mean will reveal their alarming significance. If, for instance, you should buy a house for investment purposes, and hope to earn 6 per cent on your investment, you'd have to take in $1200 a year in rent on a $20,000 house to get that return. Your investment of $20,000 would be at the rate of about 17 times earnings. If you earned 10 per cent on the house, or $2000 a year, your investment would represent 10 times earnings.

If you expected earnings of $2000 a year, and had money to invest, the chances are you wouldn't want to pay much over $20,000 or $25,000 for a house, because anything higher simply wouldn't be profitable. But if, by some wild stretch of the imagination, you decided to buy a house which would sell at 244 times earnings, you'd pay $488,000 in order to bring in earnings of $2000 a year. There are very few people who would be willing to do this—but on the stock market, they've done it.

All along Wall Street, the pros blamed the public for the tidal surge of outright speculation. Penny stocks were being gobbled in huge, indigestible lumps, and stock splits were something no well-dressed stockholder could afford to be without. Both of these factors played a big part in the champagne market of 1961. And every fashionable family corporation studied the possibility of going public. Many did.

Penny stocks, of course, are tempting bait for the sucker. Psychologically, he feels richer if he has a hundred shares at $1.00 each than if he has one share for $100. He doesn't stop to realize that even in the stock market, comparatively at least, you're just likely to get what you pay for. Since the penny stocks are picked up easily by other suckers, there is an inclination for the price to rise on them far beyond reason or value, so that they automatically become overpriced more quickly than a $500-a-share blue chip.

Stock splits are another snare and delusion, creating a wonderful false sense of prosperity on the part of the stockholder. If you take a large tenderloin steak, and cut it in half, you certainly don't create any more steak. A person with a minimum intelligence knows this. But not the misguided stockholder. He often feels that he's doubled his investment. In fact, he sometimes does, because the psychological impact of a 2-for-1 stock split stirs up interest in other optimistically deluded stockholders who in turn pay outlandish prices for the stock.

For a tightly held or family corporation to go public, there is room for all sorts of intoxicating stimulation, imparting to the buyer a feeling of getting in on the ground floor, even though the cellar hole that he might fall into might be fantastically deep.

Newsweek quotes one broker as saying that the three areas of danger in the fizzing 1961 market were (1) the new issues, (2) the glamor of growth of stocks, and (3) the formerly obscure issues. It quotes another broker: "Everyone has the idea that anything he buys will double overnight. The horrible thing is, it has happened!"

Covering a convention of stock market analysts in Richmond, Virginia, during May of 1961, the *U.S. News & World Report* came up with a grab-bag full of observations on the 1961 scene. A good many of the analysts were a little nervous about the whole situation.

Said one New York investment banker: "I think this market is crazy, just plain crazy. There are still good stocks around, companies selling at 10 to 20 times earnings and with good earnings prospects. But people seem to want to pay for stock selling at 60 or 80 times a company's earnings. I don't know why. This isn't just a thinking man's market."

A Philadelphia investment counselor told the *U.S. News* reporter: "It's an amazing market. How can stocks go up with profits no better than they are? People just don't seem to care about profits. All they want to know is: 'What's going up tomorrow?'"

Another said: "It can't go on. Actually, I am afraid this market already is 1929 all over again, except only for the fact that much less of the stock is being bought on credit now."

Others blamed the situation on emotional buying, but what buying isn't?

While the penny stocks bubbled in the Wall Street caldron, so did the blue chips. By the end of 1961 the Dow-Jones industrials, based on the averages of 30 aristocrats, pushed onward and upward to 731.51.

Companies whose assets total in the vicinity of only half a million were selling their stock at a price which would indicate to a reasonable and prudent investor that they should be worth over $15 million. Whenever a company decided to "go public," the chances were that insiders, their families, their friends, and the undewriters were able to buy the stock at rates far below what the first public sale registered.

Fortunately, the stiff margin requirements set down by the Federal Reserve, set at the rate of 70 per cent during the orgy, helped keep the romp under more control than the 1929 nightmare, in spite of ways and means devised to get around this, which will be discussed later. But instead of being grateful that such a restraint was available, the New York Stock Exchange was pushing for smaller and better margins, on the grounds that stocks were like the merchandise sold on the installment plan, and should be granted equal liberties. But the motive for buying merchandise is entirely different from the motive for buying stock on margin. Merchandise is bought to live with and to use. Stock is bought for profit and gain. There is nothing wrong with this, except for the fact that it's practically axiomatic that if you borrow money to get in a crap game, you're invariably going to get into trouble. And the 1961 market was taking on all the aspects of a crap game as the year progressed. More people lose than win on the stock market. In August of 1961, in the middle of the plushest of plush bull markets, the total stocks on the New York Stock Exchange would have brought about a 7.3 per cent loss to anyone who bought the listed stocks of that Exchange across the board. "Gullibility, thy name is Investor," said one disenchanted broker, off the record.

All through the 1961 frenetic market, the giant pincers

dangled, ready to squeeze at any moment. On the one side, the risky, red-hot issues which in spite of inflated prices could fizzle out into nothing at a moment's notice; on the other hand, the high-priced offerings of the blue chips, bid up to the point where it would take a generation for them to pay off in any meaningful way.

Meanwhile, the SEC was swamped during 1961 with registrations for new stock issues, which continued into 1962. Many of them were penny stocks, handsome shiny lures for the amateur bass swimming around the shoals of the financial world.

Over 2300 registrations were filed with the SEC, the largest in history, and almost half again as many as for the same period in 1960. And even though the SEC had augmented its staff, it was still swamped with a gigantic registration and policing job.

Without the SEC and the higher Federal Reserve margin rates around, it's impossible to tell what would have happened to the post-World War II security markets, especially as a result of the pyrotechnics in 1961. If the wild and freebooting situation which existed in 1929 were still with us, many sober and reliable experts feel that the market would have crashed worse than it did in May of 1962.

As always, there were plenty of prognosticators around, consorting with their muses and consulting their oracles. Also as always, there was considerable hedging. Predictions for 1960, in general, were wildly inaccurate. At the start of 1961 it was hard to tell just what the forecasts were, because there was more than the usual hedging. And if there is anyone more skillful than a market forecaster for hedging, he has yet to be discovered.

Typical comments by the forecasters reveal this uncanny skill, as in these early 1961 predictions:

"Frankly, the crystal ball is clouded and those who try to read it are in need of better glasses . . ."

"Investors should not forget, however, that the *unex-*

pected always is a bigger price-changing influence in securities than the *expected* . . ."

"As the year develops, the business climate may be either much better or much worse than now expected . . ."

"We are entering the New Year with a mixture of apprehension and anticipation . . ."

"Obviously, only time will tell whether the psychological impact of a change in government and a change in policies will be sufficient to reverse the present downward trend of the economy . . ."

"Goodrich has declined three points since recommended here in October. Undoubtedly, there has been tax-selling in this issue . . ."

"The economy has been undergoing a moderate readjustment but business is good in many lines . . ."

"We're in a recession, but we don't think this should be dignified by calling it a *major* recession . . ."

"In conclusion, we think that while near-term uncertainties exist and no one can really say that the decline in stock prices has gone as far as it will, we believe we are beginning to form a base which will be both fundamentally and technically sound and from which—*given the anticipated improvement in business in 1961*—we could get a stock market rise of worthwhile proportions . . ." (Italics added.)

"Even though economists are by no means unanimous on the subject, it is probably fair to say . . ."

"Some economists believe we are in a recession, others that we are not in one but are heading for one, and still others that we are neither in nor headed for one . . ."

"By and large, dividends will hold up well; however, there may be some casualties . . ."

These are statements made in just two of the most highly regarded business publications in the country. A large selection of hedging statements of this nature could be made in two hours, and could more than fill this book. It is obvious that, for the most part, the amateur investor is left with his head spinning.

What's more, nearly all of this professional advice is as cheap as a copy of an average magazine, in fact as cheap as a daily newspaper. And a broker's advice comes absolutely free. On the basis of common-sense laws of value, it is hard to see how anyone could expect to get something for nothing— especially in the case of the stock market, where the right advice, if there ever were such a thing, would make you a millionaire overnight. One well-known woman cosmetics manufacturer solved the whole problem, and came out on top.

She tacked up the *Wall Street Journal* stock market quotations every morning on the back of her office door, and threw darts at it.

Back in 1957, *Time* looked into the market advice situation and discovered that no fewer than 30,700 market letters poured out of nearly 300 of the New York Stock Exchange member firms, giving advice on what to buy or sell. The total circulation of these came to ten million or so. The consensus of opinion of their value among the Wall Street pros came to one definite conclusion: "Not worth a hoot in hell." Way back in 1933, the Cowles Commission for Economic Research made a study of the forecasters, and discovered that their predictions were 4 per cent less accurate than they would have been if the choices had been made at random. Eleven years after that they repeated the study: no improvement. Another phenomenon was the practice of many market letters quoting other market letters in an endless chain.

By the time 1961 was well under way, a good many observers felt that the ionized speculation in the air carried with it a very similar molecular structure to that of 1929. In that year the forecasters were having a field day: God seemed to be in his heaven, and all seemed right with the world.

On October 21, 1929, *Time* carried an inside-cover, full-page color ad for Fatima cigarettes. In the center is a full-length portrait of a happy, loving couple, their backs to the artist who drew them, reading the stock market section of the daily paper. Beside them is a happy, loving puppy, romping at their feet, while the young wife's high-heeled shoe is kicked up in the air in a posture of exuberance as she and her husband apparently become ecstatic over their glorious successes in the stock market.

The headline reads: WHAT A WHALE OF A DIFFERENCE JUST A FEW *POINTS* MAKE.

Further on in the musty pages of that issue of *Time* is a full-page, one-color ad headlined:

FREE STOCK MARKET BULLETINS THAT
TELL YOU THE BEST BUYS NOW

"We are this week recommending the immediate purchase of two undervalued stocks which, in our opinion, represent 'The Best Buys Now,' " the copy goes on to read, as it heralds the services of an investment research company.

Another broker's advertisement featured the picture of a midwest banker, with a headline: HE INVESTS HIS MODEST EARNINGS IN GOOD, SOUND SECURITIES.

Time itself proudly announced the first issue of *Fortune*, at "Ten dollars the year."

The Business and Finance pages were uniformly dull. The most exciting item in the entire issue was the short report on the most famous game of all the World's Series, when the Philadelphia Athletics scored ten runs in the seventh inning to defeat the Chicago Cubs, 10-8.

This was October 21, 1929, as reflected by the pages of *Time*.

Just about a week before this, on October 13, *The New York Times* was reporting some interesting things. The stock market, all during the year riding on a tide of unprecedented speculation, was twitching slightly and rather apathetic. The public, stuffed to the gullet with stock bought on incredibly low margins—down as low as 20 per cent, even down to 5, and 10 per cent—was watching the huge Cinerama-type production of the giant speculators and accepting their rigged and manipulative ballet as if this *danse macabre* were part and parcel of the fitting and proper thing to do. When you buy a refrigerator at 10 per cent down you are still taking some risk, because you will lose the appliance if you are unable to continue making payments. On the other hand, you know the limits of that payment. You know that you are not going to be asked to pay more than, say, the $200 you have contracted to pay. You might have to sweat out the payments, and you might regret your extravagance in buying such a handsome piece of machinery. But you are safe, within the $200 limit. However, if an earnest and diligent householder suddenly found that the price of his refrigerator was flexible and open-end, that he might at any moment have to "cover" a sudden rise in price, he would be as frigid as an ice tray about buying it in the first place. If he received a notice from the company stating: "We regret very much that the price of your refrigerator has risen to $300, and we must require you to increase your monthly payment as stipulated below, or surrender the merchandise at once . . . .," he might lose all he has put into it, as well as the machine itself.

Buying stock at 20 per cent margin is equally disastrous, except in reverse. If our householder bought $1000 worth of stock, he needed to put out only $200 to get it. For the moment, he feels expansive and disgustingly rich, even though he really owns only $200 worth of that stock. The rest—$800 worth—he is responsible for. But then the stock slips in value —down to one-half its former worth. His holding is now worth only $100. His margin has slipped to 10 per cent, and his broker calls on him to shell out another 10 per cent of the original price to cover. He can't do it. He loses everything— not only his golden dreams of being a big capitalist, but his cash as well. In the Twittering Twenties, nearly half of the stock market customers were buying on margin. In 1929, more margin trading took place than in any other time in history. Out-and-out manipulation was taking place everywhere. The public knew it, accepted it, even cheered it from the bleacher seats.

The big bulls, plugging for a rise in prices so they could clean up profits, gathered together in gigantic pools to buy and sell behind the scenes, "painting the tape" as it is called, so that the sucker public would think the stock was really on the upgrade; then the pools would sell out, dump the stock, and leave the public with its chin hanging out and its feathers clipped. Or the big bears, plugging for a fall in the market, would sell short—in other words, sell something which was not theirs by borrowing the stock. Then they would flood the market with the stock until the price tumbled, buy it back in at greatly depressed prices, and replace the stock they had borrowed with the much cheaper product.

Instead of rising up in anger at this sort of thievery, the public wistfully tried to figure out ways it could practice the same chicanery.

In this atmosphere, the news on October 13, 1929, was interesting mainly because it indicated a certain amount of perplexity in Wall Street, but beyond that it was undistinguished. The most noteworthy item in the *Times* on that date was a statement by Charles Dice, professor of business organization at Ohio State, and author of *New Levels in the Stock Market,* which had just been published.

In a pontifical and authoritative statement to the press, he stated unequivocally that the stock market would see bigger gains in the immediate future than in any other period of history. He went on further to say that except for minor fluctuations the present high level of prices would be constant for years to come, that the new level of prices was not fictitious.

"The public has underwritten the market," he said. "One reason why prices go up so readily is that great amounts of stocks have been taken out of the market by the people as a more or less permanent investment. Speculation is based on confidence and a readiness to support the risks of industrial progress. Industries are no longer the tools of power groups who manipulate them to their own profit through stock market operations."

Just what type of sand the professor's head was buried in is indicated by the fact that a Senate committee discovered that in 1929 over 100 stocks of the New York Stock Exchange were juggled by pools in which its own members were interested. The stocks included American Tobacco, Chrysler, National Cash Register, Montgomery Ward, Radio Corporation of America, Standard Oil of California, Union Carbide, and others. The pool organized for the Sinclair Oil deal in 1929 brought a neat $12,000,000 to carve up.

"Among the yardsticks for predicting the behavior of stocks which have been rendered obsolete," the good professor from Ohio rambled on, "are the truism that what goes up must come down, that the market will be at the end of a major advance after twenty to twenty-four months of climbing, that major declines will run from eleven to fifteen months, that stock prices cannot safely exceed ten times the net earnings available for dividends on the common stock per share."

But the Ohio professor was not alone in his feelings. In addition to hordes of other experts, Professor Irving Fisher, the Yale University economist, told a purchasing agents' meeting just two days later that stock prices had reached what looked like a permanently high plateau: "Time will tell whether the increase will continue sufficiently to justify the present high level. I expect that it will."

He later added: "I expect to see the stock market a good deal higher than it is today within a few months . . ."

But Fisher, wearing his Yale-blue varsity letter in Economics, had comforting company himself. On the same day he was speaking to his group of purchasing agents, Charles E. Mitchell, chairman of the National City Bank of New York, was leaving London to sail for America.

"Although in some cases, speculation has gone too far in the United States," he told the press, "the markets generally are now in a healthy condition . . . many leading industrial securities are now at levels which would have been considered perfectly sound and conservative even by the standards of ten years ago . . ."

Getting up more steam, he went on to say: "The market

values have a sound basis in the general prosperity of our country. All the basic industries are doing satisfactorily, and unless something unforeseen occurs, should continue to do so. I cannot see anything such as some people are warning us of, to check that continued expansion."

One of those people who was putting up storm signals was Roger Babson, the Boston crystal-ball gazer of the economic set, who was flatly predicting that stocks would tumble between 50 and 60 points in the not-too-distant future. He was preaching that the frenzy of speculation was unwarranted and unheard of, that the mass of market dabblers had better damn well get out of debt and out of the thin margin accounts they were carrying.

But Babson was hooted down both by the crowds in the bleachers and the box-seat holders as well. He never had half a chance to be heard, so great was the babble.

Saturday, October 19, was cloudy, chilly, grey, and ominous. And so was the New York Stock Exchange, which at that time had Saturday sessions. The temperature dipped, and so did the stocks. Not that this was a crash or a panic. But it was a sharp break, and an alarming one.

The New York Times headlined the fact that stocks were driven down, while a wave of selling engulfed the market. Losses were put at 5 to 20 points. The ticker, characteristically falling behind in the heavy volume of trading, left thousands of speculators wondering what had hit them, falling over like tenpins in their failure to cover the margins.

A big bear raid was one of the chief stories floating around Wall Street as the reason for the break, *The New York Times* reported. The chief sitting bull of the day was supposed to be Arthur W. Cutten, a Chicago financier who was reached by that paper in his hotel suite in Atlantic City for a quote. No more characteristic picture of the twenties could be conjured up than this—a big wheel deal, watching the ticker tape in an atmosphere of salt water taffies and bootleg whiskey, just off the Boardwalk. Close friends of his revealed that nothing had happened on the market to change his opinion that everything was rosy, and that, if anything, stocks were going to go higher.

Another big wheel deal on the other side of the fence, the bear side, was Jesse L. Livermore, the great plunger who was credited with being the biggest speculator in the country at one time. He was thought to be clawing and chewing away at the market in an orgy of short selling, whereby prices would be depressed. Livermore was supposed to have borrowed huge chunks of top-rated stocks, in the hopes that the market would go down; Cutten was supposed to have bought the same stocks heavily, pushing for a rise. The two were supposed to be ripping at each other's entrails—the bear fighting for the market to go down, the bull fighting for it to go up. No real evidence was uncovered at the time, but, as usual, the public was hardly ruffled by this report, counting it as part of the game, even though the little man was losing quarts of blood at a time from their battle.

The market opened slowly, and was expected to rally. At 10:30 A.M., the rumble of heavy artillery was heard on the selling side, and stocks began falling. In the last half-hour stocks made an anemic rally, enough to stop a runaway, at least. For the most part, investors sat around with their ticker tapes hanging out of their pockets, waiting for some kind of vague thing they called "organized support." This was, the lambs felt, the big boys rushing in to stem this tide before it got out of hand.

And by Wednesday, October 23, it began to look as if they were right. As a 52-mile-an-hour gale battered the city, stocks made a sharp recovery, in spite of a slight slip toward the close of the day. Gains were registered up to 15 points. Much of the recovery was credited to the organized banking support the public was counting on, as if these Olympian creatures were supposed to ride up on chariots stacked with gold bullion. And by now Charles E. Mitchell was back in the country, radiant with optimism and declaring that the decline had certainly gone too far. And he could have been right. Hershey Chocolate was up 10 points, Eastman Kodak up 9¼. The J. I. Case Company was up 28 points, and Columbian Carbon up over 16.

As for the spreading alarm over the extent of brokers' loans, Mr. Mitchell puffed and said: "The public is suffering from 'brokers' loanitis.' The situation is one which will correct itself if let alone . . . It is nothing to become alarmed about." Yet thousands of unanswered margin calls had been taking place, especially among the small traders who could afford it least. The big, wealthy bear traders, sniffing blood, had been coming in for more profits. And, of all things, Professor Fisher returned again with a statement, pronounced with all the authority he might have had if he had been standing by the Yale fence with a pigskin under his arm. The market has *not* been inflated, he said; it had only been "readjusted." He brushed off the market break as a "shaking out of the lunatic fringe that attempts to speculate on margin . . . ," and went on to say that he predicted within the next few weeks a "ragged market, returning eventually to further steady increases." But one wise gentleman in the audience of credit men whom he was addressing nudged him with the reminder that Fisher himself had said several months before that predicting human behavior was quite different from analyzing facts and figures.

Washington, in the meantime, was eyeing the situation gingerly. The news from there, and it could only happen in the twenties, was that a woman had taken a thermos bottle and sandwich up to the top of the Washington monument and spent the night there so that she could see the sunrise. Experts in the nation's capitol weren't too keen on signing their names to any public statements but felt that the situation was "sound," and there was nothing to worry about. They refused to take a pessimistic view, feeling that the big corporations were making money hand over fist, dividends were good, and business was high and swinging.

They could have been right. On Wednesday, October 23, 1929, the market opened slowly and calmly—and even higher than the day before in many cases. In the middle of the morning, some automotive accessory stocks began acting queerly. Nobody seemed to know why, but it was contagious. Suddenly more prices began to slip, slowly, like the hands of a trapeze artist covered with oil. At 1 P.M. the decline picked up speed. By 2 P.M. nearly every stock on the Exchange was bobbing like a miniature dinghy at anchor in a squall. In this final hour of the day, 2½ million shares changed hands. Margin accounts were wiped out by the thousands. One stock, the Adams Express Company, fell 96 points; General Electric fell 20; I. T. & T., 13. Otis Elevator fell as if a cable had snapped—down 43 points. No one seemed to know exactly who was selling, or why. The funeral parlors were draped in crepe in every part of the country.

It was said that organized banking support was held back because, even though the jolt was severe, it still wasn't a real emergency. Powerful support, though, was expected any minute. The president of one of the largest investment trusts said that many stock issues would sweep to new highs in the following year.

A total paper loss of $4 billion was recorded for the day, which ended with growing terror as the people who were totally wiped out of existence sat stunned in front of the telephones which had previously brought them nothing but prosperous messages and wishes from their kindly, local family brokers.

To most, the crumble—still not of gigantic proportions —was a total mystery. It was as if a huge dump truck had backed up the doors of the Exchange and slid an unending pile of securities on the floor—as if they came off the chute of the truck so fast that buyers, if any, could hardly grab them long enough to hold for a moment. Thousands and thousands of stockholders, all over the country, suddenly and simultaneously said to themselves: "This is it. I've had it. I'm getting out." Specialists, with their books full of stop-loss orders (orders which had been placed by wary stockholders to sell if a stock fell below a certain level), were forced to execute these orders, dumping many more hundreds of thousands of shares on the market, with the dispassionate and automatic action of a thermostat when the heat drops below a comfortable 70 degrees. When everybody decides to sell at the same time, there is no such thing as a market. It simply doesn't exist. The ticker tape, of course, fell back again, with the final quotations flickering out 104 minutes late. Total transactions came to around 6 million shares, as the final churning subsided. Bankers and insiders, themselves stunned by the avalanche, made no attempt to stem the tide. Or if they did, they pulled their fingers away as if they had touched a hot stove. But this was more than a stove. It was a Bessemer furnace. Wednesday, October 23, 1929, was a near disaster.

But out of the wilderness came a voice—a familiar voice. A voice which the caldron could not still. A voice amplified by the concrete vastness of the Yale Bowl, even though the shadows of the goal posts on the gridiron were lengthening. It was the voice—again—of Professor Irving Fisher.

"Gentlemen," he told an audience of bankers in Washington, "any fears that the price level of stock might go down to where it was in 1923 or earlier are not justified by present economic conditions.

"We are living," he continued, "in the age of mergers under the Coolidge and Hoover administrations and the old 'trust busting' sentiment has lapsed almost completely . . . These mergers have effected great economies and have therefore increased the profits of corporations to a great extent. Every merger boosts the stock of the merged companies because of this expectation. A considerable part of the rise in stock prices in the last two years has been due to the increased rate of formation of these mergers and the anticipation of future economies arising from them."

Professor Fisher got his answer to the great wave of mergers on the following day: Thursday, October 24, 1929.

It was a Thursday never to be forgotten.

It was Black Thursday.

The first sale of the day was Montgomery Ward. Six

thousand shares. Price: 83. Previous high for the year: 156.

It was to be followed by 12,894,649 other shares traded on the New York Stock Exchange that cloudy, chilly day in October of 1929. It was a volume unheard of, unprecedented, and it has never been equaled since.

It was a day of sheer, maniacal hysteria and panic.

Reporters who viewed the floor of the Exchange that day groped for words to describe it. Among the words used were "eerie" and "swaying." These are not unusual words, but in the context of a body of men carrying out their routine duties of a business day, they create a graphic picture.

In the ordinary course of human behavior, and in the line of transacting business, men simply do not cluster in groups and sway. Nor do their voices rise up in a weird and eerie roar. *The New York Times,* in chronicling the events of Black Thursday, finds itself repeating these phrases. You can sense, feel, and smell the scene. A forest of hands raised in the air, as if in supplication. Sweating, grunting, glazed clots of men around the trading posts, with their bodies literally waving in some sort of grotesque, inferno-like caldron. Outside, on the Street, the thunderous roar cuts through the walls of the Exchange like a knife through cheese, startling the crowd packing the sidewalks and Wall Street itself. It was a rumble, they say, a mammoth rumble, neither rising nor falling throughout the day. On rare occasions a singular groan or boo was heard, but for the most part it was the sound of a funereal cascade, echoing in the hollowness of the Floor.

The day started slowly enough. Shortly after the Montgomery Ward sale, General Motors was traded, but the drop in price was negligible. A good many other large blocks were put up for sale, but still there was no trend evident. For almost 30 minutes not much happened.

But by 10:30 it started, and the cascade was on. No avalanche or landslide could match it. The ticker tape slid hopelessly along, with no pretense of reflecting the current sales. At the end of this first half-hour it dropped 15 minutes behind, and only those on the floor knew any fragment of what was actually going on at the moment. A sale taking place at 11:30 would be reported nearly 50 minutes later. At 1:00 an anxious seller in the provincial recesses would have to wait 92 minutes to find out what had happened to his stock. And the last of the frantic sellers of the day picked up the information about his sale at 7:08½ P.M., just over four hours after the final gong had rung.

The roar rose and fell again, as brokers moved around the floor, dazed and in a trance. Hardly anyone knew what to make of it there, or in the board rooms throughout the country, which had literally turned into funeral parlors, with untold thousands of small speculators wiped as clean as the walls of an operating room. And they refused to go home. They hung around the gloomy boards, staring, stunned, and muttering.

A numbness, a tidal feeling of incredulity gripped brokers and investors everywhere, as the panic subsided and apathy—the closest attitude to death—set in.

It was as the panic and desperation reached its highest climax that Hero Richard Whitney shoved his way in to the Steel crowd and made his famous bid. And his ploy had its effect. The market rallied—and continued to rally to the end of the trading. As phony as the rally was, it saved Black Thursday from being the millennium itself. This was to come shortly, but not on that day. This whiff of oxygen, this massive dose of adrenalin administered by Dr. Whitney, actually floated the market with a deceivingly high buoyancy, leading to a temporary recovery at the end of the day—too late, of course, to save the wide mass of margin-holders who were unceremoniously sold out as new lows were reached. And like a dropped stitch, each new low set off a whole new batch of stop-loss orders, which in turn precipitated others, which in turn precipitated others, and so on endlessly.

Of all the pontifical statements issuing from Wall Street quarters, that of Thomas W. Lamont, senior partner of the J. P. Morgan firm, stands out as a genuine masterpiece.

"There has been a little distress selling on the Stock Exchange," he said, "and we have held a meeting of the heads of several financial institutions to discuss the situation."

The meeting was held at high noon in the hallowed halls of the House of Morgan. Four other leading financiers pushed and shoved their way through the crowds outside the Exchange to join Mr. Lamont in the hurriedly called conference. The crowd, clustered between the Exchange and the Morgan offices directly opposite, changed its tune from frantically depressive hysteria to frantically manic hysteria as word of the meeting buzzed from mouth to mouth. Here was the secondary defense moving in to save the day. The line might have crumbled, but it would take a miraculous broken-field runner to get through these billion-dollar line-backers.

Joining Lamont for the defensive huddle was Charles Edwin Mitchell, chairman of the National City Bank. He had all the proper credentials and decorations: he was an Amherst man, a member of the ultrasocial fraternity Chi Psi, a Republican, member of nearly a dozen clubs, with an office at 14 Wall Street and a home at 1 Sutton Place South. And Albert Wiggin, chairman of the Chase National Bank, joined him with a 660 Park Avenue address, a summer home in Greenwich, a dozen clubs, and a New England background. Both belonged to a club known as The Links—as did practically all of the members of that famous meeting, a badge they seemed to wear as a symbol that they had not only arrived, but had settled in. William Potter, president of the Guaranty Trust Company, contented himself with lesser status symbols. His homes were in the upper East 70's and in Old Westbury on Long Island. He was a Deke, an M. I. T. graduate, and a practicing engineer before he moved into finance. Seward Prosser, chairman of the Bankers Trust Company, was also rather unpretentious, belonging to only three clubs, and not having a college education to aid or hinder, as the case may be. He was, however, a staunch Republican, an Episcopalian, and a Union Leaguer, even though he didn't belong to The Links. Lamont himself epitomized the ultimate in material success. With Exeter, Harvard, The Links, the Union League, the House of Morgan, and everything else thrown in, he was, like the offspring of the parrot and the tiger, able to inspire the financial world to say: "When he talks, we *listen!*" And they listened, even to such statements as: "It is the consensus of the group that many of the quotations on the Stock Exchange do not fairly represent the situation."

In a way, he was right. Because Black Thursday was only the beginning. In spite of the repair job which Whitney Scotch-taped at the request of the meeting of these bankers, the precipitous downward plunge kept going out of all reason, with not even the sound of screeching brakes to lend hope that it would stop.

The Monday after—October 28—repeated the same pattern, but the panic did not seem to be there. The men on the Street had been fully anesthetized by Black Thursday, and worked through the nights with red-rimmed eyelids, with the numbness that comes from a dentist's needle in the lower jaw. The volume dropped a few million shares, but the losses were even more staggering. And this time Mr. Lamont and his defensive backfield failed to show up. Instead you could find only an advertisement in *The New York Times*, signed by P. W Chapman, which said: "We believe that the investor who purchases securities at this time with the discrimination that as always is a condition of prudent investing may do so with utmost confidence . . ."

This statement was a fitting lead-in to Tuesday, October 29. It was such a day on the stock market that even the most callous of fight referees would have stepped in and stopped the fight. It was as if a fighter were held against the ropes, limp and half-conscious, and pummeled beyond mercy by his opponent, while the crowd stood by and watched it happen and the referee looked the other way. $14,000,000,000 gushed from the economy of the country, spilled over the canvas, and was lost forever. No tourniquet could stop it. Even the conservative *Times* called it a "nation-wide stampede." General Electric, a favorite blue chip, plunged 47½ points down in a single day. John Galbraith, in his fascinating book *The Great Crash,* called it the "most devastating day in the history of the New York stock market." On the following day more stocks collapsed, but by now it was almost an hysterical joke. Thomas Lamont was continuing to reassure investors; hordes of famous names were gathering to announce that they were buying stock, and that the public should remain calm and steady.

Among them was Chase National's Albert Wiggin, who staunchly supported the effort to buy stocks now, in order to keep the economy on an even keel.

The shattering thing was that he was selling short for all he was worth at that very moment.

By November 11, *Time* magazine was looking at the entire nightmare as if it were over and done with. It eulogized Thomas Lamont and his teammates; it indicated that an "intangible change in feeling" had saved the U.S. from complete surrender to "what could properly be called a Values Panic."

But the real bottom was never reached until 1932—almost three years later. Eddie Cantor summed up the whole picture with the story of the man who asked for a hotel room. The clerk looked at him and said: "For sleeping—or jumping?"

Glaring out from behind the headlines of the times and standing as monuments of deceit are the statements of so-called responsible financiers who continued their pious pronouncements through the debacle. John Galbraith concludes his book *The Great Crash* with: "Long-run salvation by men of business had never been highly regarded if it means disturbance of orderly life and convenience in the present. So inaction will be advocated in the present even though it means deep trouble in the future. Here, at least equally with communism, lies the threat to capitalism. It is what causes men who know that things are going quite wrong to say that things are fundamentally sound."

"The Securities Act of 1933 and Securities Exchange Act of 1934 ushered in a new era in American finance ..."
—Statement by the New York Stock Exchange

CHAPTER VIII

The howls that went up from the halls of the Stock Exchange when the Congressional committees moved in to investigate the Era of the Orgy could be heard from Zanzibar to Outer Mongolia. Investor confidence had been shattered beyond recognition. As the SEC reports it, the market value of all stocks on the New York Stock Exchange had reached nearly $90 billion on September 1, 1929—just a few weeks before the Crash. In the middle of 1932, the same stocks were worth about $15 billion—a drop of nearly $75 billion, or over 83 per cent. If you had owned $1000 worth of stock in 1929, you would have watched it hit a value of $166, as you stood by hopelessly and wrung your hands. But the chances were, even if you had bought a thousand dollars worth of stock, you would have lost everything, because you had bought it on margin and you were closed out in the first wave. Either way, it was a catastrophe.

With the shattering of confidence, not entirely the fault of the stock market alone, came the Depression, the sickening wave of unemployment, the shelters for the homeless, the soup kitchens, the hopeless groans of millions of able-bodied men who wanted work, craved it, and were deprived of it.

Even a self-respecting drunk faces his moments of repentance, when the excesses of the evening before strike him the next morning with horror. Arrogance and a hangover are mutually incompatible. But not so with the Stock Exchange. It insisted that the government should keep hands off, even in the role of an outside referee. Richard Whitney, the White Knight with rusty armor, rode forth again to tell the Senate Committee on Banking and Currency that everything on the Stock Exchange was well in hand, that it could tame its own tigers, that the excessive bulls were locked in their pens and the bears chained to their trees.

What's more, the Old Guard of the Stock Exchange claimed that any government regulation would throttle new capital, ruin the investor, and thrust a plague of boils on the security market from coast to coast. It was as if the catastrophic Crash had never taken place, or, if it had taken place, such a monstrous cataclysm was natural and fitting. They wanted the football game, but they refused to consider the idea of a referee, umpire, linesman or timekeeper.

But after a quarter-century of regulation by the SEC and Federal Reserve regulation, the stocks on the New York Stock Exchange rose from their nearly $90 billion value in 1929 to just about $300 billion by 1960—hardly a testimony to dwarfism. What's more, in 1929 only $11 billion was put into new plants and equipment by investors, as compared to some $33 billion in 1959—a triple gain in the face of the so-called oppression by the SEC. According to further SEC information, the gross national product contrast between 1929 and 1959 does not seem to indicate that outside refereeing hurt the economy any. The total rested at over $100 billion in 1929, and had increased just about five times thirty years later. It is now over $500 billion.

The stage settings in 1929 before the Crash were hardly less ludicrous than those of the musical comedies of the day. The stock market was wearing a blazer-and-white-flannels mind and a roll-'em-girlies-roll-'em outlook. Busboys, batboys, bellboys, choir boys, and call girls were talking about the market as if it were an automatic elevator to financial heaven, and there were hardly such a thing as making an investment. The objective was to make a killing, and nothing less would do. The climbing curve of the Dow-Jones averages was literally a fever chart of a speculative virus which crossed all social and economic lines. Those at the top, who were ostensibly the guardians of both the flocks and the wool, were as irresponsible and immature as the rest. Regulation was long overdue, and it is not unreasonable to suppose that if the current SEC regulations had been in effect, the 1929 nightmare would have been reduced to merely a bad dream. Corporate and financial leaders thought nothing of engaging in maneuvers which were outright frauds. In the ten years following World War I, about $50 billion worth of new securities were floated, of which half sank without leaving an air bubble. These were out-and-out fraudulent securities, shoved on to a glazed-eye public with assurances that these would turn to gold in no time at all. Instead of selling gilt-edged securities, brokers and underwriters were shoveling out guilt-edged securities as fast as they could be run off the printing press.

This, combined with the massive manipulation carried on by many of the so-called respectable Wall Street figures, made the Crash inevitable. Huge pools of cynical speculators would organize themselves with such skill and cunning that they could make the weakest stock look like the hottest thing since the flanged wheel. When the psychological climate was right, they would dump the stock on the Great Unwashed and count their take. Pool operations, with carefully timed purchases and sales, would build up the prices of stocks to a totally unrealistic level, and then the pool operators would pull the plug. As they pulled it, the market would go down with a sickening gurgle. The bear market manipulators would rush in and borrow hoards of stock, then tickle the market to depress prices, buy up the stock at a dirt-cheap price, and return it to the suckers they borrowed it from. In case after case, any resemblance between actual value and market price was purely coincidental. In that great year of 1929, over one hundred stocks on the New York Stock Exchange were being put through these phony acrobatics by giant pool operators. Rumors, tips, phony press releases, and phony profit-and-loss figures were the order of the day. Corporations were not required to disclose anything; the buyer had nothing to go on but his own delirium tremens, and there was plenty of that around. Brokers, smelling bigger profits by selling as much stock as they could on margin, made it possible for the deluded sucker to overextend himself with obligations he couldn't possibly handle if the stock he bought on margin suddenly went down in price.

The corporation insiders had a heyday. Not being required to disclose vital information to the public or to the stockholder, the insider would govern his own position in the company's stock by the privy information he had at hand. If the company had something by the tail which would make profits soar, he would buy up all the stock he could get hold of at the lowest possible price before anyone else knew about it. Or if the company were losing three out of four engines, he would bail out before any of the suckers had a chance. With little or no regulation of proxy voting power, management could entrench itself securely in the face of any of its misdeeds, and the stockholder would remain helpless.

A major ulcer on the economic scene in 1929 consisted of the giant utility holding companies which grew like strangling weeds over the country. These pyramids of fictitious values bore much more resemblance to occasional outbursts of chain letters than to any economic common sense. In a chain-letter operation, the buyer at least knows that he is buying a pig in a poke, that the bubble is probably going to burst before the realizes any of the staggering potential the letter indicates might be possible. He also knows that when the chain-letter bubble breaks not much more harm is going to result than a few thousand people being left holding the bag for worthless sheets of paper. You've seen many of these chain-letter schemes, and you probably remember how they work.

"You have just bought a chain letter which can mean that you can receive up to X billion dollars if you don't break the chain," the letter might read. "Simply make five copies of this letter, after you have sent two dollars to the name at the top of the list. Drop that name off, and put your name at the bottom. Then sell five copies of this letter to your friends at the same price you paid for it—two dollars. *If* no one breaks the chain, you will receive thousands of dollars . . ," and so forth.

The stocks of the utility holding companies in 1929 were built on just about the same principle. Their value was fictitious, beyond the dreams of the wildest fiction writer. Speculators were literally buying pieces of paper, only it wasn't just the people who got in on the tail end who got stuck. Everybody did, when the Crash came.

In a chain letter, the entire population of the United States could be covered in less than ten "generations" of the letter. Millions of people would be left holding the bag. The overextended holding-company operations were hardly less ridiculous. They were top-heavy corporate superstructures which milked the productive operating companies until they withered and died. They did this through the process known as "leverage," which we'll examine in more detail in later pages. Using the common stocks of the actual operating companies which produced the electricity or water or gas, the holding companies would float billions of dollars worth of noncontrol securities such as bonds and preferred stocks. With voting control well in hand, the holding-company operators would begin their milking process, counting on their leverage securities to bring in profits to the top holding company, magnified by geometrical progression. But when the Crash hit, this magnification worked in reverse, and the whole structure crashed in like a Chinese cookie hit with a hammer. The tragic part of this is that even during the Depression the operating utilities, which were pawns of the holding companies and doing the hard work, dropped only 15 per cent in income. People had to have light and heat, and they scratched up enough to pay for it. But the 15 per cent drop was enough to topple the holding-company blood-suckers, who pulled down all their misled investors with them.

SEC reports indicate that between 1924 and 1930, utility holding companies floated about $5 billion worth of securities. Now the purpose of floating securities is, or should be, to increase the wealth of the company and the country by making more goods and services available to the consumer at a cheaper price. However, hardly any of this $5 billion pool of capital went to build turbo-generators, harness dams, create pipelines, further research, train employees, increase service, improve facilities, or make the customer happier. It went for the most part to buy up voting securities of other hard-working utility companies who had already been financed and were doing well. Like the transactions on the New York Stock Exchange today, this staggering fund of golden liquidity was not creating anything new. What's more, the big utility holding companies were buying up voting stock of companies which were as far remote from providing basic public service as they could get. Example: One holding company bought up a baseball team.

Not only was the consumer being deprived of new equipment to serve him better, but the stockholder who bought these tissue-paper securities was being pushed further out on a limb which was bending and splitting with his increased weight. SEC investigations indicate that there was no economic justification whatever for such antics. One holding company grew from $6 million to $1 billion in six years, and then crashed down on top of its stockholders. In the process it did nothing whatever to create or build as much as a new transformer.

In addition to the shadowy and ephemeral utility holding companies in 1929 were some of the wispy investment trusts, who were puffed up beyond all recognition in those gold-plated years. The same old story prevailed. They issued their own securities by the long ton in order to buy other securities, to the point where they were buying and selling their own securities, with insiders raking in profits which meant nothing except losses to the sucker trade.

Adding insult to usury were many unregulated investment counselors, who injected the lambs with anthraxial poison and cleaned up in the process.

This was the mural revealed to the onlooker of the security market when the wallpaper peeled off in 1929. As new legislation for regulation began to be drafted, more howls came up from the pits of the Stock Exchange, as loud as the ghostly rumble which shook the floor on Black Thursday. Forming a solid phalanx behind the banner of White Knight Whitney, they roared defiance. All kinds of disaster would be bound to follow any new legislation. Wholesale dumping of stocks would take place. Investors would liquidate all their securities. The market would be utterly demoralized. Utilities would face a death sentence.

But the legislation went ahead. It was enacted.

It somehow seems incredible that after the black disaster of 1929 the ailing, feverish Stock Exchange would not welcome some kind of responsible medical man to prescribe a health-building program for recovery. It had been indelibly proven to the patient that it could not possibly handle its own illnesses. When a play is failing on the road, the play doctor is called in when it becomes evident that the playwright can't handle the job himself. A fresh, outside view is almost necessary. But the Exchange resisted its medicine with the crotchety cussedness of a hospital patient who hurls his pills across the floor and thumbs his nose at the nurse.

As the legislation continued, the specific R shaped up. It was a massive dose, but it was an antitoxin for a virulent disease.

First was the "truth in securities" law, known as the Securities Act of 1933. Object: to let investors know exactly what they're buying by requiring that all essential information about the company be laid out for him. Also: to prohibit fraud and misrepresentation in offering a security for sale.

Any objections to a law which regulates against this sort of requirement would have to spring from insanity. Why shouldn't an investor know what he's buying? Why shouldn't he be legally protected from fraud? Why shouldn't he damn well have the right to study the facts and figures about a company before he puts his hard-earned cash on the line? What possible objection would a company have to presenting this information, if it wants to use somebody else's money for its own gain?

The second law was the Securities Exchange Act of 1934. Object: to keep fair and honest markets in securities. The act covered all the stock exchanges and the over-the-counter markets, concentrating on regulations to prevent fraudulent trapeze work after an issue was floated—picking up where the 1933 act left off. It also provided for supervision of brokers and dealers who were handling other people's money by the carload.

Next was the Public Utility Holding Company Act of 1935, designed to prevent the psychopathic pyramiding of the holding companies of the twenties, which bilked multi-millions of dollars from the unsuspecting public.

Next came the Trust Indenture Act of 1939, which provides minimum protection to the investor the corporation wants to borrow money from, as opposed to the stock buyer who becomes a part owner of the company. Many corporate loans had been floated in the form of bonds or debentures without any protection to the buyer.

Next was the Investment Company Act of 1940, designed to keep investment companies, which invest billions of dollars for other people, in line, after many excesses were revealed in the Crash.

Next was the Investment Advisers Act of 1940, requiring those who advise others how to invest to register, and to maintain certain standards to protect the interests of investors.

As each act was passed by Congress, the resistance on the part of many corners of the financial world grew to gargantuan proportions. Most of the larger holding corporations in the country refused point blank to register with the Securities and Exchange Commission, which had been set up to police the laws as they were enacted. They fought the Public Utility Holding Act with the passion of a wounded tiger, refusing to acept the registration requirement. They were able to stall all the way up to 1938, when the Supreme Court handed down a decision which upheld the constitutionality of the registration requirement of the Utility act. Losing ground here, they continued to fight the integration and simplification requirements of the act.

At the beginning the big holding companies, for instance, were given a chance to voluntarily set their houses in order but again they refused, making it necessary for the SEC to use the power granted it by Congress to see that the job was done. Only after long, expensive hearings and court sessions did the SEC win out.

The utility holding companies claimed that all of this would be a death sentence. Instead, the corporations involved saw their stocks rise to new highs. And those who fought the hardest have now come to look on the regulations as having a big hand in bringing them out of the doldrums.

In 1961 the regulations which the Stock Exchange, the utility holding companies, and many other segments of the securities market fought against had some force in retarding an exact repeat of history.

Every sign pointed to the same frenzy of speculative fever which swept the country like the Asian flu in 1929. But thanks to the laws which the short-sighted portion of the stock market tried to derail, conditions were at least reasonably sounder.

The flood of margin calls which shattered the 1929 market was more limited.

The incredible utility holding-company houses built of matchsticks in 1929 were not around.

The fly-by-night corporations were somewhat limited by the SEC registrations and "disclosure" requirements, although the situation was still far from safe.

The flagrant and open pools, combining for painting the tape, wash sales with manipulators entering spurious orders, and massive manipulation were not operating on anywhere near the scale they were in the twenties, although many fraudulent practices still remained.

The dangers of 1929 were greatly reduced—but they were still around, still in the background, still breathing.

In spite of the vast improvements arising out of Congressional action to protect the investor, the SEC still has its hands full. As the SEC points out, securities are distinctively different from almost any other type of merchandise a customer wants to buy. It's impossible for him to see, hear, smell, or feel them, except for the warehouse certificate which his investment gives him. It is almost impossible for him to visit a plant personally, and if he did his eyes and ears could easily be deceived.

The Commission further makes no pretense of telling a customer whether he is buying a pig in the poke or not. It in no way passes on the merit of a security, and in no way guarantees that the investor will not lose his shirt. It does, however, through its disclosure provisions, make it possible for the prospective buyer to make a decision based on some essential information, which, if incorrectly stated, can put the issuer into enough hot water to make him think twice before he issues a security. As long as a corporation discloses its basic facts properly, the investor is on his own. The security might be outlandishly overpriced. It might be shaky. It might be dubious. It might be an utterly wild and blue-sky scheme. But the buyer will at least have the privilege of looking at it in its own light through the disclosure prospectus filed with the SEC, and available to anyone on request.

What's more, the SEC requires that periodic reports be filed for all stocks listed on the exchanges, and these keep anyone desiring such information up to date. Copies of these reports can be obtained from the SEC at nominal cost.

With the surge of stock market activity swamping the small SEC staff, a lot of chinks still remain. In 1960 the SEC announced: "Unfortunately the pace of statutory violations, of fraudulent distributions and of other malpractices in our security markets has not slowed sufficiently to permit the Commission to divert to other matters the major segment of our personnel . . ."

The other matters include reviewing and modification of "forms, rules and procedures to meet and deal with new and developing patterns of securities . . . to cope with problems arising from . . . the growth of investment companies . . . ; to reach decisions as to the proper role of the Federal Government in the ever growing area of enforcement."

Present regulations and enforcement cannot guarantee against the recurrence of 1929 again by a long shot. When the public frenzy assumes manic proportions, the dike is beginning to spring a good many leaks, any one of which could become a 1929 flood.

The public is a funny animal. Few economists understand it. Many more of them would do better to study abnormal psychology than business charts, because the movement of the ticker tape in one direction or another can create more hypertensive symptoms in the emotions which make up the stock market than any economic textbooks yet written. Professor Fisher remains to this day the classic example of the economists who looked at the numbers instead of the psyche. Two kinds of blindness, academic and economic, can throw all the painstaking study ever compiled to the winds.

The tons of publicity about successful traders recently could well be one of the greatest catalysts in setting the biochemical stage for another 1929.

"Boiler-room" activity reached its peak during the early sixties, although SEC pressure has been forcing them to shift their base of operations to Canada. Boiler rooms are those establishments which set up fly-by-night salesmen on long-distance phones to con the investor on securities which are next to worthless. In spite of warnings all over the place, the public still continues to fall for them. The SEC keeps pounding away on the first law of investment: *Don't deal with strange security firms,* but apparently distance lends enchantment, and the long-distance call from a spurious boiler-room operator still casts some kind of magic veil over the buyer's eyes. High-pressure sales talks still work, and as soon as one boiler room is squelched, another one springs up. For the most part, these are so obviously in the con-man classification that it's hard to believe anyone could fall for them. One observer, looking across a hearing room at a line-up of boiler-room salesmen, whispered: "If they don't look like Murder, Inc., I don't know who does."

Part-time salesmen, not necessarily dishonest, but out to make a fast buck, are growing in numbers. Many of them will promise everything and deliver little or nothing.

Broker-dealer firms have been adding new salesmen by logarithms, with the number of salesmen of New York Stock Exchange member firms doubling in the past decade, from 11,409 to 24,898. In the over-the-counter market over the same period, the number of registered representatives tripled, going up from 29,824 to 84,648. What's more, a lot of brokerage houses are setting up branch offices, making supervision of overenthusiastic salesmen difficult.

Real estate securities have been on the increase, many of them shaky and dubious, but finding a sucker market regardless.

One of the most sensational growths in the securities market has been the investment companies, especially the mutual funds, which have been growing like ragweed all over the country. They have become one of the three principal elements in the securities market. Because of their size and the capital they represent they can almost singlehandedly affect the stock market, and there is plenty of nonsense going on among them which will be examined later.

An investment advisor remains in a handy position to influence the market if he should care to. The SEC is getting set to turn its spotlight on them and, if necessary, build up a heavier rule book to throw.

With the public attitude the way it is, with the securities market inclined to push the specter of 1929 out of its mind, and with an army of cynical stock salesmen running around footloose, and with major manipulations sneaking back into harness, the need for more adequate investor protection is obvious. The last amendments of any consequence to the securities laws were made over twenty years ago, in 1940. New situations have arisen, and old practices have been sneaking back in.

New legislation backed by the SEC to improve the situation has not exactly been received with open arms by Wall Street, any more than it was in the post-1929 period. Some of the current SEC regulations are as full of holes as a pound of Swiss cheese. In the Securities Exchange Act of 1934 there is still not specific language which would make it a violation of the act for a registered broker or dealer to embezzle moneys or securities left in his care even though he would be subject to state law. The statutory provisions of the act in regard to manipulation and the financial responsibility of brokers and dealers need clarification and stiff buttressing. The Commission needs more power to regulate the borrowing, holding, or lending of the customers' securities by a broker or dealer. The act doesn't make it crystal clear that attempts to buy or sell securities are covered by the anti-fraud provisions of the statute, nor is the SEC authorized to suspend or withdraw the registration of a securities exchange when the exchange fails to meet the requirements of its original registration. At certain times, it can be urgently necessary for the SEC to call for the suspension of trading in the over-the-counter market, and a wide loophole remains in this area.

While the Stock Exchange claims that "matched order" manipulation is a thing of the past (buying and selling the same stock to create an impression of activity), current provisions in SEC regulations make it possible. A false impression of active trading in an issue can still be engineered with impunity if the matching orders are not "of substantially the same size." The SEC is gunning simply to remove those five quoted words from the act in order to remove the loophole. Another part of the act requires proof of a series of manipulative transactions before the offender is clamped down on, whereas a single manipulative transaction can raise all kinds of hob.

These and a great many other golden opportunities for the unscrupulous security dealer are holes which critically need to be plugged. It would seem almost obvious that a customer's fully paid security should be set aside and kept for him. However, nothing in the present statute requires that his fully paid security be segregated from other securities that the broker might want to lend or borrow for his other transactions. One firm received 3,000 shares of a stock from a customer, who instructed the broker to apply 1,000 shares against a purchase of other securities, and to return 2,000 shares in the customer's name. The broker turned over the 3,000 shares to another broker to cover a short sale. The SEC secured an injunction against the broker, but the law still remains hazy.

None of the SEC regulations, of course, is designed to protect the investor from a drop in price. No statute has yet been designed to prevent a market break on the exchanges, and there probably never will be one until the laws of psychology are changed. The investor still has to keep his eyes open, still has to do his own evaluating, or find somebody he trusts to do it for him. So regardless of any improvements which might be made in the SEC regulations, there is still danger and plenty of it. The postwar trend toward widespread speculation opened up all kinds of pitfalls, and the gullible public has to accept its part of the blame if all the tinderbox conditions of 1929 should develop again.

At the present time, the SEC cannot take effective action in closing the barn door until the horse has been stolen. As Philip Loomis, Director of the Division of Trading and Exchanges for the SEC, explains it, a broker-dealer might begin to sell 100,000 shares of stock which he is grossly misrepresenting. He might be getting the word around that the company is making a million dollars a year, when the company is actually operating at a loss. The SEC begins to check up. They question investors as to what they have been told about the stock. They track down the true economic picture of the company. But then the broker gets wind of the fact that the SEC is on his trail, and he immediately stops his misrepresentations. The SEC would then be unable to get an injunction against him, because the practice wasn't carried out at the time the case was brought to court. The SEC, of course, must refer the action to the Department of Justice, and a whole year or so can go by before anything happens. Meanwhile, there is ample time for thousands of investors to get bilked.

Another indication of the hunger of the public for something which smells like a good thing has been the "when issued" or "when distributed" trading. Loomis explains this by pointing out that when A. T. & T. announced that it was going to split its stock, people began trading in the new shares before they were even issued, working with conditional contracts on a when-as-and-if basis. They bought, sold, paid for, and collected for stock which wasn't there yet. While there are controlled regulations on the stock exchanges, the over-the-counter market can run in any direction it wants with this maneuver. Some securities have been traded when no one knew whether the courts would even permit them to be issued. What's more, regular margin rules don't apply.

The New York Stock Exchange, in its position as the focal point of the stock market in general, again shows some of the same symptoms it exhibited when the Securities and Exchange laws were being formulated in the post-Crash period. Any new regulation which doesn't affect its own operation, it approves wholeheartedly. Any regulation which affects its own skin, it protests against vehemently. In doing so, the Exchange has tried to play Congress against the SEC, so that Congress would feel that the SEC was trespassing in its backyard, and vice versa.

"Some proposals trouble us," said Edward Gray, executive vice-president of the New York Stock Exchange, "insofar as they would delegate to the Securities and Exchange Commission unnecessarily broad legislative authority which we think Congress may well want to reserve for itself."

If any sentence was ever designed to put a wedge between Congress and the SEC, who must work together in order to get the proper legislative correction of the securities laws, this is it. "We think Congress should not be asked to abandon reasonably precise statutory standards in favor of broad powers inviting government by men," Mr. Gray goes on to say. However, in contrast to the protests of the 1930's the new protests have been milder.

The scanning of investment advisors by the SEC radar has shown that there is much to be done in this area. This is a variegated group of individuals, including those who advise individuals as to where to put their investments, those who publish information as to what to buy and when to buy it, and those who analyze the market and come up with all kinds of recommendations. Regardless of their status, if they get any kind of circulation at all, they can affect the market —some of them seriously. Prices can jump up and down if an influential adviser comes out with an important pronouncement, whether it's right or wrong. If they felt so disposed, they could act as fraudulently as anybody else, and the market could receive a high-voltage jolt, while they profited.

The confusion as to who is an investment adviser, as

contrasted to an investment counselor, still remains high to-day. Under the 1940 Investment Advisers Act, anyone giving investment advice about securities is considered an investment adviser, with few exceptions. As Hazen Ayer, president of the Investment Counsel Association of America points out, this includes people who publish bulletin services, statistical organizations like Standard & Poor's, Moody, and firms which supervise individual clients on the investment front. But brokers and dealers who receive no special compensation fee for their advice are not considered in this class, which is confined to those whose major business is the furnishing of advice. The general broker, who only hands out suggestions as part of the sale he hopes to make, is therefore excluded from the club. A little over 1500 dyed-in-the-debenture investment counselors are registered with the SEC.

Of this group, only those who tend to give clients continuous investment advice are referred to as "investment counsel." In other words, investment counselors are the supervisors of clients who pay them to handle estates and funds. Only about 350 of these are registered with the SEC, and they consider themselves as professional as doctors and lawyers. Mr. Ayer's organization distinguished itself by supporting SEC measures to bring stricter control in this field. It is a refreshing stand, as was that of Frederick Stahl, president of Standard & Poor's, on the same subject. The resistance of much of the financial world to any form of refereeing, even if it is to its own advantage, has been so marked in the past that such examples of co-operation stand out in contrast.

Another problem nipping at the SEC lies in those companies who manage to have themselves placed under another, more liberal, government commission, although for the most part they are actually investment trusts which do little or no managing of the real assets involved. An example is the Allegheny Corporation—famous for its proxy fights between the Murchisons and Allen Kirby, in addition to the stir created by Robert Young's battle for the control of the New York Central, which Allegheny controls. Here is a giant investment company, exempt from many SEC regulations because it claims that most of its securities—which are its only assets—are railroad stocks. In this way, the Interstate Commerce Commission carries the authority on most of Allegheny's financial structure.

The SEC claims that Allegheny is ducking its major responsibilities through this ploy, trying to escape into the easier realm of ICC regulation. Allegheny considers itself a carrier holding company, although it controls an out-and-out investment management company known as Investors Diversified Services, Inc., with assets valued at over $64 million, and which represents five mutual funds of its own, plus an insurance company. In addition, it holds a $20 million bite in Webb & Knapp, the real estate empire evolved by the gingery William Zeckendorf.

Out of these and other SEC problems has come the interest of both houses of Congress in the entire, over-all security market picture, especially in the light of the public's almost hysterical passion for stock market "killings," much of which bears entirely too close a resemblance to 1929.

Representative Peter F. Mack, chairman of the Subcommittee on Commerce and Finance, has propelled much of the Congressional action for looking into the Market, putting a micrometer on it, and assessing its values and problems. Through him, House Joint Resolution 438 was introduced, authorizing $750,000 for the SEC to make its major study and investigation, covering an entire year. As the preliminary hearings on this resolution shaped up in June of 1961, several noteworthy things were in the wind.

Keith Funston, president of the New York Stock Exchange, had issued two sharp warnings against the speculative influenza sweeping across the country. The SEC was beginning its investigation of Amex in the wake of the Re, Re & Sagarese defection. The Commission also found itself in the middle of more manipulation cases than ever before. The NASD, as Representative Mack pointed out, had written to all its members with great concern about a large total of undelivered securities, which it refers to as "fails." Many million dollars worth of over-the-counter contracts were undelivered. The biggest brokerage firm in the country was running ads for two months, telling investors to take it easy and calm down.

One brokerage house issued a memo to its employees which expressed in very realistic, concrete terms the kind of atmosphere in and around Wall Street:

"To any of you who were in the securities business in 1930 the above-listed items would be sufficient to alert you and tell you that there could be very rough times ahead for the securities business. To those of you who have recently entered this profession, I will tell you flatly that the warning flags are flying, and it behooves every one of you to recognize this signal and to conduct yourselves accordingly.

"The Congressional investigations of 1930–31 were bitter ones as far as our industry is concerned. Out of these investigations came the Securities Act of 1933, the Securities Exchange Act of 1934, and the SEC, but something far worse than that [Note the basic, almost unconscious attitude toward the SEC] came from the investigations. Our entire industry was cast in an unfortunate role insofar as the public was concerned and we became the most popular whipping boys available. Our entire industry suffered for many long years. It is only recently that the public has again come back into the market in strength and has made it possible for many of you to earn handsome salaries and live as successful business men.

"I for one do not care to go through the early 1930's again. There are several things that all of us can do right now.

"1. The rules and regulations of the SEC, NASD, and the New York Stock Exchange are clearly written and are available for study by each one of you. It is the policy of this firm to abide by all of these rules. During the recent active markets—which of course have caused the events described in the first paragraph—many registered representatives have been critical of some of the rules under which we operate and work, and newly-acquired customers have agreed with the criticisms. We do not write these rules but we do propose to abide by them and we can tell you that it is to your own advantage if you also accept and abide by these rules. At this stage of the market and for the reasons outlined above, acceptance of the rules can be your major contribution toward your profession.

"2. Our network with busy wardroom offices provides a perfect workshop for manipulation of the securities market. Manipulation and rigging of markets is as old as our business. At the present time it is against the law. Let each one of us make absolutely certain that we are not being used by irresponsible persons for the purpose of manipulating or affecting the price of any security. Be extremely cautious about entering orders for any group of speculators. We must carefully guard against being 'used' by irresponsible and avaricious groups or individuals of any kind."

This is a very revealing memo. It reflects the atmosphere in and around the board rooms throughout the country, the same tensions and proclivities that characterized the 1929 market. It reveals the fact that the responsible members of the New Guard accept the SEC regulations and what they have done to help provide an orderly market. At the same time, through several Freudian slips, the memo also reveals the unconscious resentment which still smoulders. But most of all, it reveals the general conditions backstage during the active performance of the stock market in the recent scene.

Representative Mack, along with others, feels that the more than twenty-year-old regulations of the SEC could stand a good going over at this stage of the game, especially since a program for revision was interrupted by World War II.

SEC Chairman William Cary feels that the most significant change in the market has been the sheer, staggering increase in its size, plus the growing participation on the part of the public. He notes that the volume on the New York Stock Exchange jumped from an average of 1,980,000 shares per day in 1950 to an average of 4,500,000 in 1961. A similar increase in the over-the-counter market has been taking place.

In addition, many innovations have been taking place in the sales and distribution of securities. The increase of branch offices of brokerage houses, and the addition of the many part-time salesmen, add to the confusion. Branch offices of New York Stock Exchange firms have almost tripled in the past ten years. The part-time employees often operate far from office supervision, or out of a hat or a bedroom. The heavy volume of trading has swamped brokerage offices with paper work, burying them under a pile of figures, and causing deliveries to be made late or even overlooked.

The full details of the over-the-counter market remain a mystery even to the expert. No one knows, for instance, exactly how much volume this market handles. The information simply isn't there. It is not even known how many securities are being traded which are not required to be reported under SEC regulations. Many of these companies, Mr. Cary notes, are not even listed in standard financial reference works. He also points out that there are many gaps in the "full disclosure" requirements of the SEC which urgently need to be plugged.

The growing tendency of over-the-counter securities in a bull market to jump like a jack rabbit in price, just moments after being issued to the public, is a major problem for the SEC, which it would like to investigate in minute detail in its massive study.

As far as the stock exchanges go, the SEC has been leaving it to them to police their own members, and to set their own standards of conduct, which often go beyond minimum SEC requirements but at the same time leave a lot to the exchanges themselves to handle through self-discipline. The Amex explosion showed that this mechanism can be dangerous and threatening to public investors.

Another big gap is the extension of credit by banks on over-the-counter securities, which, unlike those listed on the exchanges, is not regulated. Further, a lot of credit by money-lenders other than banks is being extended, all of which serves to make the margin requirements set by the Federal

Reserve Board totally ineffective.

It is in this area that a critical problem exists. The crushing cascade of 1929 was violently precipitated by margin calls and the slim 20 per cent margin requirements of the day. Wave after wave of stock was dumped on the market by brokers who could not collect the required amount of additional money from customers who bought on the slim thread of low margin. Today, even with a 70 per cent margin set by the Federal Reserve Board, credit can be extended by lenders other than banks to destroy completely the protection of the higher required margin. The Sutro case, which later will be examined in detail, showed clearly how margin dodgers operate to get around the present requirements, thus giving speculation a chance to spread far beyond conservative limits—or even 1929.

The $750,000 which Congress authorized to pay out for the investigation is peanuts in contrast to the amount of money which plugging the loopholes will save the investors who might otherwise have become hooked in a dozen varied schemes to relieve them of their cash. Wisely, Commissioner Cary has asked Congress not to withhold the results as the investigation goes along. Any urgent need which is revealed to require immediate attention can thus be brought sharply to light, and appropriate legislative action can be taken.

"Many buyers and sellers in the market are uninformed," says Commissioner Cary, "except in a vague general way, about corporate financing and market operations. We believe that an investigation of the character contemplated is necessary and appropriate in the light of changing conditions in the securities markets."

Congressman Robert Hemphill of South Carolina, one of the House subcommittee members, feels that the biggest problem is the large number of investors who don't know anything about the market, but are persuaded to put their money into securities they know nothing about and have no control over after they invest in them. "The question in my mind," he says, "is whether or not the American public is getting the protection it thinks it should have, since we have the regulatory agency, and the next question in my mind is whether or not this investigation or study would produce as the American public thinks it should produce. I am concerned because I think the average person thinks that because we have an SEC that he has much broader protection than he actually has."

But from the start the study began to have repercussions. The stock exchanges, many of them claiming that their houses were completely in order, were nervous and jumpy about what clamps might be put on the specialist, who happens to be the most vulnerable of all the exchange members because of his inside information on the condition of the stocks he handles, and because of his unique position in trading on his own account and as a broker for other brokers. Never before has the SEC had the luxury to let its own staff continue on in the work of administration, while it has a fresh, new department devoted solely to study and survey. A spotlight of this sort is bound to show up a few wrinkles which were never noticed previously. The more active the market, the greater the possibilities for manipulation, and even the exchanges might not know where all the skeletons are hiding.

Over 1000 full-scale investigations were on the docket at the time Congress approved the SEC study in 1961. The sheer job of handling this biggest work load in the SEC's history would make it impossible for the Commission to conduct its special study without the $750,000 Congress appropriated for the job.

Even before the inquiry started, the SEC knew, for instance, that manipulators were covering their tracks by operating through dummy accounts, through banks in Switzerland, and other nominees, so that the actual manipulators would look as pure as Snow White at a church picnic. The SEC's Philip Loomis tells about one case which involved a promoter who took over a mining company, which for all intents and purposes had gone out of business. A front man acting for the promoter bought all the stock of the company for a mere $5,000; then the promoter conveniently split the stock some 100 to 1, and arranged for a score of people to act as further fronts to carry the stock up to Canada. Then a broker-dealer firm in the United States, which the promoter controlled, bought the stock at a fictitious price of between two and three dollars per share, and resold it to the American public. The mining property was practically worthless, but the stock maneuver turned over a pretty penny until it was uncovered. Eventually, the broker-dealer firm was put out of business and the promoters were indicted.

It takes the SEC an average of 16 months before it can process a case like this. All of this slows down the machinery and dilutes the protection the average investor counts on. With the work-load increase, another factor hampering the Commission, the problems are bound to multiply.

"I think we have had perhaps more manipulation cases in various stages of administrative and criminal proceedings than I ever recall," says Mr. Loomis. "It is difficult to say how much is going on at this time. There is one indication on that. In addition to our formal investigative proceeding, we have what is known as quizzes where we suspect something is wrong by reason of a market movement and we go in to the various brokers and identify who bought the securities and who brought in the various orders, to see if there is any manipulation going on.

"During the last fiscal year we had 88. In the last nine months we have had 89. There are more in the last nine months than in the entire fiscal year. This compares with 53 cases for the comparable period last year."

These quizzes may or may not lead to formal investigations. The serious cases must be referred to the Department of Justice, which itself is overloaded with case work, and more delay ensues.

Merely keeping an eye on the lurid advertising of some investment advisers is a considerable chore in itself. In November, 1961, new restrictions were put into effect which banned testimonials in such advertising, and eliminated specific recommendations which the adviser had made in the past. This was a neat trick, because all an adviser had to do was to cull out his successful previous recommendations to come up with a record which made him look like the oracle at Delphi. It was important to squelch these ads, because they used to lure many innocent investors into the shoals.

The other problems needing a thorough going-over are many: the buying and selling of stock by insiders; the many questions of adequate disclosure; the group of companies, many of them large, which are not listed on any exchange and have not issued any securities in recent times, so that they have remained exempt from SEC scrutiny. Most important is the need for requiring corporate insiders of over-the-counter corporations to report their transactions in their own stocks.

The time for the investigation is not only ripe; it is over-ripe.

With the need for action so clearly indicated, both the NASD and the American Stock Exchange, the latter in spite of its critical problems, both endorsed the SEC study heartily.

But true to its colors, the New York Stock Exchange hemmed, hawed, and balked, stating that it did not believe that any special investigation into the rules and procedures of the New York Stock Exchange would be necessary.

"We think it unwise," said President Keith Funston, "to direct the Securities and Exchange Commission to undertake broad new studies if these will divert its energy from the inquiries presently under way. It seems to us that it is more important to reach conclusions regarding presently known problems than it is to delay those conclusions in the search for new problems."

In other words, ignore what is going on now. Look into past history. Avoid the obvious. Leave things as they are. Don't make waves. Remember the Alamo, but forget the headlines. The utter predictability on the part of the Stock

Exchange sharpens the comic-opera aspect of its pontifical statements, and, if it were not involved in such a critical area of hitting America where it lives, might almost be written off as humor. Apparently Mr. Funston chose to ignore the fact that Congress was appropriating some three-quarters of a million dollars later increased), so that the SEC could carry on the investigation without impairing the current work of its staff.

When asked by Congressman Mack whether he thought the new investigation would divert the energies of the SEC, Funston replied: "No, sir. I am really in no position to evaluate that."

In his position as the head of the New York Stock Exchange, Funston's words carry a lot of weight. When he made two statements warning stock buyers to be careful of what they were buying in April and May of 1961, the market fluttered and even dropped a little at the sound of the trumpet. As Congressman Mack points out, one article headlined: DROP LAID TO FUNSTON WARNING.

With such a statement, even though it is totally unintentional or deliberate, and given with the best of motives, a considerable number of insiders are going to have an educated guess as to what the market is going to do, and prepare their own plan accordingly.

Before making his first statement in April, Funston went to the Exchange Board and told them that he was considering making a warning statement. The advisory committee agreed with him that the statement was necessary and timely, and it may or may not have even crossed their minds that such a pronouncement could enhance the halo around the Stock Market securities and dim the glow around the less stable stocks and bonds. It may or may not have given them a flash insight that maybe *all* securities might be affected adversely to some degree, and it would be an inhuman paragon who could refrain from passing such information along to his friends, family, or business associates. All this could happen with no ulterior intent whatsoever. It is the make-up of the human psyche which makes it almost irresistible for those who are privy to forthcoming information to spread the good word around where it counts most, either from the point of view of benefiting personally or of becoming an Olympian hero in the eyes of others.

Funston attributes the timing of his statements to the tremendous blizzard of stock-market activity which began with the opening of 1961. Wild tips and rumors were being swirled about and piling into uncountable drifts. He felt that the speculation fever was not centered in what he calls "Aunt Janes"—the rather unflattering term he uses for the unsophisticated investor—but rather in the semi-pros who were in for a killing and prepared to get out again as soon as they bagged a neat profit. He was a little fuzzy about why he chose to warn about securities of new companies and low-priced "penny stocks," neither of which the New York Stock Exchange handled.

Following his second announcement, there was a general decline in the prices of stocks on both national exchanges in New York, especially those on the rival American Exchange.

In spite of the fact that Funston was putting up storm signals about speculation, he was vociferously plugging for smaller margins at the same time. "Our feeling is that the margin requirements in general are higher than they need be," he said at the time, and continued to say it even in the face of the snowballing market at that time.

As the full-scale investigation began to get under way, the New York Stock Exchange made it plain to everyone that it was smugly and completely satisfied with its rules, procedures, regulations, and operation, and had no plans whatever to re-examine them.

Even if it is correct, it is this sort of attitude, this unyielding inflexibility which makes venerable institutions fair game for the termites they refuse to admit exist, and which they have to eliminate before they can have a sturdy structure.

"The speculator is frequently described as a gambler. Nothing could be further from the truth . . ."
—STATEMENT BY THE NEW YORK STOCK EXCHANGE

CHAPTER IX

On one fine May day in the twenties, a certain stock found itself hitting a mark of 500 points, and investors were so excited about it that they were converting even their government bonds in order to buy it. All through April and May of that year, the stock had been rising, and its buyers included everybody from chambermaids to the highest government officials. In the financial district, the buzzing about the stock continued long after the exchanges had closed. It was reported that the stock would be sold within seconds at a price ten cents higher than the previous sale. Just three days after it hit 500, it soared to 890, and the profit-takers began sniffing the air and started unloading. By the third of June, the stock plummeted from its snow-covered peak down below the timberline, falling to 640. The directors of the company began feeling uncomfortable around the neck, and set out to buy the stock back. They were successful. Slowly the issue crawled

186

back up under the impetus of this whiff of oxygen, and by nightfall it was up to 750.

It stayed at this level through most of June, with the public fingering its pulse as if it were its dearest relative in a convalescent home. By August, it reached 1000 points, but by September 2, it teetered and clumped down to 750. Public confidence teetered along with it, and a special stockholders' meeting was called, with directors, officers, and stockholders jammed inside the building with a shoehorn.

The usual patter took place, the mutual back-scratching of the officers, and the reassurance of the audience at the prayer meeting that everything was well in hand under the guidance of skillful directors and officers in whom the stockholders could have complete confidence. The secretary moved that the assemblage extend a vote of thanks and confidence to the directors for their magnificent skill in handling the corporation, and that they should be permitted to continue in any way they wished for the "interest and advantage of the corporation."

One major stockholder said that he had seen "the rise and fall, the decay and resurrection of many communities of this nature," but in his opinion "none had ever performed such wonderful things in so short a time as our company."

The meeting ended without accomplishing much more than the back-scratching.

By the next day, the stock sank to 540, and then continued sliding. Soon it was down to 400, and thousands of misled investors were wiped out and penniless. Milling crowds around the financial district threatened the directors of the company, and it looked as if actual rioting might break out any minute. By September 29, the stock was down to 135, and the whole structure of the company, as wispy as spun sugar, fell to pieces.

The inevitable government hearing followed and revealed scandal and infamy, compounded by the wide number of public suckers who were engulfed in the mirage, all of it due to widespread gambling and speculation which had created an utterly unattainable image of lush prosperity.

But all of this did not take place in the 1920's—it happened in the 1720's, and it was that towering monument to insanity known as the South Sea Bubble, which swept the senses out of the English people into the North Sea and left thousands of families unshod and financially impotent. Most important, though, it demonstrates vividly what happens to people when they are seized with the desire to grasp and to win something for nothing in an atmosphere of pseudo-dignity created by pontifical official statements and blessings from high quarters, and documented by ledgers, quotations, and accountants' statements which seem to make a mirage look as if it were carved out of granite.

All speculating is gambling. There's not an honest speculator on Wall Street who won't admit it. History is constantly recording the waves of gambling mania which sweep through the financial world at regular intervals. They have done so in the past. They continue to do so today and tomorrow.

Such phenomena as the South Sea Bubble, when examined in contemporary light, show that the gambling instincts of the speculator never change. For much of the time, the harm comes only to the speculator himself. But when the mass hysteria sets in, then the real danger appears.

Charles Mackay, in describing what happened in the South Sea Bubble mania in his book *Extraordinary Popular Delusions and the Madness of Crowds,* says that "the public mind was in a state of unwholesome fermentation. Men were no longer satisfied with the slow but sure profits of cautious industry. The hope of boundless wealth for the morrow made them heedless and extravagant for today. A luxury, till then unheard of, was introduced, bringing in its train a corresponding laxity of morals. The overbearing insolence of ignorant men, who had arisen to sudden wealth by successful gambling, made men of true gentility of mind and manners blush that God should have power to raise the unworthy in the scale of society . . . In the parliamentary inquiry, many of the directors suffered more for their insolence than for their speculation."

The South Sea Bubble was the active ticker tape stock and "tronic" hot issue of its time. Both the people who were swept up by the mania and the South Sea Company itself were equally to blame. The insiders pushed, tugged, and inflated the values of the securities, smelling the public's taste for gambling blood. Like a dog chasing its tail, both the public and the company spun around on each other's idiocies until the dog—both head and tail—collapsed. The public bought—as it does today—not for reasonable return for the use of its money, but for unloading, making a killing, and getting out while the getting was good. No values are created, no real wealth produced. The cynical gambler feeds heartily off the dreams of the Great Unwashed, sucks them dry, and finds that he has fed on a poison which ruins them both.

Mackay's book, published in the middle of the nineteenth century, is loaded with such examples. Bernard Baruch claims that the book saved him millions of dollars. By clearly recording the susceptibilities of man to the gambling instinct, and the contagious qualities of it, Mackay provides a shocking mirror which could be dusted off today to good advantage.

Take the great and unbelievable "Tulipomania" which gushed up in Holland in the 1600's and almost left the entire country bankrupt. By 1634, the tulip gained so much popularity as a flower that it was considered sheer bad taste for any gentleman to be without a collection of them. It was a passionate thing, a snob-appeal thing, and since the bulbs of the innocent tulip at first had to be imported from Constantinople, their price was stiff, even for a gentleman.

Eventually, what the gentleman has, the shopkeeper wants. And so it was with the tulip. Prices were absolutely ridiculous. One trader in Haarlem dished out half his fortune to pay for a single bulb, just to have it on display. It's a shaky, nervous flower, constantly acting temperamental; yet the

Dutch went all out for it, spending hours to keep their bulbs in shape and safe from the ravages of disease.

Soon the whole country was forgetting about its own industry, and getting itself knee-deep in tulips, for no apparent reason other than snob appeal. A tulip called *Admiral Liefken* was sold over the counter for 4400 florins. When you consider the fact that four hefty oxen cost a mere 480 florins, you can get some idea of how the rage was taking hold. As a matter of fact, the Dutchman could buy himself 55 suits of clothes for what a single *Admiral Liefken* tulip bulb cost him. As the gambling fever shot up on the chart, a single bulb in Amsterdam brought in exchange a new carriage, two grey horses, a complete set of harness, and 4600 florins thrown in to boot. One sailor accidentally ate a bulb, thinking it was an onion, the price of which would have fed the crew of his ship for a complete year.

The tulips soon moved into the Stock Exchanges of Amsterdam, Rotterdam, Haarlem, and other cities, and at this point the gambling fever really took over. "The stock jobbers, ever on the alert for a new speculation, dealt largely in tulips," says Mackay, "making use of all the means they so well knew how to employ to cause fluctuations in prices. At first, as in all these gambling mania, confidence was at its height, and everybody gained."

And they did. Sober, reliable Dutchmen all over the country sold their real estate, their produce, and everything else in order to get in on the thing. A new batch of millionaires began blossoming out of the innocent tulip bulbs. People were not buying them for beauty, for love, or for country. They bought them to turn them over for a fast florin, to unload, to make a killing. It couldn't last, and of course it didn't.

When it all collapsed, many speculators were saved by an interesting attitude on the part of the courts, which may well be an historic definition of speculation: the judges refused to press claims against the speculators on the ground that debts contracted in gambling were no debts in law.

It would be hard to reason that the speculation of these

historical wild times is any different from the speculation in the present era. When reason is replaced by frenzy, when prices soar absurdly, it is purely and simply the gambling instinct that makes them that way.

Walk into any hundred living rooms during a bull market, and the chances are that the chatter over cocktails in a large percentage of them will center around the inside dope or around one stock or another which is sure to make a quick killing. The motivation: pure, straight, dyed-in-the-dice gambling. No one tries to deny the fact, with the possible exception of the New York Stock Exchange's official proclamations.

"I hear Cubicle Copper is buying up Centrifugal Forge," you'll hear a voice say.

"That's right," comes the answer. "And I've got it all doped out. Cubicle is going to lose a little by the deal; Centrifugal is going to be jacked up. So what you do is sell Cubicle short and go long on Centrifugal. You can't lose."

You'll hear constant patter about mutual funds, growth stocks, puts and calls, stock warrants, splits, and options—and never hear such a thing as dividends mentioned once in the conversation. The zenith of success in such cocktail conversation is to say: "Boy, I tell you, I just got out in time."

Or: "I really got in on the ground floor on that one."

Or: "I'm holding on until she hits 80. Then I unload fast."

About the only axiom you can count on in Wall Street is the old saw which says: "There is one thing certain on the stock market: It will fluctuate." Operating on a base like this can mean only one thing: Speculation is gambling. Even if the market is played by the sober student, he cannot possibly probe the unseen tides underneath the surface to make it any less of a gamble.

The late Jesse Livermore, one of the biggest admitted gamblers of Wall Street, points up a critical area when he says that a man has to give his entire mind to speculation if he wants to succeed. Though he later goes on to say that no man can consistently and continuously beat the stock market (he may, however, make money in individual stocks on certain occasions), his first statement brings out an important angle on the gambling story. Not only is the gambler himself losing, and causing others to lose, but he is also putting all the energies that might well go into something creative into an empty and vacuous life. Livermore emphatically felt that the real pros know that acting on "inside" tips is the surest way to go broke, that there is no road to success on Wall Street, in spite of the illusion that there is. He emphasizes that no one is going to let a good tip out if he can help it, that any advice which is printed is worthless, that many insiders can't be trusted at any stage of the game, that others might not lie but they accomplish the same thing by saying nothing.

Livermore had no respect whatever for the gullible public, believing that it always wanted to be told what to do, and always acted on tips which are of no use whatever in the long run. He claimed that brokers have to make their money by commissions, and therefore think mainly of making the immediate sale.

The emotional immaturity of the American public en masse is reflected everywhere. With few exceptions, those television shows which attract wide mass audiences reflect the stunted emotional status of large segments of the population. The "vast wasteland" referred to by Commissioner Minow of the FCC could not exist if the public didn't swing toward it. The upsurge in stock gambling in many ways reflects this same neurotic immaturity. The fact that the obsessional search for profits and money is a neurotic compulsion is well established. As the late psychiatrist Edmund Bergler has pointed out, the money neurotic is one who secondarily shifts the values stemming from the nursery to money. The child struggles for exclusive possession of a doll or his parent's love, and this is later shifted to the money spectrum where his immaturity is given long pants and adult clothing.

For the most part, Bergler traces the compulsive drive for money as reflected by the stock gambler to psychic masochism, a deep, unconscious wish for disappointment. Without knowing it, he seeks punishment, moral reproach, and guilt. Unaware of why he is doing it, he takes extreme pleasure in pain and discomfort. As a result, money becomes an end in itself. Automatically, everyone knows that this can never produce anything but unhappiness. The fear of being taken over the hurdles in money matters becomes a giant threat—a painful enjoyment which only the gambler can understand. All the common enjoyments and genuine pleasures of life become subordinated to the urge to possess more money, and again the masochist gets his unconscious wish fulfilled. In sum, Dr. Bergler concludes that for the immature psychic-masochist, money becomes a blind for existing and repressed infantile conflicts. The wish for unconscious self-damage makes the gambler a glutton for punishment, and clinical experience has made this almost axiomatic.

The gambler continues his frenzied drive for making fast money not only to satisfy his unconscious desire for self-damage, but also to impress everyone else but himself. To him, the formula for success is impressing others, rather than a deep inner tranquility and satisfaction with himself. The infantile desire to get something for nothing, as reflected in the wild desire on the part of the public for hot tips, hot issues, hot stock, and hot profits can often take hold of otherwise mature and intelligent people who get caught up in the mass wave, as reflected in such phenomena as the South Sea Bubble, the Tulip Craze, and the manic market of the 1920's and 1960's. The same psychological basis is there, but it becomes contagious and takes over temporarily, at least, people who in normal times would not respond to such stimuli. Everyone has at least a small amount of psychic masochism in him. The times and the atmosphere can bring it out in greater or less proportion. While the honest and steady profit motive cannot be challenged as neurotic, it is the exaggerated stage which becomes pathological. Investment in American industry is important and vital, and must continue to grow. However, it now turns a solid mechanism into a casino, which creates the danger today as it did in 1929.

The gambler always loses in the long run, and unconsciously even he knows it, though he'll rarely admit it. He also knows that his compulsion will never lead him to any stage of contentment, even if he could win. The hot-shot successes of the financial world are seldom happy in any degree. Many psychiatric cases have indicated that for the most part their sex life is miserable, their relationships with friends and family are worthless, their worries are enormous, their tensions almost unbearable, their insecurities greater than ever. The reason for such a prevalent condition lies in the fact that the drive is based on neuroticism rather than ordinary ambition. With such a root, the plant can't be anything else, because it stems from a false premise to begin with. The gambler always has with him his unconscious desire to lose, and he will only get his exquisite pleasure-pain when he ultimately does lose.

The difference between a risk to create something which will provide a genuine service and the gambling tone of a large portion of the stock market is clear. It is the motivation behind the drive. The investor doesn't watch the tote board for every tick, wondering when to unload, to get out, to dump his stock on some sucker. He doesn't try to overextend his credit, or make a killing on every deal. He is careful, methodical, and if he doesn't know the ropes, he makes sure that he gets his information from someone who does know the risks and potential return. He holds on to his emotional maturity in the face of widespread sound and fury. And he doesn't get into a crap game when it looks pretty obvious that the dice are loaded against him.

A floating crap game and the House of Monte Carlo are basically no different, except in texture. The same relationship exists between the penny stocks and the listings on the Big Board. One operates on the sidewalk, as the Curb Exchange literally used to, and the other operates in marble halls. Both benefit by gambling fever at the time, and both fail to take active steps to try to reduce it. When the New

York Stock Exchange raises its voice in an attempt to create easier margin requirements, it is hardly less different than selling the chips at Monte Carlo on credit. They both lead to the same place: gambling on money which isn't yours.

One of the most flagrant aspects of straight gambling in stocks lies in the practice of short selling. If you were to ask 15 different brokers, as we did, the direct question: "What is the basic economic function of short selling?" you will be greeted by an open jaw and a look of awe. Experienced brokers hem, stall, and stutter, and over half of them will say something like "to make yourself some money." Not one of the 15 we talked to could find any social gain accomplished by the practice, lending more evidence to the conclusion that short selling (except in a few technical cases) is pure out-and-out gambling, and nothing else. Again, the more honest brokers will tell you straight from the shoulder that gambling is the main function of selling short. The latter group make no pretense about it, and accept it as a matter of fact.

Yet the New York Stock Exchange has this to say about selling short:

"The farmer sells his wheat and, at the same time, contracts to deliver it to the miller at harvest time. The farmer doesn't know at the time whether wheat will be abundant or scarce. He makes, in effect, a short sale—a sale of something he does not own. His judgment, based on experience, is that he will be able to produce the wheat for less than the miller agreed to pay him for it . . . "

This little fable of Stock Exchange wisdom could stand some serious scrutiny. Although it is obvious on the surface that the comparison of a farmer (who sweats out a 12-hour day in the fields to create the wheat which he has planted) to a funeral-parlor addict who sits and stares at the Trans-Lux ticker tape is absurd, there are many other aspects to look at.

A speculator who sells short is doing it for one reason: to make a fast buck out of something he doesn't own, never intends to keep, and has no interest in whatever except for hoping that the price goes down, resulting in somebody else taking it on the chin.

The procedure of selling short is very simple, and not the least bit difficult to understand, in spite of the aura of mystery which sometimes surrounds it. The gambler goes to his broker. He borrows, say, 100 shares of Adulterated Steel Common, which is on the tape at the price of 80 at the time. He sells it to some poor sucker at 80, promising his broker that he'll replace the stock at a later date. He now goes to his prayer rug, and bows toward Wall Street, praying (or in some cases manipulating) for the stock to go down so that the sucker will get stuck, and he himself will get rich. At this precise moment he has sold $8000 worth of stock which isn't his own to sell. He is obligated to replace it, but he wants to replace it at a price as far below the market as possible. Let's say his prayers work, and the stock sinks to $50. He goes out and buys 1000 shares at this price, for a total of $5000, replacing the stock he borrowed, and making a neat $3000 on the deal.

That's about all there is to it, except that if the price goes up, he is still committed to replace the stock he has borrowed and sold, and he'll end up stuck for whatever over $8000 he has to pay for the stock on the open market. He will argue that he deserves to make money on this gamble, because he is taking a big risk.

But what about the motivation? Does his action in any way compare to a farmer producing food for people to survive on? Does his hope that the stock will fall in value help the economy any? Is he doing anything more than playing games with himself, on the basis of somebody else's misfortune? Is there any real excuse for this kind of motivation in the final analysis? No wonder the old war cry around the financial sector still holds true:

> *He that sells what isn't his'n*
> *Must buy it back or go to prison.*

There are all kinds of rationalizations to make short selling a socially acceptable thing. Dr. George Leffler, in his book *The Stock Market,* reports that short sellers are for the most part professional traders and members of the Exchange itself. He found that in the year's period ending October 31, 1949, 68.8 per cent of all round lot short sales were made by members of that organization, with only 31.2 per cent of the general public engaging in the practice. From an SEC study, Leffler quotes that much of the short selling is concentrated in a few stocks, most of them blue-chip market leaders. In AT&T and U. S. Steel, short sales accounted for over 30 per cent of all sales.

All the technical discussion in the world can't disguise the fact that short selling is the result of motivation directed toward the wish for bad luck on the part of somebody else. This is the simple, primitive analysis of the practice, and, as such, cuts through all the red tape and makes it clear what practically all of short selling is: gambling.

Of the hundreds of books written about the stock market, very few concentrate on the motivation behind the phenomenon. It is as if business were business, and nothing else, floating in a limbo. The motivation behind most short selling is obvious. The motivation behind buying on margin is equally so, and another part of the gambling picture.

When stocks are bought on margin, they are bought with the hope that the speculator will get something for nothing. If a speculator in the 1920's was able to get $1000 worth of stock for $200, and the stock was paying dividends of 6 per cent, the return on his investment could equal a gross return of some 30 per cent, since the dividends on the amount of stock he has would come to some $60. His cost of borrowing the money from his broker would be much less. Also, if the stock goes up, he can unload at a neat profit with very little risk of cash. If the $1000 worth of stock went up to $1500 in value, he could sell out for a gross profit of $500, or a profit of 250 per cent.

Again the question of *intent* comes up. If the speculator were seriously interested in buying stock on an installment plan, and creating new wealth, and pledging future earnings to create it, margin buying could provide a useful service. But in the vast majority of cases, this is not so. The margin buyer is in for the kill again. He is buying, for the most part, the stocks of large corporations which are already financed and don't need his money to create new wealth. He is pushing the stock he buys to an inflationary value. He is susceptible to a call for higher margin if the market goes down, and when this is compounded with overextended margins of others, a serious stock break might well follow, as it did in 1929, and later in 1962. What's more, the loan that the broker makes to finance the margin gambler takes good money out of productive industry and puts it into the hands of a nonproductive principal.

The wide extension of margin accounts cannot help but jack up the price of stocks beyond their value. Buying pressure is automatically increased by whatever amount of margin is permitted by the Federal Reserve. In 1961, 70 per cent margin was required, meaning that 30 per cent of extra pressure on market prices existed. Fortunately, it was nowhere near as low as the 20 per cent margins of the twenties. On the surface, low margins create a bull market, but it's as safe as an inflated rubber bull in a Macy's parade hit by a blow torch. Speculation takes time and energy away from turning out goods and services, and when the bubble breaks there is nothing left but a coast-to-coast hangover.

The gambler's mind is wild and uncontrollable when it gets up to full steam, and none of us is exempt. The argument that margin buying for stocks is the same as other installment buying, which the New York Stock Exchange likes to extol, couldn't possibly be further from the truth. The intent, the motivation, for buying a refrigerator is functional use. The intent and motivation for most margin buying is to gamble. When the rubber balloon bull caused by the overextension of margin pops, the live and very real bear market steps in to claw every other part of the economy along with it.

The gambler—or the speculator, take your choice of terms—is constantly pushing for easier margin requirements so that he can make bigger killings in the market. What's more, the less margin to put up, the more he can "pyramid" his holdings so that he can clear even more profits without creating any wealth in return for it. Back in 1929, this personal form of pyramiding, along with the giant holding-company pyramids, helped make the Crash even more sensational. The speculator put up 20 per cent to buy 100 shares, which might be quoted at 50. In this way, he'd get himself $5000 worth of stock for a mere $1000. The stock rises to 70, meaning he now has $7000 worth of stock without putting up any additional funds, or a profit of $2000. He takes this $2000 and applies it against the purchase of more stock on the same 20 per cent margin. Although the price has gone up a little, he can still get $10,000 worth of additional stock, so that now he has $15,000 worth of stock for the cash investment of his original $1000. If the stock should happen to rise to 100 points per share, he could put down his new profit of some $9300, and buy 240 more shares at the new price, giving himself total holdings on margin of over $48,000, all for the price of a single grand.

Pyramiding can still be done today, although on a much lesser scale because of the Federal Reserve regulations requiring the gamblers to put up 70 per cent of the price of the stock before they can buy.

When Regulations "T" and "U" came along, in the wake of the 1929 Crash, to curtail speculation, there was barely a dry eye on Wall Street among the gamblers. Each of these regulations was designed to prevent the uncontrolled use of credit in the purchase of securities. Regulation T of the Federal Reserve nips the tendency to extend too much credit to the speculators at its source: among brokers, dealers, and members of the national securities exchanges.

As of July 28, 1960, and continuing through the frenetic market of 1961, the maximum loan value of any stock, whether registered on an exchange or not, was set at 30 per cent by the Federal Reserve, under Regulation U. This means that no bank is permitted to make any loan which is secured directly or indirectly by any stock for the purpose of carrying more stock in excess of the 30 per cent loan value. In other words, the would-be speculator is blocked from going to the bank and getting money to build up more pyramids of phony value to the extent that he used to be able to do in that golden halcyon of 1929.

But like a junkie in search of a fix, this won't satisfy him by a long shot. He's got to figure out ways to get around it, and he has. He is turning now to "factors"—moneylenders who have not yet been clamped down on by the Federal Reserve, although the Securities and Exchange Act of 1934 clearly prescribes that it is unlawful for such activity to take place.

With the 1961 margin rules still in effect, both banks and brokers can lend a security buyer up to 30 per cent of the price of the security, as long as the buyer puts up 70 per cent in cash. But the factoring concerns, who are not under direct Federal Reserve control, have been having a field day by extending margin up to the hilt, recalling the Roaring Twenties. A whole rash of speculators has been swarming to the factoring concerns where they have been indulging their appetites to the tune of putting down a mere 20 per cent of the purchase price, and borrowing the 80 per cent needed to nab the stock. It's 1929 all over again.

The factoring concerns enjoy a peculiar position. They do not have to report to either the federal or state government, and yet they remain in the critical area of moneylending, where public protection and interest is high. The Federal Reserve has been taking a laissez-faire attitude toward them and the short-handed SEC is just now getting ready to put the spotlight on their activities. Section 7 (d) of the 1934 act says clearly: "It shall be unlawful for any person [aside from the broker or security dealer] . . . to extend or maintain credit or to arrange for the extension or maintenance of credit for the purpose of purchasing or carrying any security registered on a national securities exchange, in contravention of such rules and regulations as the Board of Governors of the Federal Reserve System shall prescribe to prevent the excessive use of credit for the purchasing or carrying of or trading in securities in circumvention of other provisions of this section . . ."

In other words, the Federal Reserve has it in its power to issue regulations which would clamp down on the factoring moneylenders. It has not yet done so, but the widely publicized SEC case against the brokerage house of Sutro Brothers, members of both the New York and the American Stock Exchanges, may soon change that picture.

The Christmas party in December 1960 at the 49th Street office of Sutro Brothers, members of the New York Stock Exchange, had more than the usual repercussions. It was there, for instance, that young Barbara Schwartz, bookkeeper for the First Discount Corporation, saw many of her old friends at Sutro, and met some of the key partners. In describing the party, Miss Schwartz says: "I met all my old friends from Sutro there—and a few others, but they, now they were too ossified." And she reports that one of the leading partners said to her: "You are the fabulous Barbara. My boys have been talking about you."

Badinage such as this is bound to be heard at any office Christmas party, but in this case there is particular significance to Miss Schwartz's words. It would, in fact, have been better for the staff of Sutro Brothers not to be on such familiar terms with Miss Schwartz. The reason is that she handled all the "clearance" transactions at First Discount steered her way by the Sutro customer's men in direct violation of the Securities and Exchange Act of 1934, which prohibits brokers and dealers from arranging credit for customers in excess of the current Federal Reserve margin requirements. It would have also been better for the staffs of such front-line brokerage houses as Kidder, Peabody, du Pont, E. F. Hutton, Shields & Company, Pershing & Company, Carl M. Loeb, Hemphill, Noyes, Schweickart & Co., and others to have kept their proper distance from Miss Schwartz. Not that she wasn't personable and likeable, and doing her job. Or that she herself was involved in any wrongdoing whatever. She was merely the device through which the customer's men could increase their sales, and hence commissions, by providing up to 80 per cent of the cost of stocks through the First Discount Corporation, which happened to employ Miss Schwartz.

Since there is no Federal Reserve regulation yet in force to control the factoring houses, they were enjoying a free ride on the horns of a bull market. The only illegality involved is on the part of a broker or dealer who facilitates the use of the factoring houses in setting up a margin deal reminiscent of the 1920's. But beyond the evasion of the Federal Reserve margin requirements is the even fancier scheme of buying stock with no money down at all. This is the "clearance" operation which Miss Schwartz handled for the now-extinct First Discount Corporation. It's a risky operation for all concerned, but it helps build turnover and commissions, and with the usurious interest rates charged by First Discount, it helped that organization until they faltered, stumbled, and collapsed with a million dollars in checks due Sutro Brothers as they did so. First Discount has since been indicted for larceny.

It worked like this: A customer would consult with a broker in the employ of any of the houses named above. If the broker knew him well enough, and trusted him, he would surreptitiously guide him to First Discount (or one of the other factors active in this kind of operation), trying not to let his left hand know what his right hand was doing. On the theory that the customer felt that a stock was certain to go up within a few days, he would buy, say, a hundred shares from the broker, who would deliver the securities out to a bank as collateral for a loan from First Discount to pay for the deal. Since it takes four business days for the transaction to be completed, it is quite possible to sell the stock on that precise day, and pocket the difference if the stock has gone up. And this is exactly what the "clearance" operation did for the speculator who wanted to make a profit without putting a cent of his own money up, to say nothing of the 70 per cent required by Federal Reserve regulations for banks and brokers. This was not just 1929, this was worse than 1929. In the meantime, the factoring house would take its hefty ½ of 1 per cent of the buy figure for a flash loan of only a few days. Or if a straight loan was made by a factor like First Discount on a stock purchase with a margin of 20 per cent put up (less than a third of the Federal Reserve requirement) , the factoring house would charge anywhere from 12 to 18 per cent on the loan.

Take the actual case of a Sutro customer's man whom we'll call Lester Debenture. Lester first learned of factoring and of the First Discount Corporation at the famous Sutro Brothers Christmas party of 1960, where he met not only the disarming Barbara Schwartz, but also the executives of First Discount. He was told, he says, that this firm would lend money against securities, and discussed the process in relation to his own personal accounts in the presence of some of the Sutro Brothers partners. He talked again to one of the partners and a representative from the margin department about getting more margin for his customers because of a declining market, in which he didn't want to sell some of his stocks at a loss. The margin man said this was all right to do, but the partner made no comment. Later, both the partner and margin department representative warned him against the practice, saying that it was dangerous and risky. It wasn't until early in 1961, Lester claims, that he realized that it was illegal for him as a broker to facilitate loans in excess of the Federal Reserve specifications. Meanwhile, he had been factoring with relentless consistency several of his own personal accounts, and those of his customers. Like several other Sutro Brothers brokers—and brokers in other New York Stock Exchange houses—he made all the arrangements necessary with First Discount, preparing or suggesting the proper letters to be written to authorize the factoring. In spite of the fact that one of the Sutro partners seemed to be quite familiar with the First Discount operation, a memo from the top brass was circulated in the spring of 1961, which said:

"We have repeatedly warned all of our account executives not to effect tradings in accounts which are factored. Last week we found such an account and the account executive [a new, more fashionable term for a customer's man] was dismissed. It is impossible to believe that there are any in our organization who don't know whether an account is being factored. Please review all of our accounts carefully and if you are in doubt, please contact our branch office manager or partner in charge. We intend to dismiss any employee who is doing business with such an account."

Lester Debenture (which, again, is not his real name, or anyone's name) explains a clearance transaction in these words: "You buy a security, have it delivered out to a bank by the fourth day. The bank redelivers it back for the firm that you purchase it from or another firm, within four days. If a customer buys a stock on Monday, he must pay for it by the fourth day—Friday. But he sells it on Friday in order to pay for it. Now to make this possible, we'd call the First Discount, and arrange for it to receive from Sutro the securities purchased Monday. First Discount would pick it up Friday, and the customer would give the order to sell. Sometimes the factor would use a bank to mask these activities."

Lester finally was overwhelmed by the practice, and found himself short on some securities which he couldn't cover. When he was called up on the carpet, the firm wanted him to sign a note, a process he didn't take too kindly to. At this point, he is reported to have told the firm that they shouldn't fire him if they didn't want the SEC to find out all about the factoring process which was taking place throughout the organization.

Or take the case of another account executive at Sutro. We'll call him by the improbable name of John Interim Earnings, which again is not his name, or anyone else's. John checked one of his associates in the firm to find out if the factoring process, with its evasion of the standard margin requirements, was permissible. He was told, he claims, that the practice was prevalent all through Wall Street, and that there didn't seem to be any reason why he shouldn't get the business. He was further told that he'd have to be careful. "You are not in the business that long," the associate said. "It is highly technical. You have to know your customer."

John figured that he'd stand to lose a lot of business if he turned down the opportunity to factor some of his more active speculative customers. So, like the others, he went ahead to set up the routine.

One of Sutro's customers claims that he got wind of the fact that there was a way of buying a stock with a factor in the middle, so that he wouldn't need any money at all for the transaction, simply through general scuttlebutt. When First Discount folded he was on the short end of several thousand dollars. In one transaction in December of 1960, he had bought 200 shares of Flintkote, 100 of Johns Manville, and 100 of Burroughs at a total of $11,595.82, borrowing $8,500 from First Discount and $985 from Sutro, and putting up less than 20 per cent for a healthy chunk of stock. His Sutro broker saw to it that all this transaction was taken care of smoothly for him. What's more, the broker was kind enough to let the customer eat lunch at his desk for over a year, where they chatted amiably about politics, girls, marriage, and securities. On one particular day, this customer noted some big blocks of stock going by on the tape and remarked philosophically: "Where do people get the money to pay for all this?"

The Sutro broker told him: "You never can tell. Those securities may be wash sales by a 'plater,' or they may be purchases by some big factoring operator, by operators, big operators with factoring. They don't necessarily reflect honest purchases." The broker went on to tell him about various con games people play on brokers.

Relations between this particular broker-customer team were fine until the First Discount tumble. When it collapsed, so did their relationship, with the customer going to the SEC to spill the whole story.

Another Sutro customer admitted that his Sutro account man didn't force him into using a factor. "They didn't put a gun in my hand and tell me to go to First Discount. They just said: 'Call this number.' " Reflecting further on the operation, the customer said: "You know it's like shooting crap when you buy stock. In my opinion, it's legalized gambling, the market is."

A third customer came right out and asked his Sutro man to help him factor some of his speculation. He was referred immediately to First Discount, not altogether sure that it was a violation of the law for a broker to arrange a loan on such favorable terms. In April of 1961, the customer bought several hundred shares of a hot electronic issue, at a total cost of $13,549.14. The Sutro man made all the arrangements for him, and he put down the difference in cash. The stock was to be delivered to the North Jersey Trust Company, which was a front operation for First Discount. But the stock was never delivered there, and there was never adequate cash in the customer's account at Sutro to cover the transaction between the dates when he bought and sold the stock.

As the factoring practices began to snowball under the pressure of high-gambling speculators, some brokerage houses began running scared. Miss Schwartz, the First Discount bookkeeper, sums it all up by saying:

"I believe Sutro and a couple of other houses on the Street stopped doing business with First Discount because the SEC started to suspect something was going on that was prohibited in their eyes. But Sutro turned around and started doing business again with First Discount."

The result has been anything but profitable. The SEC staff is pushing hard for the suspension of Sutro from both national securities exchanges.

Only a thin protection against overextended margin buying is provided by Regulation U, in regard to banks lending money for buying listed securities. Under the regulation, both a bank official and a borrower must sign a statement that funds borrowed by a speculator will not be used to buy securities. To dodge around this paper curtain of resistance, all a speculator has to do is to sign the statement, take the money, and use it to pay his son's tuition at prep school or for putting a new roof on the house. He can then turn around and yank the money he has previously put aside for these purposes and plunk it down on the stock he craves, with a totally free conscience. He will of course make sure that the bank doesn't find out that he bought more stock with the money borrowed to replace his son's tuition fund. Or if he wants to take a big risk, the speculator will sign the statement that he's not using the borrowed funds for a listed security, and simply go ahead and use it for that purpose anyway. This is in direct violation of the law, and he's bound for real trouble if it is discovered.

Theoretically, an eager-beaver speculator, intent on getting around the margin rules, could take $10,000 worth of stock, and borrow from a bank, say, $5000 on it to buy more securities, giving him $15,000 worth of stock. He could then take his new stock and use it for collateral for another loan of, say, $2500, which in turn would be used for buying more securities. Under such a process, the self-leverage speculator might go through something like this:

ORIGINAL STOCK ON HAND — $10,000.

Borrows $5000 on this to bring stock holdings up to $15,000.
Borrows $2500 on new stock, to bring holdings to   17,500.
Borrows $1250 on new stock, to bring holdings to   18,750.
Borrows $600 on new stock, to bring holdings to   19,350.
Borrows $300 on new stock, to bring holdings to   19,650.
Borrows $150 on new stock, to bring holdings to   19,800.

In other words, the margin-happy speculator, through a lot of red tape and headaches, could conceivably double his holdings if he wanted to put his mind to it. Admittedly, he would have to be rather crazed with lust to go to these extremes.

The factors, or specialized-finance houses, who require nothing but blood, are safer. They cost a lot more in interest, but the speculator figures that if he gets more stock for his money the extra dividends he reaps will more than compensate for this. But no matter how it is done, it does nothing more than set the stage for another 1929.

The more stock that is bought on margin, the more chances are for stocks to become overrated, overvalued. One look at some of the yields of stocks on the Big Board of under 2 per cent at the height of the bull market showed how many of the blue chips carried such a slim return on a common stock risk. Back in May of 1961, Addressograph had a yield of 1.1 per cent; American Machine and Foundry, 1.4 per cent; Bristol-Meyers, 1.5 per cent; Corning Glass, 1.1 per cent; Dow Chemical, 1.9 per cent; Eastman Kodak, 1.9 per cent; General Foods, 1.9 per cent; and the classic "growth" stock of all times, I.B.M., 0.4 per cent.

From the point of view of common sense, which seems to be somewhat unfashionable these days, a stock exchange should primarily exist for only one reason. That is to provide a place where someone owning a share of stock could go and find a buyer for it if he absolutely had to. The dubious blessing of the fast ticker tape, the plush accommodations of the brokers' funeral parlors, the instant purchase, the instant public recording of the sale make the setup for the gambler a thing of beauty and a joy forever.

The claim of the Stock Exchange that sober investors would not invest their money if there were not a powdered, ready-mix, super-sud market for their securities can be seriously challenged. Small industry still gets a tremendous amount of capital, even though it is being chiseled away by the concentrated industries. Real estate continues to be a popular investment. Thousands of companies not on any exchange are well financed. In addition, a big percentage of the real, down-to-earth financing is provided through bonds and preferred stocks. As J. T. Flynn wrote in the *Christian Century*: "The speculative mechanism of the Stock Exchange does not assist in supplying capital funds to industry. The Exchange has expended hundreds of thousands of dollars to prove that speculation is not gambling. The reason is obvious. There are laws covering gambling and speculative contracts which would not be enforced if they were gambling contracts. But, while they may succeed in evading the legal consequences of gambling, they cannot evade the economic and social."

A favorite gambling device centered almost exclusively on the stocks of the New York Stock Exchange are those options advertised with monotonous regularity in the financial pages known as "puts and calls." The most typical and frequent transaction of the option trader, according to the SEC, is for speculation.

A "call" is an option to buy stock at a specified price on a future day. In this way, a speculator pays a set fee (or premium) in order to be assured that he'll be able to buy the stock at the agreed-upon price. If the stock goes up, he can exercise the option and he wins. If the stock goes down, he loses only the premium.

A "put" is an option to sell stock at a specified price. The holder of a put contract can unload his stock during the agreed-upon time period at a specific price. If the stock goes down, he can get his money back at the former price. Again, he must also pay a premium for this privilege. Both the put and call options run anywhere from 30 days to six months.

In an intensive study of the put and call market, Helen Steiner of the SEC uncovered many interesting facts.

As speculation grew and flourished from 1949 up through 1960, the total sales of put and calls grew with it. In 1943, they were only .49 per cent of the New York Stock Exchange volume. By 1960, they had increased to 1.12 per cent. Almost half of the volume of put and calls deals was in 50 stocks, and more than four-fifths of the options sold were on the stocks listed on the New York Stock Exchange. The options for the most part were centered on highly active, volatile stocks.

In 1959, for instance, 360,900 calls were purchased, for which the public paid a total of $1,544,000 in premiums. In addition, it paid $19,000 in taxes and $116,000 in commissions for the stock purchased. This resulted in an over-all net loss to the public of $647,000. Because there are many small, uninformed investors in the field, this is not a very encouraging picture. And while the industry continually points out in its literature that calls can be used as insurance protection against price fluctuation, the SEC study definitely indicates that only a small number of options are bought for this reason. By far the largest amount of transactions are done on the gambling motive.

The premiums paid for options are high. In one month treated by the study, the public paid $472 on the average for a call option. Again, the gullibility of the public comes into play. The dreams seldom pan out, the money goes down the drain, and the buyer might have been just as well off at the race track.

The gambler or the speculator is the greatest fall guy for "inside information" there is. He is always operating on that tenuous basis. And while it is true that the only way ever to be really sure in the stock market is to be directly and completely in on "inside" information, the amount of this information actually available is about as rare as radium in the first days of Madame Curie.

You can count on it almost as an inflexible rule that no genuine and bona fide insider is going to let you in on a hot deal unless you hold a gun to his head or have him in a frenzied blackmail situation. The insider will never discuss publicly any real information prior to its proper release time, when it will be too late. He is interested in two things: the company he represents, and himself and his own profits. Any statements he will leak out, unless he's an absolute idiot, are those which will only show the company in the best possible light. Any profits he might make from his own stock options would be badly seared by premature public knowledge, and he is loath to part with any such information. What remains is rumors and gossip which have little or no relation to reality.

If his company is on the rocks, and he knows that the stock is going to take a fast tumble, this is the last information he would leak out. He's got enough to worry about. If there is a stock split in the wind, and the profits are going to soar, he's bound to keep his mouth shut so that he can benefit to the maximum in this sort of a situation.

What's more, the genuine insider is in the limelight constantly as far as his own stock purchases and sales are concerned, because the SEC requires him to list all his activity in the stock of his company each month. He has as much privacy as a goldfish in a bowl. Each month the SEC issues its "Official Summary of Security Transactions and Holdings," which shows how many shares an officer, director, or beneficial owner of more than 10 per cent of any registered security has bought or sold during that month. And while this offers considerable protection against insiders doing tricks with stocks, it doesn't prevent them from teaming up with selected outsiders who can benefit from such information, and splitting the excess profits thus realized. In cases like this, there would be a leakage of inside information, but under carefully controlled, test-tube conditions. By the time the outsider receives the reports of insider trading through the SEC publication, the clues are as stale as last week's bread crust.

The thirst for inside information* is compulsive in the type of gambler who wants to throw off the shackles of his masochistic neurosis and go in for a sure thing. The intensity with which he follows this chase is of course as neurotic as any masochistic complex he might have, but there are enough speculators on the track of inside information to make up a good-sized army.

Insiders include directors and officers of a corporation who are able to create stock increases or decreases of value through their control of the company, and who are in on every activity which might affect the market for their stock. Often, they own considerable chunks of the company stock,

---

* *Note:* As this book went to press, the story of Edward M. Gilbert had cracked wide open. As an insider, he attempted to get control of the Celotex Corporation, and drew out nearly 2 million dollars from E. L. Bruce Company, which he headed, to engineer the deal. As the first major casualty of the '62 slump, he illustrates the dangers of margin-buying graphically. Said one broker: "He's not the last casualty, by a long shot."

and they have their eyes out for making extra money through any number of actions they might take. Along this line, many illegal actions have taken place, but some of them are perfectly legal. A merger might be in the wind, involving an exchange of stock, which might enhance the value of one company's stock and lower the value of the other. Or it might make both stocks go up. To be in on information like this in advance might change the gambling aspect to a sure thing, but it's working with loaded dice and often—but not always —is just as crooked. Corporate insiders might know that an unexpected stock split is in the wind, that profits are going to be astronomical, that the company has hidden assets which are about to be revealed—whatever. And while the knowledge of this might change the gambling aspect to a sure thing, the net result is that it often leads to gambling with the nation's economy on the part of the outsider who doesn't stand a chance.

One recent book on the stock market claims that the current trend in investment advice should be called "the vogue of the chicken-hearted." It goes on to blare out in large letters: "ANYONE CAN SPECULATE AND, IF HE'S WILLING TO TAKE THE TIME AND EFFORT TO STUDY THE SITUATION, HE CAN BE A SUCCESSFUL SPECULATOR IN THE NORMAL COURSE OF EVENTS." Adding a higher thermometer reading to the gambling fever, it adds: "Every man deserves at least one attempt at freedom. That's why we hold to our conviction that speculation is for *EVERYBODY!*"

Contrasted to this is the statement of Nicholas Darvas, recent king of the speculators: "There is no sure thing in the market . . . I was bound to be wrong half the time." There could hardly be a clearer definition of the gambling arena. But Professor F. W. Taussig of Harvard went considerably further when he wrote:

"The immense majority of transactions have in view no bona fide business. The machinery which has been devised for the easy and rapid transactions of business is utilized for gambling on a large scale."

"Member firms of the Stock Exchange handle about thirty per cent of all mutual funds. The mutual funds, in turn, constitute one of our members' most important customers . . ."
—STATEMENT OF THE NEW YORK STOCK EXCHANGE

CHAPTER X

The theory of mutual funds represents one of the most hopeful signs on the investment front. Through them, the small investor can take advantage of diversification and professional handling of investments which he could never afford otherwise. What's more, the investor's dollar remains liquid, and he can get his money back on demand. But like everything else in the sensitive area of finance, mutual funds are open to abuses which are being uncovered at an alarming rate.

In August of 1946 a mutual fund known as Managed Funds, Inc., was founded in St. Louis, Missouri, by two cousins, Hilton Slayton and Hovey Slayton. Hilton was the dominant figure in the company, serving as president and making pretty well all the decisions. Nine men served on the Board of Directors, including "nonaffiliated" directors who were named by Hilton Slayton and a close friend of his. It is required by law that mutual funds have some "independent" directors, since there are many avenues open for intramural monkeyshines which could provide an uncontrolled management with a lot of questionable profits at the expense of the investors. Often, however, the nonaffiliated or independent directors are little more than figureheads who will go along with anything the active directors and management suggest.

There are only two main functions of a mutual fund, as with most investment companies: (1) to acquire participants in enough quantity to create a large, pooled fund for diversified investment; and (2) to invest the funds so accumulated in the most profitable way, through professional selection of the securities bought for the fund. The first function, then, is one of sales: Sell enough people on joining the project to make it a profitable operation. The second function is one of management: Invest the funds carefully so that they will produce either assured growth or a decent income, or a combination, depending on what the objectives of the mutual fund are.

But it is frequently the habit of mutual funds to farm both these processes out to other companies, known as "management companies." Just how or why this habit grew is rather obscure, but it amounts to the total abdication by the mutual funds of all their responsibilities. The mutual fund doesn't need to set up, train, and carry a large sales department; it farms the job out. It doesn't need to go to great lengths in setting up a staff of professional investment advisers, researchers, and analysts; a fee is paid to an outside company which does the job for the fund.

This fee is not inconsiderable. It often amounts to a half of 1 per cent of the average assets of the fund. On a $500 million fund, which is not uncommon, this fee would run to $2½ million a year. For paying out this fee, the participants in a mutual fund could well expect a considerable amount of service and energy expended on their behalf. Instead, many mutual fund directors make themselves the recipients of a glorious and incestuous windfall.

Managed Funds, Inc., grew and prospered along with many other mutual funds in the expansive post-World War II era. By 1959 its assets were valued at over $80,000,000.00.

In 1952, seven years before this, Hilton and Hovey Slayton joined together to form their own "management company" to handle the chore of recommending and purchasing the investments of the fund which they had organized as the dog to be wagged by their management company tail. The stockholders of the fund approved of the action—as good stockholders always do—and a contract was signed between the fund and the firm of Slayton Associates, in which the latter was to furnish ". . . advisory, research, and statistical services as required . . ." For this service, the Slaytons would receive the usual half of 1 per cent of the value of the company's assets. With assets at $80 million, this fee would amount to $400,000 per year.

In return for this fee, the investors in Managed Funds, Inc., received the full-time services of exactly one employee, who was a security analyst at a blushingly modest salary. In addition, they received the services of the Slayton cousins, who were already on the payroll of Managed Funds itself. As an additional bonus, a contract was thrown in with an outside economist.

For the Slaytons, there could not have been a more pleasant setup. For hiring one employee and making a contract with an outside consultant, they had the benefit of a magnificent fee for practically no work. It was somewhat of a fiscal nirvana, but apparently even this began to pall.

In the autumn of 1953 Hilton Slayton made a contact with a brilliant and knowledgeable security analyst by the name of Stephen Jaquith, who was employed by the New York Stock Exchange firm of Model, Roland & Stone. Jaquith was in the process of setting up an investment advisory department for the firm, for which he was to receive a substantial salary and bonus, plus 40 per cent of any brokerage fees he was able to produce.

By December of 1953 Hilton Slayton was able to persuade

Jaquith that a bit of mutual back-scratching between them would be of extreme profit to both. Slayton's management firm would be gaining Jaquith's services, and Jacquith would be gaining some sturdy commissions if a deal could be worked out.

It was.

On the first of December in 1953, Jaquith was given a contract which would put his talents to use in selecting, buying, and selling securities for the Slayton management firm, which in turn simply meant that he was doing the job that Managed Funds, Inc., was paid $400,000 to do. There was no payment to Jaquith. The contract provided that in place of any fee, the Slaytons would direct the commission business of the entire fund to Jaquith for a five-year period.

Jaquith was now sitting on top of an attractive package, and, possibly out of embarrassment, he didn't disclose the attractive contract to the partners of Model, Roland & Stone, his employers. He did tell them that he had a new customer in St. Louis—a large mutual fund, from which he hoped to get a considerable amount of brokerage commissions. He also failed to disclose some other tie-ins, whereby his wife made a convenient loan of considerable proportions and advanced over $40,000 for Hilton Slayton to buy some land which was to be used for building an office building, which in turn would be leased to Managed Funds, Inc.

On the other side of the fence, Hilton Slayton made sure that his nonaffiliated directors didn't learn about his deal with Jaquith. The transaction was muffled from beginning to end, and even Hovey Slayton didn't learn about it until later.

During the first part of the arrangement, Jaquith made more or less general recommendations, and Hilton Slayton was content to keep his one full-time analyst on the payroll. But by the spring of 1954 the analyst was dispensed with, and the outside economist's contract was terminated. The "management company" of Slayton Associates now consisted officially of the two Slayton cousins alone, neither of whom was a securities analyst.

At this point Jaquith was carrying on a detailed operation for the Slayton interests. He had a direct line to the Model order room, set up for daily confirmations of purchases and sales. Between 1954 and 1959, Jaquith practically ran the entire operation at no cost to the Slaytons. The guaranteed commissions were more than enough to make him and the Model firm happy. In order to make everything look a little less slanted, Hovey Slayton gave Jaquith orders to divide the commission business up among a few other brokers, allocating 30 per cent to Model, and the rest to other brokers in lumps varying from 10 to 15 per cent.

To present a more impressive picture to Managed Funds investors, Jaquith would be instructed as to how much money was needed to distribute annual capital gains, and he would pluck the ripest flowers in the Managed Funds portfolios at the most strategic times. He was left on his own as to how to accomplish this, which was a direct violation of the contract the Slaytons had with the Managed Funds organization.

In an outburst of nepotistic generosity, the Slaytons also requested Jaquith to see if he could get a relative of theirs on the Model payroll, and in return the Slaytons would see to it that the brokers picked up a little more commission business. Since Jaquith would supervise the new employee, his firm gave him a 10 per cent override on the new man's commissions, provided he brought in $50,000 worth of commissions a year.

By this time Model was appreciating more and more the volume of business brought its way by Managed Funds, and finally agreed that it would hire and pay for a full-time research assistant for Jaquith, if the gross commissions reached $200,000 a year from this account. In addition, Jaquith would get his own take raised from 40 to 50 per cent of the Managed Funds commissions.

By 1958 Jaquith's firm had provided him with five more analysts and a battery of secretaries, although Jaquith himself did pick up part of the tab for this. He had also lent a hand to another friend of the Slaytons, for which he picked up another 10 per cent override on commissions.

There was nothing sluggish about the volume of business. Between 1953 and 1959, the commissions paid by Managed Funds' "management" company came to $2,300,000, of which the Model firm received $1,940,806.72.

But an SEC investigation brought all this to a halt in 1959, and the New York Stock Exchange stepped in to take severe action against some of the partners of Model, although the firm was not a party to the misleading registration statement of Managed Funds which was the cause of the SEC's action.

When all this came to light, the investors in Managed Funds were justifiably indignant. For many years they had been paying out of their own pockets an enormous fee for a "management" company which had been farming out all or the major burden of its work for no cost at all. Nothing in the Slaytons' contract permitted them to do this. One of the investors, a Nettie M. Lutz, brought action against the Slaytons and the partners of Model who went along with the arrangement, and her initiative finally inspired the entire Managed Funds, Inc., organization—now under independent management—to turn against its creators—the Slaytons—and to file for heavy damages.

Abraham L. Pomerantz, the prominent New York attorney who likes to take up his sword and shield in favor of the underdog, attacked the case vigorously in the Delaware courts, where the St. Louis company was officially incorporated. He was able to prove that Jaquith's power to purchase and sell securities held in the Managed Funds portfolio was an unauthorized grant of power, that the Slaytons had no right to make such an agreement. Hilton Slayton, at that time president of both Managed Funds, Inc., and his own "management" company, had signed the agreement with Jaquith as president of both companies, but had no power to compensate Jaquith by guaranteeing him the brokerage business. The Slaytons, of course, were already being paid handsomely for the work Jaquith was doing. Their arrangement with Jaquith was never disclosed to the stockholders of Managed Funds, who of course would hardly be enthusiastic about it if they knew. No group of stockholders would be in the mood to go along with an executive who took massive chunks of their money for services which he didn't render. The court found that the Slaytons were jointly and severally liable for all management fees they received from June 1954 on, in addition to being liable for all the commissions paid the Model firm after they made their contract with Jaquith in December of 1953. However, since the Slaytons had few or no assets by the time the decree went through, it was a Pyrrhic victory for Managed Funds.

The Model firm, which hired Jaquith, was strongly censured by the court, and ordered to pay the differences between its properly allocated expenses and commissions received after June of 1954. It was at this time that the firm became aware of the fact that the Slaytons were taking in their lucrative fees and that its own firm was doing most of the work.

"The public interest and the interest of the investors are adversely affected when investment companies are operated in the interest of brokers," the court said. It went on to say that the handsome overrides for Jaquith amounted to little more than a payoff for the business, as well as the hiring of the Slayton figureheads. What's more, the firm was severely rebuked for excessive trading in the Fund's securities, with figures showing that the turnover of its securities went as high as 97 per cent in 1958.

The one "independent" or "nonaffiliated" director who came under the Delaware court's jurisdiction suffered along with the Slaytons, although he had never been filled in on the fantastic web of the operation. The court found that he was grossly negligent by not giving full attention to his job, and that liability rested on him as well as on the overactive Slaytons.

The passive acquiesence of the "nonaffiliated" or "independent" director of mutual funds seems to be apparent in a recent trial involving the stockholders of Fundamental Investors, Inc., against the directors and executives of their own advisory management company, claiming that the directors of the management company controlled the fund for their own purposes. The issues at hand included the question as to whether the directors of the fund failed in their duty to the stockholders; whether the compensation to Investors Management Company was far out of line with the actual service rendered; and whether the nonaffiliated directors took their responsibilities seriously in the light of what happened over the years.

And it is a tidy fund. Its assets at the beginning of 1961 totaled nearly $600,000,000. Fundamental Investors also has three younger brothers, which are specialized mutual funds all run by the same board of directors, and handled by the same management company. One had assets of some $92 million; another over $100 million; and a third about $80 million. Out of all this, the Investors Management Company took in fees totaling $4,500,000, with Fundamental Investors shouldering $3,000,000 of the cost and its brothers kicking in the rest.

The key man in the over-all operation was Hugh W. Long, who served as president not only of the fund, but also of its three other specialized funds. In addition, he was president and director of the management company. In his operation of the vast and complicated network of mutual funds and management companies, the stockholders charged him and his fellow directors with failing to reduce the burden of the management company fees, selecting "ornamental" independent directors who would go along with his whims, concealing vital information from them and from the stockholders, using the advisory fees for other functions, and paying another investment advisor not to compete for the management of the fund. Some of the same charges revealed in the Managed Funds case may be true here, and the practice of appointing do-nothing independent directors, who fail to assume the responsibility of the public's trust in them, may be equally marked.

No directors can get away with exorbitant fees unless they have other directors studiously looking the other way. Long and his active associates were charged by the stockholders with picking men who would be deferential, indulgent, and compliant, and not inclined to look underneath the rug. While their characters were not challenged directly, their lack of attention to duty was. Long and his associates were charged with making it a point to keep the independents in the dark about the astronomical profits the management-advisor company was raking in. Several of the independent directors appeared to know amazingly little about what their management-advisory company was doing.

One so-called independent or nonaffiliated director happened to be the son of the chairman of the board of the management company. He was made a director when he was 25 years old. He couldn't explain just why he was selected. He didn't know by whom he was recommended, unless it might have been a friend of his father's. In his position of trust, he would, oddly enough, be forced to keep a neutral and critical eye on his father, to whom he was obligated for a $150,000 house, on a mortgage which bore no interest. He had scarcely any knowledge of the operations of the management company in handling the millions of dollars of the fund's investments. He had no idea where the security analysts of the management fund worked, or how many of them there were. When informed that the management-advisory company had been merged with the Hugh W. Long Company, which handled the selling function of the fund, he thought that it was perfectly all right for selling and promotion costs to be taken out of the so-called advisory fee. He raised no objection to the fact that the fund was supporting its newer splinter funds, or that, as the fund moved toward the billion mark, a sliding scale of management fees might be an equitable arrangement for the fund stockholders, as was done in other funds. He knew little about other fees charged to other mutual funds whose assets were over $300 million.

Another "independent" director thought that the management company's expenses increased proportionately as the fund grew in size, where no such increase existed. He never made independent inquiries about the fees other mutual funds of comparable size were paying.

A third independent director of the fund made no inquiry about the actual costs of the management company's service to the fund. He never knew that certain personnel of the management-advisor firm were doubling in brass for the management-underwriter or selling firm. He didn't attempt to find out whether advisory fees were going for sales promotion fees. He didn't know how little of the management company's fees were going toward building up a staff of securities analysts, as the fees of the management-advisors grew in 1961 to five times the amount they were in 1954.

Still another "independent" director attended just one out of 36 meetings of the board.

In the face of the fact that these men were responsible for nearly three-quarters of a billion dollars of the public's money, this is rather strange behavior, or lack of it.

As these independent or nonaffiliated directors looked the other way, the management-advisor company was building up its fees to the fund from a little more than half a million in 1952 to $3,700,000, as it collected its constant ½ of 1 per cent of the fund's average investment value. As the amount of the fees rose, a small group of a dozen or so security analysts and five to seven officers continued to handle all the investment services needed. In the over-all picture, the nonaffiliated directors failed to make any real inquiry into the costs of handling the management services for the fund, and voted for renewal of the management contract year after year. When one of the later funds was assigned to the management-advisor, only three employees were added to handle an $88,000,000 fund. The total personnel in 1960 was approximately the same as it was in 1954.

In discussing the case, Stanley L. Kaufman, one of the attorneys handling it on behalf of the stockholders, said: "I think this is a shocking expenditure of entrusted funds. The mutual funds industry has become so large that the public and the stockholders have a right to know that the directors to whom they trust their money are going to give them every possible break in keeping operating costs reasonable—and that the independent directors on the board act as something more than Christmas tree decorations."

Win, lose, or draw, the case dramatizes the importance of mutual funds' protecting their shareholders against unreasonable, back-scratching fees to management advisors, which are engineered to fatten certain members of the very board of directors who are appointed to serve the stockholders' interests. Many mutual funds have recognized this necessity, and have taken steps to correct the intrinsic evils of the system.

The Affiliated Fund, for instance, has net assets of nearly $650 million, but its advisory fee is the customary ½ of 1 per cent only on the first $50,000,000 of assets. After that, it drops to ⅜ of 1 per cent for the next $50,000,000, and down to ¼ of 1 per cent on the balance. The MIT Fund, which has net assets of over a billion and a half, has a variable formula, which results in the payment of 2.52 per cent fee on *gross earnings*, not total asset value. The Wellington Fund's advisory fee drops down in a pattern similar to Affiliated's. The only other funds in this gigantic class are two funds controlled by the Allegheny Company, who maintain the straight ½ of 1 per cent fee regardless of how high the assets get, and they are under sharp attack for so doing.

With one mutual fund in a position to grant over $10 million in commissions a year, and with many others in a position to offer tempting largesse to the broker to handle the job without any fee except commissions, the situation of "management" companies for mutual funds has been under the scrutiny of the SEC for several years. The Managed Funds case dramatized the need for this sharply.

In March of 1962, the SEC indicated that it may request new laws to keep mutual funds and investment companies in hand. The key area in its studies—one of which is the special study made by the Wharton School of the University of Pennsylvania for the SEC—lies in the arrangements between the mutual funds and their management companies, some of which handle their stock advisory service; others, their sales; and some, both. The unscrupulous manipulator can have a heyday in this field, as the Managed Funds case and others have shown. Also interesting to the SEC is the tremendous impact that mutual funds can have on the market, because of their power.

In January of 1962, over $360 million worth of mutual funds shares were bought by investors in that month alone. The total holding of 166 mutual funds in 1961 came to $22,000,000,000. All of this money to be used for purchases and sales on the market leaves a tremendous amount of power in the hands of relatively few experts. What they do—with no intent of manipulation at all—affects every investor in the market, both large and small. The management of mutual funds, and that of other investment companies, becomes a heavy public responsibility.

Mutual funds, of course, are investment companies, and as such come under the Investment Company Act of 1940, which tries to see to it that malpractice in the control, management, and operation of the companies is kept down to a minimum. It is also designed to give security holders a substantial voice in the company affairs. But as Joseph Woodle, director of the Division of Corporate Regulation, puts it: "Experience has shown gaps in the fabric of investor protection."

One of the gaps is that which leaves an investment company free to change its objectives overnight, without the approval of its stockholders. A fund could promote itself as being built on the objective of bringing in maximum income rather than growth, then suddenly switch to being a speculative growth company. Since the investor has more or less picked his mutual fund on the basis of a specific objective, whether it's a "balanced fund" or a "growth fund" or an "income fund," he might well be consulted before such a drastic change in policy is made.

Another gap is that which permitted the Slaytons to enjoy their maximum prosperity for the minimum of work and expense. Section 10 of the Investment Company Act was supposed to prevent such maneuvering, to a degree, by providing that not more than 60 per cent of the board of directors could be officers, employees, or investment advisors of the investment company. Another part of this section states that the majority of the board cannot be made up of regular brokers or principal underwriters of the company. The objective is to gain independent members of the board who would be less inclined to permit such goings-on as those of the Slaytons. But loopholes remain here which are not plugged, and the general public as well as the SEC would like to see them taken care of. There is still little to prevent straw members of the board being appointed—friends or relatives of the management—who would only be prevented from going along with such things as the Slayton syndrome by the chance that they might be held responsible and liable for the activities of their benefactors.

Since the investor is putting his cash into the hands of the investment companies and forgetting about it, and since so many small investors look to them for performance they could never accomplish themselves as single investors, the attention of the SEC will continue to be directed toward them. Although they will not receive a major portion of attention in the SEC's 1962 investigation of the market, they are bound to be involved on the periphery. As the study went into action, there were a great many lawsuits against mutual funds bearing a close similarity to the Managed Funds case. Allegations that certain investment companies were paying excessive fees to investment advisers (or management companies), and that the independent directors were not following up their responsibilities were popping up all over the scene. At least 50 cases were in progress in 1961. The main common complaint was that the funds named in the suits were being operated in the interests of almost anybody except the direct shareholders of the funds. In its own case against Managed Funds, Inc., the SEC proved gross abuse and gross misconduct on the part of the officers and directors of the company. In other cases, it is maintaining the same interest and concern.

In the Investment Company Act there is no actual provision for the SEC to deal directly with the fees charged by the investment advisers or management companies of the mutual funds. Its power is limited to making sure that the stockholders know exactly what the managers of the fund are up to, and that they have the right of approval. The right of the stockholders to approve the renewal of such contracts, however, is limited. As Congressman John Dingell of Michigan points out, the board of directors can continue to ratify the fee paid to the investment adviser or management company without further scrutiny by the stockholders. This condition, and others, has led to Wharton School-SEC combined review of the practice.

With the SEC able to assure that the investor will have only disclosure of facts, rather than being able to approve or disapprove the outlandish fees the mutual funds are often charged with, the Commission has to rely on whether such fees are violations of other sections of the act. This leaves effective action against such flagrantly generous practices with other people's money dependent on whether gross misconduct or gross negligence can be proved. As Congressman Dingell further points out, the average investor doesn't bother to read his contracts very carefully.

The questionnaire sent out in the Wharton study to get more detailed information was formidable. It would know, in addition to basic general information, the amount of securities owned by the officers and directors of the investment advisers and their immediate families, the total number of employees of the investment adviser (in the Managed Funds case, it was one lonely analyst, and he was finally dropped), and the gross compensation paid to the investment adviser over the previous year. It would also know what services are supplied, including office rental, clerical, accounting, auditing, salaries, and so forth. Further information is requested about the broker or dealer participating in commissions on the transactions of the investment company, plus a good many other penetrating questions about the directors of the investment company, and its advisers or management company. The answers received will have a strong bearing on further legislation which the SEC might recommend to Congress.

The more than fifty lawsuits which were in process in 1961 were brought by individual shareholders on behalf of the investment companies, and against the investment adviser, or management company, just as the Managed Funds case was handled. They were not part of the SEC program itself, although the SEC is of course interested in the outcome.

In referring to the part of the Managed Funds case where excessive trading, or "churning," was involved, Manuel Cohen, Director of Corporation Finance of the SEC, points out that this practice produced a profit picture which would look good when the salesmen of the fund presented its sales story. This practice is receiving particular attention in the review of the field. In addition, a sharp eye is being turned toward the promotional practices of selling mutual funds and other investment companies to the public.

Former SEC Commissioner Richard McEntire summed up the hopes and problems of the vast growth of mutual funds after World War II by saying: "The development of mutual funds, if kept reasonably free of abuse, may well point toward a further broadening of the base of American capitalism. At the same time, it places a great responsibility on our doorstep, for the expansion has not been accomplished without high-pressure salesmanship, and the new investors to whom the mutual fund has appealed are, as a whole, somewhat inexperienced and naive as compared to those who have traditionally invested in American enterprise."

Given half a chance through enlightened management and adequate monitoring (as opposed to government control), the funds can offer the public one of the best buys on the investment scene. But they will have to put their houses in order, and they will have to improve their performance. *The Analyst's Journal* reports that the majority of the leading mutual funds in the country failed to do as well as the Dow-Jones stock average. If the investment advisers and the management companies are going to continue to siphon off such a generous fee, it would seem that they should be able to do better than throwing darts at the stock tables. The Dow-Jones average is essentially a random choice, and as Julian Huxley has always contended, even a monkey at a typewriter can come up with a random selection. He might also work for bananas instead of a management fee.

"By bringing buyers and sellers together in one open market, the Exchange becomes a living reflection of the Founding Fathers' creed that we all have the right to hold property . . ."
—STATEMENT BY THE NEW YORK STOCK EXCHANGE

CHAPTER XI

As the full-scale investigation of the securities market by the SEC moved into high gear at the beginning of 1962, the picture presented was one of a strange paradox. On the one hand, there had been the wild and feverish pressures on the part of a speculating public, eyes glazed by the get-rich-quick success stories reminiscent of 1929. Few of them could afford the risk. And although the 1962 dive sobered up a great many, the hangovers were widespread and intense.

On the other hand, there was continuing evidence, as reported by the conservative National Bureau of Economic Research, that the concentration of ownership of corporate stocks was becoming more and more narrow and confined, that not enough people could basically afford to become stockowners in any degree which would make them genuine partners in America's industrial growth.

The wild and chaotic speculation had been most apparent in the American Stock Exchange and in the over-the-counter market, whose lax regulations led to all kinds of excesses. The New York Stock Exchange listings were not exempt from this by any means. With its daily newspaper listings and ticker tape dominating the interest of the public, the fluctuations, as usual, constantly nourished the speculative instinct of many people who couldn't afford to gamble. Complicating the picture was the gullibility of a large new portion of the public, whose manic proclivities had been stirred to the boiling point through the contagious fever which sweeps the investment scene at regular intervals.

Standing by with its finger in the dike has been the SEC —understaffed, underpaid, and misunderstood by both the general public and the securities market itself. Without it, and without the regulations which grew out of the 1929 crash, the 1962 slump would have been greater, swifter, and more damaging. Enough evidence is available to show how much illegal manipulation and fraud is extant in the face of its regulations to suggest the damage which would have been incurred in a totally unregulated market. Emerging from the picture was the need for a safer securities market, through better and stronger regulations, and the need to provide more Americans with the chance to invest wisely and soberly.

In spite of all its faults and chaos, the securities market is essential to America's growth and progress. It supplies the nourishment for the entire economic complex. But pontifical and misleading statements cannot correct its deficiencies. And certainly smugness and self-satisfaction cannot. For the most part, the securities market has had to be prodded by outsiders to set its house in order. In spite of all the grandiose statements by its leading spokesman, the New York Stock Exchange, the market has never welcomed change, and in fact resists it wherever possible.

The flow of investment capital into American industry being urgent and vital, the need for proper incentives for the investor to invest is equally so. The long-term trend of the economy and the securities market, disregarding monthly or annual spasms, is up and it is healthy. Even the Big Crash of 1929 could not shake the foundations. People who held on to their paid-up stock at the height of that overvalued market found that they eventually reaped fantastic rewards, in the wake of their temporary ruin.

Allied Chemical, for instance, reached a high of 44 in 1929. By the middle of 1932 it rested, weak and exhausted, at 6. Those who had bought the stock on margin, and who were unable to cover, of course lost everything. Those who owned it outright and held on to it felt crushed and defeated. An investor who had put $44,000 into the stock at its high point now held equities worth only $6,000. But by 1937, the stock was up as high as 32. After another dip, it climbed back up to that price in 1950. And at this time, the stock was split 4-to-1 —and it kept right on climbing. In 1950 the shattered investor of 1929 had $128,000 in equity. In 1959, the stock moved up over 65, and again was split 2-to-1. Even with severe bear market jolts, the rise in value over the years makes it a top investment through its frequent splits.

The story of Allied Chemical is typical of many blue chip stocks which looked so hopeless after the Crash. Alcoa hit a high of 43½ in 1929. It dived to under 2 in 1932. The stock has split a total of seven times since then, which helps protect the investor from heavy drops in value, if nothing else.

Bethlehem Steel looked pretty sick to a holder in 1932, when it dipped almost to zero from its 1929 high of 13. It has been worth over 130 times its depression low, through two stock splits and a ragged but steady climb. The same story holds for duPont, G.E., General Motors, U.S. Steel—almost any reliable company in business. As they say on Wall Street: "You can make more money sitting on your tail than any other way."

The long-run trend cannot help but be upward. Yet the carnival atmosphere prevailing in recent years tends to make a mockery of an otherwise vigorous economy. The securities market thrives on and must have commissions in order to exist. The more churning in securities, the more commissions. Registered representatives of brokerage houses must by the nature of their job create business, whether they are on salary or commission. Under this pressure, it is a rare man who at one time or another would not move a customer in or out of a security, rationalizing the process as he was doing so. The practice is not necessarily devious or Machiavellian, and for the most part an attempt to improve the customer's position is made. But the holy worship of turnover and volume is hardly the criterion of a sound investment plan. The groans and the misery expressed by Wall Street on low-volume days have little or nothing to do with investments. But they have everything to do with a dismal outlook on commissions. Whether the values go up or down makes little difference to the broker in this particular regard. The more turnover, the more fluctuation. The more fluctuation, the greater the temptation to speculate rather than invest. The more speculation, the tougher the road for the more sober investor who is interested in a fair return on his money, and the hope of future long-term growth rather than false and inflated values he can jump in and out of. The most seasoned securities speculators admit that, in the long run, the speculator can't win. The inside trader who works on an inside deal is not a speculator. He is betting on a sure thing, through inside information in which his profits will be gained at the expense of a gullible public. None of this churning in any category is creating better economic health for the country.

The need for discipline and control in such a situation is obvious, as it was in 1929. At that time there was none, and the tragedy struck with the force of a hurricane. There were no weather stations to give warning. Today, there is better financial weather equipment, but there is no guarantee that warnings will be heeded, nor have they been.

The Securities and Exchange Commission, except in the cases of outright fraud, is equipped to do little more than post weather warnings. It is still up to the investor to look out for himself; the SEC can only demand full disclosure of the facts about a security. These are hard for the investor to interpret, and sometimes distorted beyond reality.

Because the securities market is in the most sensitive area of the economic scene, it must face the fact that it is under much greater public scrutiny than any other routine business. It is entrusted with the public's money, and it has a super-responsibility for it. Experience has shown that when it has been permitted to run wild, not only the public has suffered, but the financial community as well. Its public responsibilities are no greater than its responsibilities to itself.

In spite of the resistance of the bulk of the securities market to government regulation, its own practices seem deliberately to invite more government scrutiny rather than less. And at times there has been evidence that the SEC has been instrumental in saving the market from its own folly. Justifiably, the market has a legitimate fear of government control. But it fails to distinguish between government regulation and government control. A referee or an umpire is an absolute must in any game of football or baseball. Without them, there would be nothing but chaos. Yet this doesn't mean that the referee is permitted to drop his regulatory role and make a flying tackle. He is not a participant, and the players are permitted to play the game—within the rules—as they see fit.

At the moment, the SEC as a referee is the only thing which stands between the investor and a totally chaotic market. A large portion of the public doesn't understand that it is a referee with very limited powers, and that the noise of the crowd is sometimes so loud that the whistle is not heard. Many members of the public think that the SEC can ban shaky and unsafe investments. Of course it cannot do this. Many have the feeling that if a security is registered with the SEC it has been checked over by the SEC staff and found to be all that the prospectus says it is. Since the Commission can only require a full disclosure of facts in new issues, it can only act when a distortion of these facts is brought to light; the investor has to do his own checking. In buying an existing issue, the investor has little SEC protection.

However, various states have their own securities laws which buttress SEC regulations, and sometimes go beyond them in order to protect the investor. One of the most aggressive states is California, whose Division of Corporations is headed by Commissioner John G. Sobieski, whose popularity with Wall Street in general is rather slim. He is responsible for administering the California securities or "blue sky" laws (so called because a jurist at one trial remarked that some securities laws give the investor about as much protection as a "patch of blue sky"), some of which have been in existence since 1879. In addition to requiring full disclosure, the Division of Corporations in California must find that the "proposed issuance of securities are fair, just, and equitable..." before any permit is allowed to issue them. State jurisdiction is limited, however, to those securities issued in the state.

In a recent case, about 30 per cent of a common stock to be issued consisted of options and warrants. Under SEC requirements, the issuing corporation was required merely to disclose this fact, which would indicate that the stockholder's equity would be considerably watered down. On the other hand, the Division of Corporations in California refused to grant clearance for the issuing of this security at all, regardless of the disclosure, because the amount of warrants and options appeared to be excessive and to create an unsound capital structure.

"The California legislature," says Mr. Sobieski, "requires this office to make judgments as to the fairness of securities, which judgments Congress has not authorized the SEC to make. There are substantial theoretical arguments which can be made in support of either line of approach. If our staff believes an issue is basically unsound, or the terms are unfair to investors, this office has authority to deny the company the right to sell its securities in California. This authority is exercised, in proper cases. Nevertheless, with this type of regulation, which California has had since 1913, our securities industry has flourished and it is generally believed that more stocks are sold to residents of California than to residents of any other state."

New York has more total sales, when you include both resident and nonresident investors, but California stands second in importance, representing 11.9 of all United States shareholders. Under its laws, the investor has far greater protection than under the SEC regulations.

"Adequate voting procedures and adequate reports to stockholders and sound financial structures," says Mr. Sobieski, "appear to be basic to the continued success of our capitalistic system. Experience has shown that the financial community needs policing the same as all other segments of the community. Experience has also shown that here, as elsewhere, the police are most effective when they have the co-operation and good will of the community in which they operate. The administration of the California Corporate Securities Law has been immeasurably helped by the co-operation it has received from the responsible elements in the financial community, from the Governor, the legislature, and from other state agencies."

The California laws are among the most stringent in the country, yet this hasn't prevented the investment business there from enjoying a leading position in the country. In addition to its tough registration requirement, the Commission there looks with acute disfavor at noncumulative voting common stock (which prevents the stockholder from putting all his votes on a favorite director), and at underwriters who make exorbitant charges for floating an issue. The securities laws of Illinois, Florida, Oregon, Washington, Missouri, Michigan, Ohio, and New Mexico are equally tough.

The question whether the federal laws should be changed to provide this type of protection to investors on a national scale can be answered better after all the results of the 1962 SEC investigation are in. Certainly the investor has much to gain. Certainly, the SEC would have to extend its staff considerably and its fees would have to be increased. On the other hand, there are members of the financial community who would be more than willing to have the SEC raise its fees a reasonable amount if it would mean speedier action in clearing the registration statements submitted to it.

The New York Stock Exchange, as the standard-bearer of the financial community, has a meticulous and admirable set of rules and regulations. But not only has it at times failed to do an adequate policing job, it is also in no position to regulate other nonmember portions of the market where its activities do not apply. Self-policing is one of the most difficult jobs in the world in any area. Where other people's money is concerned, it is doubly difficult.

Progressive American capitalism doesn't need defense; it needs rendition. It has proved its capacity to produce for the benefit of the mass of people far better than any other system, and yet still maintain the rights and privacy of the individual. But it cannot let itself lose its dynamic energy in the face of sweeping changes in the modern scene. It cannot let the distortions and anomalies of its basically sound foundation lead to its own destruction.

The $750,000 which Congress has appropriated for the full-scale SEC investigation is a small price to pay for the protection of the public investor, who in turn often works against his own interest. The bulk of the regulations for the securities markets was laid down over a quarter of a century ago. There has not been a major over-all study since that time, yet market conditions have changed radically. The loopholes need to be defined and plugged. New statutes and regulations to fit the new situation need to be shaped and put into effect. Confidence in the securities needs to be maintained and strengthened, not through noble pronouncements, but through sensible, up-to-date regulations which will correct the new abuses which have grown up in the new era.

As Representative Peter Mack noted, the growth in the size of the securities market, in the trading volume, and in new types of investment media has been prodigious, along with that of skimpily trained registered representatives. Violations have been piling up higher than ever. Because of its heavy office load, the SEC has not had a chance to back away and look at its problems from any kind of perspective, which the Congressional appropriation has now permitted it to do.

The need for the prevention of the increased fraudulent and manipulative acts and the safeguarding of the public against unreasonable profits, commissions, and unethical practices is obvious. Reluctantly, even the New York Stock Exchange released a statement: "However, if the Securities and Exchange Commission believes the current resolution [to conduct the study] can best meet its needs, the New York Stock Exchange would be glad to accept the Commission's judgment."

Final results of the study will not be available until January of 1909. If, as a result of it, the SEC can be made more effective, the public can only benefit.

The regulation of the market is only part of the picture. The other side of the seeming paradox is the incapacity of the great bulk of the households in America to become genuine owners of American industry in enough numbers and with enough equity to create a genuine capitalistic democracy. With 1½ per cent of the adult population controlling over 80 per cent of all the corporate stock, as the National Bureau of Economic Research studies show, and with the concentration of the ownership of production tending to increase, there remains a danger as great as a wild and uncontrolled securities market. And there is no easy answer to this. The danger of the abuse of its power by concentrated industry is equaled by the danger of power of bigger government and bigger labor unions. Not only the consumer but also the large stockholder himself can benefit by a genuinely broad ownership of industry, in a growing but stable securities market.

The success of private free enterprise has been accomplished through the use of vigorous imagination and the stimulation of competition to prod competitors into doing the impossible. Behind all this is the profit incentive. Without it, such astounding progress would have been sluggish if not impossible. In its earlier stages, private enterprise responded with the enthusiasm and yeastiness of youth. In its maturity, it has lost a tremendous amount of this verve. Business and industry are tending for the most part to settle back and relax, allowing administered prices or the "conscious parallelism" of prices to take over, so that the consumer has to pay for its inefficiencies. It often is blind to its own shortcomings, and unable to utilize imagination or vision to determine what can be done to bring modern capitalism into more dynamic form. And the greatest danger which exists is that by failing to utilize fresh energy, imagination, vision, and high industrial statesmanship, it is inviting government to step in and change things its own way.

There is no question that the problems are extremely involved. If too much money is diverted from the consumer to investment purposes, the sales of goods are bound to drop off, leaving a glutted market and a recession. If purchasing power on the part of the consumer is reduced through exorbitant taxes, inflation, or price-fixing, the same thing could happen. If dividends fail to show a decent return on investment, the industrial growth needed for an expanding population cannot take place. The average wage-earner or salaried employee has little concern for the profits of his company as long as he gets his steady paycheck and keeps his job. Heavy taxes hit both the consumer and the corporation, removing the profit incentive all along the line.

One reason for the speculative mania hitting the securities market is the lack of incentive in other areas. The successful businessman can no longer keep his better salary. The sound investor gets little out of his dividend yield. The rank-and-file employee gets little or no extra return from his company if he contributes to a profitable year.

There is nothing more stimulating to creating a good job on the part of anyone than a healthy and non-neurotic profit motive. Yet where is it evident today? A handful of top executives enjoy profit-sharing and restricted stock option plans, and represent the most extensive area where profit means something. If moderate and fair, this is good for the company, good for them, and good for efficient business. It should not be discounted. Good management deserves good rewards, or else total apathy could set in. But the problem is this: Aside from this group, and that infinitely small percentage of stockholders who are able to hold large and significant quantities of securities in their portfolios, the profit motive—on which our entire greatness is based—is almost nonexistent. It does not apply across the broad spectrum of the American population. And unless this incentive is increased all across the board—to the stockholder, executive, office-worker and wage-earner all together, there is grave danger it may disappear from the scene. One reason why the coffee break has become so popular and more frequent is because of this fact. One reason for unreasonable labor demands lies in this area. Employees who know what a profit is, and who participate in it, don't take time off for coffee breaks, or for demanding more wages without an equal increase in production.

The profit motive—now largely dormant on a wide scale —is just as important to the lowest employee as it is to the executive and stockholder. It can stimulate, prod, encourage, and inspire the lethargic and apathetic employee to produce more and earn more. But Big Business, on whom the responsibility has to fall, has not been taking adequate steps in recognizing this or in doing anything about it. On the other hand, Big Government is intent on penalizing the profitable, efficient concern through heavy taxes, which in effect is taking money out of the pocket of the efficient operator and awarding it to the inefficient. Big Labor is intent on seeing that all workers—efficient and inefficient—get the same rates of pay. Each of the legs of the tripod has its own justification for this.

The awarding of money by government subsidy to non-producers (aside from obligatory and urgent emergency measures for deserved relief) is just as bad as corporations failing to broaden the base of profit incentive and stock option plans to its rank-and-file employees. Yet neither Big

Business nor Big Labor nor Big Government has been willing to give up something in order to get something better back.

Concentrated wealth can never produce a sturdy economy, whether that wealth is concentrated in government or business or individuals. The velocity with which money is spent is just as important as the amount of money in circulation. Two fast nickels do more for the economy than a slow dime. One dollar spent fifty times is geometrically more advantageous to the economy than fifty dollars spent once. This is axiomatic. The major problem seems to be to put money into wide and high-velocity circulation, so that the economy can produce enough margin to permit more people to become participants in a sober investment market. This can not only increase our rate of industrial growth, but provide the mass purchasing power necessary to support that rate of growth in doing so. In the long run, both large and small investor benefit.

The ancient countries of Europe have so exceeded our rate of growth in the recent past that there is genuine cause for alarm. Competition from abroad can no longer be brushed off. Yet a symptom of arrogance gargantuan in its implications was the action of United States Steel in raising its prices at a time when foreign competition was making its greatest inroads. Attitudes are often more important than facts. With the attitude of U. S. Steel so obviously revealed in its ill-considered action, it's a wonder that the American economy has been able to hold up as well as it has. A child running a lemonade stand knows that you cannot meet competition by raising prices. Yet this is what U. S. Steel attempted to do, with the excuse that it needed new working capital.

It can get that working capital by helping to see to it that enough buying power is placed in the hands of the American consumer that he can buy more goods, invest in stock on a realistic basis, and increase the demand for steel, so that the company can operate at the efficient full-capacity rate.

Edward Dale, the *New York Times* staffer, writes in the

New Republic that the reason for the faster economic growth of Western Europe lies in the fact that the United States does not have enough *real* demand in the hands of the consumer. It's important to recall that real demand is not simply desire or want on the part of the consumer; it is the combination of the desire and the cash-in-hand to go along with it. Dale quotes a still-secret report by the Organization for Economic Cooperation and Development, which reached the unanimous conclusion that United States growth in the last half of the decade was slow because of "insufficient pressure of demand." The small proportion of the population who own significant amounts of stock, and derive major income from it, cannot possibly create the demand needed to enable companies like U. S. Steel to operate at the profit they deserve and need. Houses, bridges, television sets, bobby pins, automobiles, nails, and wire need mass purchasing power to produce any kind of profit for steel or any other industry. The urgently needed velocity of money cannot come from a small group of people. Both industry and large stockholders can benefit themselves by helping to create the greater "pressure of demand," not only for buying goods and services but for investing in the working capital necessary to increase the gross national product.

Nearly five million unemployed representing nearly 12 million family members won't enhance the value of the common stock of U. S. Steel or any other corporation. Nor does it make any sales manager's job easier. "Demand pressure" starts with eliminating the unemployed and extending the ability of the consumer to spend and invest, both at the same time and in sensible proportion.

For some obscure reason, both management and stockholders generally fail to realize just how handsomely the wider extension of the profit motive can pay off for them. Ever since the "Hawthorne Experiments" at Western Electric, there has been glaring evidence that the average employee responds to recognition, even if it is token recognition. The experiments were set up only to study different groups of employees and their working conditions. The main discovery made, however, was that whenever a group of employees was made the center of attention or interest, production went up regardless of the variables used in the tests. The participation of an employee in something beyond his paycheck obviously is an emotional involvement rather than an economic one. But it is incredibly important in effecting economic profit.

The Hawthorne experiments took place more than twenty-five years ago, yet the response of industry on a wide scale has been dismal and disheartening. There are some bright spots on the horizon, however, although the growth of a really significant amount of understanding on the part of management and directors for extending the profit motive and employee stock ownership is still too small to bring a fresh new outlook to the economic scene.

Sears, Roebuck, for instance, has been a rewarding example of how enlightened management can bring greater profits to itself and to its stockholders through recognizing the important relationship between employee incentive-beyond-salary and profitable productivity. For the main part, the stockholder is interested in profit alone. He is not an integral part of the labor-management combination which actually turns the machinery from which his profit is derived.

The stockholder's stake in helping the rank-and-file employee to learn about and experience profit is more than he sometimes realizes. As a result of the efforts on the part of Sears, Roebuck management to broaden equity ownership among its employees, its profits have been enhanced and the nonemployee stockholder has materially benefited. While its rival Montgomery Ward stumbled all over the map, Sears prospered handsomely. Since 1945, its stock has been split twice—once on a 4-to-1 basis, and again on a 3-to-1 basis. Its earnings have reached the highest peak in history.

As Sears' Vice-President James C. Worthy says in his enlightening and intelligent book *Big Business and Free Men:*
"One of the worst sins a corporate management can com-

mit is to make a high rate of profit at the cost of jeopardizing the company's long range interest." Worthy goes on to point out that the genius of Henry Ford lay not only in his concept of mass production; his most lasting contribution was his recognition of the fact that the best way to expand the markets for mass production was to improve the capacity of workers to consume.

While a large part of management and boards of directors continues to ignore this essential fact, Sears has discovered in completely realistic terms that it means long-run profit, better employee relations, and greater benefits accruing eventually to the stockholder. Sears' Employee Profit-Sharing Plan, as Worthy points out, began in 1916 when such plans were practically nonexistent. At the end of 1958, the assets of the fund stood at over $1 billion. As a result of the plan, over a quarter of the company stock is held by the employees, which is the largest stockholder group in the company. Worthy cites some typical examples which demonstrate clearly that the plan is far from meager in extending free enterprise. One woman had participated in the fund for nine years, and had deposited in the profit-sharing plan as she worked with the company. When she left, she was able to draw out $4,025. Another woman was with the fund for 25 years. From her deposits of $3,450 she took out $47,125. Another employee who had been a charter member of the employee plan had deposited $4,820, and on retirement his share of the profit-sharing fund was $174,980.

"Unquestionably," says Mr. Worthy, "the profit-sharing plan has had a highly-favorable influence on the attitudes of Sears employees. It is the most talked-about of all company policies. Employees are not around for long before they begin to hear about the plan from their fellow-workers."

In spite of all the practical benefits the employee receives from such a plan, Mr. Worthy feels that the "symbolic" value is even greater than the economic. This symbolic value has further assets for the nonemployee stockholder, who often doesn't take the time to realize that practical idealism in business can turn out to be extremely profitable to him, and be reflected on the stock ticker in no uncertain way.

The unconventional policies of the colorful and dynamic William Black, founder of the highly successful Chock Full O'Nuts firm, further demonstrate the power of positive employee relations. His capacity to understand the motives of the average employee has enabled his company's stock to blossom and grow, with enough left over for him to give Columbia University a donation of $5,000,000, the largest single sum ever contributed by a living person to the institution.

A look at his employee relations program—administered without paternalism—tells a good part of the story. In addition to generous sick benefits, Blue Cross, life insurance, pensions and medical care—all without cost to the employee—Black's rank-and-file employees get a Christmas bonus amounting to a flat 10 per cent of the company's earnings before taxes, while the managers and assistant managers get 2 per cent and 1 per cent of their store sales, respectively. The employee bonus alone has amounted to more than five weeks' extra salary each year in recent times.

But in the face of all this, the stockholder too has been prospering through high and healthy earnings.

There are other encouraging signs of advanced statesmanship in other companies throughout industry which serve to broaden the profit motive among the wide mass of employees. Active in profit-sharing plans have been Proctor & Gamble, Eastman Kodak, Lincoln Electric, Pitney-Bowes, Bell & Howell, Lever Brothers, and others. But in the total picture they fail to represent enough of the industrial scene to create a better and growing "people's capitalism." According to an estimate of the National Industrial Conference Board, there were 10,000 plans in effect by the end of 1956. The plans are growing, but not fast enough. Employee stock plans, as contrasted with executive stock plans, are few in comparison to the total number of corporations in business. Ironically, labor unions have opposed such plans, on the grounds that the worker should get his total pay in wages, a strikingly short-sighted attitude.

The avoidance of a welfare state—and nearly every American earnestly wants to avoid it—depends on the capacity of industry and finance to recognize their own shortcomings. The blindness of institutions to their own faults is the severest danger the country faces in this direction. No one can rest easy or be the least bit satisfied with the nearly five million people out of work at the height of prosperity. No one can be satisfied with a "people's capitalism" which finds nine out of ten of American households not holding any stock at all. No one can be satisfied with a securities market which, in spite of some earnest effort, cannot keep its own house in order. A healthy dissatisfaction with the way things are is the most satisfying attitude to have. Anything else represents a head-in-the-sand policy.

The less government interference, the better—but there must be enough government regulation in the sensitive areas of finance, where its institutions have consistently proved themselves unable to handle their problems in the past or present. A very great man in history said:

"The only use of government is to repress the vices of man. If man were today sinless, tomorrow he would have the right to demand that government and all its evils should cease."

He was neither a politician, nor an industrialist, nor a labor union leader. He was Percy Bysshe Shelley, who as a poet could cut through the cluttered abstractions of economists and statesmen and get at the heart of the matter quickly and effectively.

A journalisic report such as this book can offer no panaceas, but it can offer a point of view from an outsider not involved in or blurred by the everyday action of the financial maelstrom. Those who operate on the inside of any field find it very hard to stand back and look at the picture at arm's length. Conflicting responsibilities are bound to press hard on the insider, and make it impossible for him to focus sharply.

Out of the Wall Street jungle, whether it's loaded with bulls (as it was in 1961) or bears (as in 1962), certain obvious basics emerge, each of which has been reviewed in the previous pages.

First, it is obvious that the circus-and-carnival atmosphere of the stock market must be reduced and cut down. Anything as important as the basic economy of the country cannot remain on the plane of semi-fantasy, such as the unrealistic prices in 1961 seemed to reflect. Because of this, the 1962 investigation by the SEC assumes an importance that should cause it to be backed fully by the public and the financial community. The hopes of full support by the latter are slim. The public, however, can make itself felt by notifying its Congressmen of its full support, and by demanding further investigation, if necessary, in order to keep itself protected. It is doubtful if there will ever be a foolproof system which will prevent fraud and manipulation in the securities market. But the effort to reach toward that goal should never be relaxed.

Second, the public itself must realize that it shares the blame for the three-ring circus when it tries to make a fast dollar on a quick killing. Not too many people get burned when they don't try to get something for nothing. There is no cure for this except wisdom.

Third, the mass of the public must be put realistically in a position where it is possible for them to participate in the equity ownership of industry on a conservative investment basis. It must be more than a token ownership. In spite of all the talk about it, this trend is not growing to the point where such terms as profit, free enterprise, or capital mean anything to a significant number of households in this country. Without such meaning, free enterprise is likely to fight a losing battle with socialism—accompanied by the loss of the dignity of the individual, his rights, and his incentive. The only sensible avenue through which broad ownership of enterprise can be achieved is through the extension of profit-sharing and employee stock option plans, so that the demand pressure of the public can be increased on the basis of real wealth created. Industry itself must give this objective a front seat, instead of leaving it in the trunk. But beyond that, the government through taxation incentive should risk some of its current corporation tax to encourage business in this regard, just as it is attempting to do in its capital investment and depreciation incentives. The increase in gross national product may compensate the government for what it loses temporarily, and avoid a government handout program which no one of any initiative and enterprise desires.

Fourth, the new and the old-line investor must have the greatest possible protection for his investment in a stable market kept in line by improved securities laws and regulations, which recognize frankly that the market as a whole is unable to police fully its own activities, in spite of the protests that it can. The concept of disclosure alone, which is the whole basis of the SEC operation, has demonstrated many weaknesses in protecting the investor. Some of the California "blue sky" laws have shown great advantage to the public, which, if adopted on a national scale (and surely under the wailing protests of a large bulk of Wall Streeters), could help bring greater confidence than before to the securities market. And, in spite of Wall Street's fears, such laws could lead to a stronger and more profitable securities market—on a non-fantasy basis.

All of this might be wild-eyed and visionary, but unless new imagination is applied to the economic scene, however visionary, there will inevitably be a choking of incentive, which will seriously affect the stockholders, executives, employees, and the public.

If genuine incentives to all participants of the economy can be stimulated, fostered, and maintained, then perhaps the present-day myth of Bill and Grace Richards (in the New York Stock Exchange fable), may possibly not be so far-fetched. At the moment it is something out of Hans Christian Andersen. The sooner it can come true, the better off America—and the stock market—will be.